CW00866760

The Peacock Committee and UK Broadcasting Policy

Also by Tom O'Malley

CLOSEDOWN? THE BBC AND GOVERNMENT BROADCASTING POLICY 1979–92 (1994)

A JOURNALISM READER (*with Michael Bromley*)

REGULATING THE PRESS (*with C. Soley*)

THE MEDIA IN WALES: Voices of a Small Nation (*with David Barlow and Philip Mitchell*)

RECONSTRUCTING THE PAST: History in the Mass Media 1890–2005 (*with Sian Nicholas and Kevin Williams*)

Also by Janet Jones

BIG BROTHER INTERNATIONAL: Format, Critics and Publics (*with E. Mathijs*)

The Peacock Committee and UK Broadcasting Policy

Edited by

Tom O'Malley
Professor of Media Studies, University of Wales, Aberystwyth, UK

Janet Jones
Principal Lecturer in Journalism, University of the West of England, UK

Introduction, selection and editorial matter © Tom O'Malley and Janet Jones 2009
Individual chapters © contributors 2009

All rights reserved. No reproduction, copy or transmission of this publication may be made without written permission.

No portion of this publication may be reproduced, copied or transmitted save with written permission or in accordance with the provisions of the Copyright, Designs and Patents Act 1988, or under the terms of any licence permitting limited copying issued by the Copyright Licensing Agency, Saffron House, 6-10 Kirby Street, London EC1N 8TS.

Any person who does any unauthorised act in relation to this publication may be liable to criminal prosecution and civil claims for damages.

The authors have asserted their rights to be identified as the authors of this work in accordance with the Copyright, Designs and Patents Act 1988.

First published 2009 by
PALGRAVE MACMILLAN

Palgrave Macmillan in the UK is an imprint of Macmillan Publishers Limited, registered in England, company number 785998, of Houndmills, Basingstoke, Hampshire RG21 6XS.

Palgrave Macmillan in the US is a division of St Martin's Press LLC, 175 Fifth Avenue, New York, NY 10010.

Palgrave Macmillan is the global academic imprint of the above companies and has companies and representatives throughout the world.

Palgrave® and Macmillan® are registered trademarks in the United States, the United Kingdom, Europe and other countries

ISBN-13: 978-0-230-52474-3   hardback
ISBN-10: 0-230-52474-5   hardback

This book is printed on paper suitable for recycling and made from fully managed and sustained forest sources. Logging, pulping and manufacturing processes are expected to conform to the environmental regulations of the country of origin.

A catalogue record for this book is available from the British Library.

Library of Congress Cataloging-in-Publication Data

The Peacock Committee and UK broadcasting policy/edited By
    Tom O'Malley, Janet Jones.
        p. cm.
    Includes bibliographical references and index.
    ISBN 978-0-230-52474-3 (alk. paper)
    1. Broadcasting policy—Great Britain. 2. Broadcasting—Great Britain.
    3. Great Britain. Committee on Financing the BBC. I.
    O'Malley, Tom, 1955- II. Jones, Janet, 1963-

    HE8689.9.G7P43 2009
    384.540941—dc22   2009013645

10   9   8   7   6   5   4   3   2   1
18 17 16 15 14 13 12 11 10 09

Printed and bound in Great Britain by
CPI Antony Rowe, Chippenham and Eastbourne

Contents

Preface

This collection and the conference on which it draws ('The Peacock Legacy: turning point or missed opportunity?') could not have taken place without the support of a number of institutions and individuals. We would like to thank Aberystwyth University and the National Sound and Screen Archive of the National Library of Wales for their support in the form of grants and facilities. The conference benefited from a Conference Grant awarded by the British Academy. In addition to the people who gave up their time to attend as witnesses, we would also like to thank those who attended the conference for contributing to the discussions and the debates. We extend our gratitude to the following individuals who, in one way or another, have helped us with either the Conference or the collection: Dr Peter Catterall, Jiska Englebert, Ceris Medhurst-Jones, Professor Noel Lloyd (Vice-Chancellor of Aberystwyth University), Joan Miller, Rod Munday, Robert O'Malley and Dafydd Sills-Jones.

Thanks are also due to the staff of the library and information services at Aberystwyth University and the University of West of England, at the National Library of Wales and at the University of Wales Conference Centre Gregynog, who at various stages provided valuable assistance with conference organisation and research.

We gratefully acknowledge the permissions to reprint the articles from the *Royal Bank of Scotland Review* (Peacock, 1987) and *The Political Quarterly* (Brittan, 1987) which appear in Chapters 5 and 6.

A note on the text

Sir Alan Peacock and Sir Samuel Brittan received their knighthoods after the publication of the report. We have included their titles at the head of chapters, but not in the body of articles where reference is made to them.

References to the transcriptions are to the transcriptions held at the National Library of Wales. Where quotations from the transcripts in the chapters cite material that can also be found in the edited extracts in Chapter 12, a footnote is provided guiding the reader to where these quotations can be found in that chapter.

Where authors have referred to the original copies of the publications by Sir Alan Peacock and Sir Samuel Brittan, reproduced here in Chapters 5 and 6, the reader can consult the versions published here if they wish to trace the precise reference.

Janet Jones
Tom O'Malley

Introduction

Tom O'Malley

This introduction sets the scene for the material in this collection. After explaining the genesis of this publication it outlines some of the context from which the Peacock Report emerged and sketches developments thereafter.

The Peacock Legacy: Turning point or missed opportunity?

The Peacock Legacy: Turning point or missed opportunity' conference was organised to mark the twentieth anniversary of the establishment of the *Committee on the Finance of the BBC* in March 1985 between 18 and 20 March 2005. The organisers were pleased to welcome participants, ranging from three members of the Committee, to academics, practitioners and trade unionists all of whom had either been central to the Peacock process or had, since, been closely monitoring either the history of the Committee or its consequences. These included Sir Alan Peacock, who chaired the Committee, Sir Samuel Brittan and Jeremy Hardie, members of the Committee, as well as Alwyn Roberts, who was on the BBC Board of Governors in 1985–6 and Sir David Nicholas who was at ITN during the period of the Committee and afterwards. Professor Peter Jay, a key figure in the debates about broadcasting in the 1970s, not only attended and chaired sessions, but played a pivotal role in organising the conference with the two editors of this volume.

The Conference was divided into sections: establishing the Committee; the conduct of the Committee; the view from the BBC and the influence of the Report. The proceedings were recorded and transcripts have been deposited in the archives of the National Screen and Sound Archive at the National Library of Wales.

This collection comprises a number of specially written essays, based on the themes of the conference, plus two reprinted pieces by Sir Alan Peacock and Sir Samuel Brittan written shortly after the Committee reported in 1986. The essays are organised in a broadly chronological fashion. They start with a consideration of the history of the ideas underlying the Report, which argues that most of the main ideas and recommendations in the Report had been developed over the preceding 30 years (Chapters 1–3). There follows a personal take by Professor Peter Jay on the thinking behind the Report, and defence of the conception of negative liberty which arguably underlies the document and which makes its propositions so controversial. The reprinted essays by Sir Alan Peacock and Sir Samuel Brittan provide insights into both the thinking behind the conduct and the reception of the Report, from the perspectives of the two dominant members of the Committee. These are followed by a revealing assessment of the micropolitics and history of the process from the perspective of the BBC and the central government in Professor Jean Seaton and Dr Anthony McNicholas' ground-breaking chapter.

Professor Richard Collins argues that the Report's 'claim to our attention lies in its advocacy of citizenship entitlements and ability to hold to account' rather than in terms of its arguments about technological change as a route to the creation of functioning broadcasting markets. Professor Kevin Williams takes a close look at the impact of the Report on the nature of broadcasting for the nations and regions of the UK, and brings to bear some telling points about the negative impact of the increased competition that flowed from the Report on the provision of programming for these areas. Janet Jones focuses on the way in which the Peacock Report helped create an environment, which by the early part of the twenty-first century was, along with the technological changes associated with the Internet, challenging ideas about how public service communications should develop. Sir Alan Peacock contributes an afterword, which comments on both the BBC and aspects of the issues raised by the Report. The collection also contains edited selections of the transcripts, where perspectives on the Report are given by key participants at the Conference, Professor Steve Barnett, Jeremy Hardie, Tony Lennon and Sir David Nicholas. Finally we print the key recommendations of the Report.

While all participants recognised the historical importance of the Peacock Report, and while the discussions were lively and courteous, divisions about the values underpinning the Report and over interpretations of its influence were pronounced. This is apparent, for example, in the different perspectives adopted by Sir Alan Peacock (Chapters 5 and 11) and Professor Seaton and Dr McNicholas (Chapter 7), differences of which the authors were made aware by the editors, and which provide an impetus for further reflection and debate. These divisions are reflected in the contributions to this book. They testify to the fact that the Report developed a controversial and sustained case for restructuring broadcasting.

Context

The British Broadcasting Company was established in 1922, and became the British Broadcasting Corporation in 1927.[1] It was, and remains, funded by the licence fee. The BBC ran radio services at first, adding television in 1936. After World War II (1939–45) the Conservative government under Winston Churchill (1951–5) introduced advertising-financed television through the terms of the 1954 *Television Act*, but the new service, known as Independent Television (ITV), was regulated, in the image of the BBC, so as to preserve standards. Commercial radio or Independent Local Radio (ILR) was introduced by another Conservative government under Edward Heath (1970–4) via the 1972 *Sound Broadcasting Act*. The first ILR station went on air in 1973.

The BBC, ITV and ILR were expected to provide a wide range of informational, educational and entertainment programmes. Public service TV and radio were phenomenally popular with the public. There were, however, periodic controversies between the broadcasters and politicians and increasing levels of public debate about the social purposes, organisation and accountability of broadcasting in the 1960s and 1970s (O'Malley, 2007; Sandbrook, 2006). The system was widely recognised as managing to produce high quality broadcasting in popular and minority forms of programming.

The developments in broadcasting were subject to periodic review by government-appointed committees after 1945. These included the Beveridge Committee (Report, 1951), the Pilkington Committee (Report, 1962) and the Annan Committee, (Report, 1977). Each one generated analysis and proposals for the development of broadcasting, and each one exercised, in different ways, influence over the development of broadcasting in the UK. They all, however, accepted that broadcasting, be it funded by licence fee or advertising, should be organised, primarily, as a public service.

The 1981 *Broadcasting Act* was the high water mark of this tradition. It extended commercial public service broadcasting by establishing two new commercial TV channels. Channel 4 (1982) was designed to serve the interests not catered for on the main TV channels. Sianel Pedwar Cymru (S4C) (1982) was the product of a generation of campaigning in Wales and was created to provide Welsh language TV (Barlow et al., 2005). The Act also made Channel 4 a commissioner, rather than, as was the case with the BBC and ITV, a producer of programmes. The introduction of independent producers was the result of demands from a broad coalition of reformers in the 1960s and 1970s for the opening up of broadcasting to new voices. It found a place in the legislation of the radical Tory government of Margaret Thatcher (1979–83) in part because it chimed with that government's support for entrepreneurship (Darlow, 2004).

A number of factors converged in the early 1980s which led to the establishment of Peacock.[2] Technology was changing and the potential of satellite, computers and fibre optic cable to recast the organisation of broadcasting was on the political agenda. The election in 1979 of a Conservative government led by Margaret Thatcher brought with it a political preference for seeking market solutions to industrial problems. So, for example, in 1982, the Hunt Report on cable advocated the development of a market-driven cable system in the UK (Hollins, 1984). The early 1980s also witnessed a number of clashes between the Conservative government and the BBC, most notably over the coverage of the war in the Falkland Islands in 1982, and the coverage of the ongoing war in Northern Ireland (Miller, 1994; O'Malley, 1994).

The re-election of the Conservatives (1983–7) meant that the BBC's request for a renewal of its licence fee in 1984 was handled by a government which was sympathetic to a rising chorus of criticism of the Corporation and of public service broadcasting. Sections of the newspaper and advertising industries saw rich pickings in lowering barriers to entry into the UK broadcasting market and developing more competition, and so helped orchestrate a high profile public campaign against the licence fee and in favour of placing advertisements on the BBC. The BBC came under sustained attack in sections of the national press, particularly in publications such as *The Times* owned by Mrs Thatcher's close ally Rupert Murdoch and also in a string of reports issued by the advertising industry. Simultaneously the government was receptive to the liberal economics of bodies such as the Institute of Economic Affairs (IEA) and the Adam Smith Institute (ASI) which were committed to extending the reach of the market and rolling back the State's involvement in economic life (Cockett, 1995). In 1984 the Adam Smith Institute published a report advocating an increase in competition in UK broadcasting (Adam Smith Institute, 1984).

The Peacock Committee emerged from this context. Leon Brittan, the Home Secretary, and the Minister responsible for broadcasting, was faced with a request by the BBC for a licence fee increase in a context of intense, high profile, public debate about whether the BBC should take advertising, and with a Prime Minister who was known to favour advertising on the Corporation. The solution he opted for, in an announcement on 27 March 1985, was to establish a committee to examine the finances of the BBC, with the following terms of reference:

(i) To assess the effects of the introduction of advertising or sponsorship on the BBC's Home Services either as an alternative or supplement to the income now received through the licence fee, including

(a) the financial and other consequences for the BBC, for independent television and independent local radio, for the prospective services of cable, independent national radio and direct broadcasting by satellite, for the press and advertising industry and for the Exchequer; and
(b) the impact on the range and quality of existing broadcasting services; and

(ii) to identify a range of options for the introduction in varying amounts and on different condition of advertising or sponsorship on some or all of the BBC's Home Services, with an assessment of the advantages and disadvantages of each option, and

(iii) to consider any proposals for securing income from the consumer other than through the licence fee.

(Report, 1986: para. 1)

The first two elements of the remit formed the core of the Report's deliberations, and the third provided the springboard for a consideration of subscription, pay-TV and electronic publishing. There was no basis in the remit, however, for the libertarian thrust of the recommendation on lifting controls over programme content. The appointment of Alan Peacock as Chair, a distinguished welfare economist and member of the IEA, signalled that the inquiry would have the economics, rather than social and cultural issues at the centre of its concerns. The other major appointment was Samuel Brittan, the financial journalist who, at the *Financial Times* in the 1960s and 1970s, had played a key part in winning political support for monetarist economic policies (Cockett, 1995). Together these two brought considerable economic expertise to the Committee.

The Committee's Report rejected the proposition that the BBC should take advertising, and instead proposed a vision of broadcasting in which consumers and producers would engage in direct transactions for programmes:

> Our own conclusion is that British Broadcasting should move towards a sophisticated market system based on consumer sovereignty. That is a system which recognises that viewers and listeners are the best ultimate judges of their own interests, which they can best satisfy if they have the option of purchasing the broadcasting services they require from as many alternative sources of supply as possible. There will always be a need to supplement the direct consumer market by public finance for programmes of a public service kind (defined in paragraph 563) supported by people in their capacity as citizens and voters but unlikely to be commercially self-supporting in the view of broadcasting entrepreneurs.
>
> (Report, 1986: para. 592)

The instrument that was seen as enabling the development of consumer-driven market was technology, in the form of subscription, or pay-per-view television. This, combined with freedom of entry for producers into the market, without the panoply of regulation that existed in the 1980s, would allow consumers to choose for themselves what they watched, rather than have the bulk of their viewing presented to them by State-sanctioned broadcasters. Regulation would therefore be reduced to a minimum and measures taken to finance some public service programmes which the market could not, or would not, produce. It recommended a staged shift to consumer sovereignty, with a series of recommendations addressing the immediate context, building up to a situation in which direct payment by consumers for programmes, rather than the licence fee, would fund the BBC and the bulk of other programming.

The initial response to the Report in government circles was not uncritical, as the chapters by Sir Alan Peacock, Sir Samuel Brittan and Professor Jean Seaton and Dr Anthony McNicholas detail. Yet it is clear from subsequent developments that the Report exercised increasing influence over policy thereafter, throughout the period of the Conservative governments of the 1980s and 1990s (1979–97) and those of New Labour under Tony Blair (1997–2007) and Gordon Brown (2007–). The Conservative governments of the 1980s and early 1990s accepted the proposals to index the licence fee, a version of the quota for independent producers and the auctioning of ITV franchises. Regulation of radio was eased and the 1990 *Broadcasting Act* established a new 'light touch' regulator for commercial TV and satellite, the Independent Television Commission. Thereafter new commercial services came on stream with a minimum of regulation and the ITV system was allowed to become more commercial in outlook, shedding its regional organisation in England and Wales and becoming one company, ITV plc. At the same time ITV was allowed to drop significant amounts of its public service programming on the grounds that it was facing intense competition for revenues, especially after the late 1990s when digital television began to spread such that by 2008 the majority of households in the UK were multichannel homes (Ofcom, 2008:49).

The 2003 *Communications Act* established a new regulator for commercial broadcasting and telecommunications, the Office of Communications (Ofcom). Although it had a duty to promote public service, its main role was, in the tradition of Peacock, to promote competition and remove unnecessary regulations across its areas of responsibility. It also took on the role of policing the BBC, ensuring that, in its view, the Corporation did not act uncompetitively or unfairly. These developments were accompanied by the spread of the Internet as a means of distributing programming, and offering alternatives to terrestrial and digital broadcasting.

A combination therefore of technical change and policy development meant that in 2008 the nature and structure of UK broadcasting had shifted considerably towards a more market-orientated position. It was clear, however, that, in 2008, the BBC remained the most important broadcaster in the UK, and that, where viewing practices were concerned, public service channels retained a dominant position, in spite of the fact that competition had eaten into their audiences (Ofcom, 2008:39–41). The ideal of a consumer-driven market place had not been achieved, but there had been considerable moves in that direction since 1986. By 2008 the debate had shifted such that the option of using elements of the licence fee to fund public service broadcasting in the commercial sector, or even establishing a Public Service Authority to oversee the BBC and public service commercial broadcasting was seriously under consideration (Gibson, 2008). In that sense Peacock marked a break with what had gone before and provided the intellectual justification for the shift that has been gradually taking place ever since.

Yet the report, in spite of its influence, remains controversial, not least of all because of its articulation of questions about the role of the state in broadcasting and the notion of consumer sovereignty.

The development of public service broadcasting in the UK was, in part, a product of technological constraints – that is, a shortage of spectrum limited the number of services. It was also based on attitudes, held by politicians, civil servants and broadcasters, about the purposes of broadcasting. Rightly or wrongly successive governments considered broadcasting a peculiarly powerful social force which needed to be both supervised for negative reasons and harnessed for positive social ends. In essence broadcasting was seen as one area of mass communications which could be organised outside of, or, in the case of commercial TV and radio, in a disciplined relationship, to the market, unlike the book, newspaper and cinema industries. That this should be so testified, in part, to a view that held that the State had a responsibility to stimulate the cultural capacities of the population, a view embodied in the austere approach of the BBC's first Director General, John Reith (1927–38) and his increasingly liberal successors. Over time, programming relations between the State and broadcasters and the public and broadcasters, as well as the institutions evolved within a framework of public service broadcasting, such that by the time of the 1981 *Broadcasting Act* the system was radically different to that which had obtained in the 1930s and the 1950s. It was more open, more diverse, less patronising and was committed to broadcasting different voices, reflecting the pluralism of UK society.

This public service approach to broadcasting dominated policy up to the 1980s, but did not go unchallenged. A critique emerged, most notably from the 1940s. It was rooted in liberal economics, was critical of the role of the State in broadcasting and asserted the need for developing market forces in society and in broadcasting. This represented, at its best, a belief in the moral value of individualism as an organising social principle. It was also associated with right of centre politics, highly critical of the Welfare State and the post-war economic and political consensus (Cockett, 1995). It remained, until the 1980s, a marginal approach to broadcasting.[3]

The Peacock Report brought these two approaches into open and sharp conflict with the result that the older approach began, thereafter, to give ground to the one that had been formerly on the margins of public and policy debate. The conflict was in part a result of sum of the controversial approaches and assumptions embedded in the Report. The Peacock Report, in essence, sits within a tradition of a nineteenth century liberalism;[4] stressing the freedom of the individual to act with minimal constraint in matters of economics, politics and culture, except where there is a compelling case for some kind of public intervention. It stands four square against a view that society should, in matters of culture, allow government to intervene to sustain a high level of general cultural awareness in society on the grounds that such intervention not only interferes with market and individual freedoms, but also holds out the possibility of State censorship. It views the State through the prism of eighteenth and nineteenth century debates about Press censorship, equating these with the role of the State in relation to twentieth century public service broadcasting. By collapsing two different sets of circumstances, and assuming the former applies to the latter, the positive elements of State intervention are not explored in any detail and the panoply of measures to promote high quality public service broadcasting is equated with vetting.[5] There is an idealistic stress on the value of consumer sovereignty, which assumes that it is both the best guarantor of freedom and the best way of organising the economics of a future communications system.[6] This approach to the State and economics arguably amounts to a resurgence, in the context of the history of social change since the nineteenth century, of conservative prescriptions for social organisation, a conservatism rooted in its neglect and implicit dismissal of the positive economic and cultural benefits that have accompanied the expansion of the democratic State in the twentieth century.

These considerations point to some of the issues that generated controversy around the Report and which are reflected explicitly and implicitly in the chapters in this collection. The Peacock Report is a profoundly important and, as it has proven, intellectually challenging document. It has provided a key justification for allowing economics to dominate the framework of broadcasting policy in the UK in a way which echoes developments in the USA.[7] There are considerable differences of opinion about the value of the arguments and prescriptions in the Report, not because they lack integrity or are anything but highly professional, but because of the way they advocate applying a particular set of values to the analysis of the system and to the recommendations for change. It will take some time and more research, before the place of this crucial intervention in UK political and cultural history can be more fully assessed. This collection is a contribution to that process.

Notes

1. For the history of British Broadcasting, see Briggs (1961, 1965, 1970, 1979, 1995); Sendall (1982, 1983); Potter (1989, 1990); Bonner and Ashton (1998, 2003).
2. For more details on the context and consequences of Peacock in these years, see O'Malley (1994), on which this and subsequent paragraphs draw.
3. See Chapters 1–3 in this volume.

4. Useful approaches to understanding the context from which some of the key ideas underlying Peacock arose can be found in Eccleshall (1986:1–66) and Tomlinson (1990:125–51).

5   The equation of regulation with censorship and vetting is in the Recommendations, printed in this volume, and more explicitly in Brittan (1987), reprinted as Chapter 6 in this volume. Evidence of public service broadcasters regularly challenging the state on political, social and cultural issues in the post-War period can be found in the histories cited in note 3 above, and in summary in Curran and Seaton (2003).

6. For a closely argued criticism of markets in communications see Baker (2002). The anti-socialist tradition that underpinned much of the neoliberal economics that influenced the Peacock Report is explicit in the work of Hayek and Coase, for which see Chapter 8, note 21 in this collection and Tomlinson (1990). See also Chapters 1–3 in this collection.

7. See McChesney (2000).

1
Attacking Collectivism

Tom O'Malley

This chapter outlines aspects of the underlying themes and ideas which have shaped UK politics since the nineteenth century, but more specifically, since the 1930s. It does so in order to illustrate the importance of placing debates about broadcasting in the context of ideas about the balance between individual and collective economic and political liberties, ideas which relate directly to the Peacock Report.

The long view

The political scientist W. H. Greenleaf has argued that 'modern British politics' may be portrayed in terms of two contrasting extremes', that of libertarianism and collectivism:

> The basic contrast . . . is that between, on the one hand, the notion of a natural harmony in society achieved without recourse to state intervention and, on the other, the idea of an artificial identification of human interests resulting from legislative or other political regulation.

Libertarianism, he argues, has four features, the first of which is 'a stress on the basic importance of individuality . . . on the rights of the individual and his [sic] freedom from both social supervision and arbitrary political control'. Secondly, it entails the idea that 'the role of government . . . must, in principle, be limited'. Thirdly, it recognises 'that any high concentration of power is likely to be dangerous to this sacrosanct zone of individual choice and activity'. Finally, 'libertarianism demands the Rule of Law,' that is people must be free from arbitrary constraint or abuse of power by government and 'there is the principle of equality before the law which is to say that no person or class of persons is above it.'

Collectivism, he argues, 'is simply the tendency in British political life which stands in contrast to this stress on individuality'. The 'collectivist attitude brings to the fore rather the interests of the community which are regarded as primary claims morally superior to any individual demand.' Collectivism stresses the importance of social justice, with the aim of creating conditions that mitigate social suffering; it seeks equality of outcome as a goal of social policy rather than equality of opportunity; and, it also contains within it the idea that its aims can be achieved through government intervention. Having outlined these two extremes, he points out that they 'are simply extreme and opposing paradigms; there is in reality an array of intermediate possibilities, varying responses to the matter of the proper role and office of government' (Greenleaf, 1983:14–24).

Greenleaf provides a useful aid to interpreting the development of politics and political ideas since the nineteenth century in the United Kingdom. Richard Cockett has added to this perspective by arguing that, in a very broad sense, modern UK political history can be viewed in terms of three 'ideological cycles'. The first, lasting from the 1760s to the 1880s, saw the triumph of economic liberalism over feudalism and mercantilism, such that after 1820 economic liberalism became the orthodoxy of governments. The second cycle ran from the 1880s until the mid-1970s. Between the 1880s and the 1930s the ideological battle against economic liberalism was fought and won so that from the 1940s to the 1970s collectivism, based on Fabianism and Keynesianism, was the ruling orthodoxy of all parties and governments. The third cycle ran from the 1930s onwards. From the 1930s to the 1970s, the ideological battle for liberalism against collectivism 'was again fought and won'. From the mid-1970s onwards, liberal political economy became the ruling orthodoxy of all political parties and of governments after the election of the Conservative government led by Margaret Thatcher in 1979[1] (Cockett, 1995:6).

The frameworks described here are just that, frameworks. They identify the boundaries of debates about politics and the economy, but they do not account for cross currents and variations of views between and within parties over issues of collectivism and individualism.[2] Yet they do map onto the history of the UK in that they illuminate the growth in the twentieth century, in particular, of government intervention in the economy and the social world. This culminated after the election of the first majority Labour government in 1945 under Clement Attlee in the creation of a welfare state, providing social security, health and

educational benefits, and a heightened level of peacetime public ownership of key industries, including the coal, electricity, gas and rail industries (Fielding et al., 1995; Clarke, 2004). Broadcasting, established in
1922 in the form of the British Broadcasting Company, was created by
government intervention and sustained, once the organisation became
the British Broadcasting Corporation (BBC) in 1926, as a major, state-
regulated and publicly funded political and cultural institution (Coase,
1950; Briggs, 1961).

The assault on collectivism from the 1930s

World War I (1914–18) had given a boost to collectivist measures, in
the shape of intervention in health, housing and industrial arbitration
machinery. The BBC was created in this context (Curran and Seaton,
2003). According to Richard Cockett the 1930s witnessed the 'low point
of intellectual interest in liberalism' in the UK (1995:21). The depression
of the 1930s had stimulated government interest in planning and state
intervention. The USA, Nazi Germany and the Soviet Union all used the
power of the state to intervene in the economy in the interests of economic development. In addition to the UK's tradition of liberal political
economy the voices of the economists Ludwig Von Mises (1881–1973)
and Friedrich Hayek (1899–1992) were particularly articulate in their
criticisms of interventionism. In 1935, Hayek, who had been appointed
to a chair in economics at the London School of Economics (LSE) in
1932 (Brittan, 2004), edited a book on *Collectivist Economic Planning*
critiquing planning and, in 1936, Von Mises published *Socialism*. In
that book he argued that socialist planning could not work because it
did without the price mechanism, the vital source of information on
which any effective forward planning relied. He denounced mixed economic systems, arguing that planned and market economies could not
work side by side. Lionel Robbins (1898–1984) at the LSE also criticised
interventionism. Indeed the LSE was a particularly important centre for
liberal economics in the 1930s and 1940s (Cockett, 1995:21, 23, 26–37,
53; Brittan, 2004).

Economic liberals criticised the work of economists like John Maynard
Keynes, whose advocacy of state intervention to sustain higher levels
of employment was viewed as allowing politicians to avoid confronting
the economy's underlying weaknesses (outdated industries, trade union
restrictive practices) in the interests of social harmony. In August 1938
a gathering of liberal philosophers and economists met in Paris at 'Le
Colloque Walter Lippman'. Lippman's 1938 book, *The Good Society*, was

one of a number of publications which criticised the apparently unstoppable advance of collectivism since the end of World War I (Cockett, 1995:9–12, 44–5). The use of planning by totalitarian regimes in Nazi Germany and the Soviet Union, plus the dramatic extension of state regulation of the economy and everyday life in the UK during the Second World War (1939–45) led to growing concerns about the threat that collectivism posed to individual liberty.[3]

In 1944 Hayek published *The Road to Serfdom*. He was prompted to write it:

> by his alarm at the number of well-intentioned English writers who naively wished to continue wartime planning systems to direct the economy for conscious purposes in times of peace. He saw such centralised control as a threat not only to prosperity but to freedom.
>
> (Brittan, 2004)

He attacked all parties for their investment in collectivism. There was no middle way between collectivism, a system which would decrease freedom and was inherently undemocratic, and a liberal, competitive economic system. The influence of this publication, popularised by republication in the mass circulation American magazine *Reader's Digest* was profound. In the UK it ultimately 'transformed the nature of the political debate, not as Hayek had vainly hoped, in the Liberal Party, but in the Conservative Party' (Cockett, 1995:79, 87, 97).[4] Other economists at the LSE in the 1940s, notably Arnold Plant, shared and articulated the economic arguments against collectivism; but within this tradition, according to Alan Peacock, 'one turns to Hayek for the rejection on normative grounds of collectivism as a solution of post-war economic problems'. Hayek's contribution was to show that the fact that collectivism is inefficient

> was a proposition which might be accepted or rejected on the basis of reasoned argument and empirical analysis, but that it was totally undesirable on moral grounds whether as Fascism, Nazism, or Socialism was a different order of argument.... In short collectivism in the end cannot tolerate freedom of thought and the associated reconciliation of differences by compromise and toleration.
>
> (Peacock, 1982:36–7)[5]

Nonetheless the interventionist approach epitomised by the economic policies associated with Keynes was, by the 1940s, 'the new intellectual orthodoxy in Britain and its universities' (Cockett, 1995:50; Thompson, 1996:55). For, as Alan Peacock has argued,

> The economic organisation required by total war . . . seemed to provide a concrete case for the longer-term introduction of economic planning on collectivist lines.
>
> (Peacock, 1982:5)

It was the economics department at the LSE, under Lionel Robbins, which was to act as a countervailing influence to collectivism, becoming 'the outstanding centre of economic liberalism in Europe'. In the 1940s and 1950s the department included Hayek and Professor Arnold Plant (1898–1978), R. H. Coase, Frank Paish and Alan Peacock (Cockett, 1995:24–5, 30; Peacock, 1982; Tribe, 2004). The LSE's economics department 'so far as macroeconomic questions were concerned . . . clearly conformed to the . . . Classical Economics tradition in which analysis was closely wedded to the pressing problems of the day' (Peacock, 1982:39). These included attacks on post-war financial policy, by Frank Paish, critiques by Alan Peacock and Jack Wiseman on 'the inefficiency and arbitrariness emanating from a social policy based on public provision of social services at zero cost' and an analysis of the 'brutal tyranny of monopoly' in the public sector in the form of R. H. Coase's work on the BBC (Peacock, 1982:38). Indeed one of the first articles Alan Peacock had to read, as assistant editor of *Economica*, was by Coase on wire broadcasting, which, he has said, 'stimulated my interest and I read his great work on the BBC as a study in monopoly, which was a classic' (Conference Transcripts, 2005: Establishing Peacock).[6] Although there was never 'a concerted attempt by anyone at the LSE to promote a "party line" on policy matters', according to Alan Peacock, those who worked there saw

> their task as that of destroying illusions about the attractiveness of collectivism and dispelling myths surrounding the historical record of capitalism and its alleged 'lackeys' – the Classical Economists. I shall not attempt to measure the influence of their view; sufficient to say that collectivist views are today widely rejected, and if this is so, it is at least partly the result of their writings in the period from the late 1940s to the mid-1950s.
>
> (Peacock, 1982:36, 39–40)

Some of the people at the LSE were directly involved in party politics. Alan Peacock, along with Frank Paish, helped devise an economic policy for the Liberal Party (Peacock, 1982:40). Evan Durbin (1906–48) had trained under Hayek, taught at the LSE and was a member of the Labour Party. He 'was prominent amongst those trying to reconcile classical economics with Socialism', and though he 'sympathised with much of what Hayek had to say', thought 'Hayek had been unfair in his characterisation of Central Planning British style, and asserted that in fact the growth of State interference during the twentieth century had gone hand-in-hand with an extension of liberalism and democracy' (Cockett, 1995:88–9; Peacock 1982:36; Ellis, 2004). Equally, James Meade (1907–95) who had been involved with the Labour Party in the 1930s and who worked at the LSE after World War II developed work which, although Keynesian, also contained 'a liberal position on pricing' which 'did not appeal to a large section of the Labour Party, brought up on the view that market forces were there to be suppressed at the earliest opportunity' (Peacock, 1982:39; Howson, 2004). Alan Peacock eventually withdrew from party politics. The work of Durbin and Meade, however, was to have lasting resonance in the Labour Party, in that they provided a bridge, in the immediate post-war era, between the ideas of the liberal economists and the more collectivist traditions in the Labour movement (Thompson, 1996).

Thus, by the early 1950s the economic liberal critique of collectivism was firmly planted in the academic soil of the UK, and, in particular, in the work of the LSE economists. This work included Coase's on broadcasting (Coase, 1947, 1948, 1950, 1950a). During the 1950s and 1960s recurring economic problems in the UK and a growing body of work among economists in the UK and the USA, promoting anti-collectivist economic policies, contributed to the erosion of confidence in collectivist policies among economists, opinion formers, Whitehall mandarins and politicians. One important factor in promoting a more critical perspective on government intervention and in disseminating an economic critique of public service broadcasting was the work of the Institute of Economic Affairs (IEA).

The Institute of Economic Affairs

The IEA was an important part of post-war pressure group politics and of the post-war critique of collectivism (Cockett, 1995; Denham and Garnett, 2006; Mulgan, 2006; Miller and Dinan, 2008). It developed contacts with politicians, civil servants, academics and journalists to disseminate economic liberalism as a general approach to economic organisation and as an approach to specific areas of the economy, such as broadcasting. It was part of a complex array of factors which, by the mid-1970s, was forcing politicians and civil servants to reappraise the effectiveness of Keynesian approaches to economic management (Thompson, 1996).

Anthony Fisher, a former RAF pilot and businessman, was instrumental in founding the IEA. He read the *Reader's Digest* version of *The Road To Serfdom* and sought out its author, who suggested Fisher should

> join with others in forming a scholarly research organisation to supply intellectuals in universities, schools, journalism and broadcasting with authoritative studies of the economic theory of markets and its application to practical affairs.
>
> (Cockett, 1995:103, 123–4)

The idea was to influence 'those who Hayek had called the "second-hand dealers" in ideas, the journalists, academics, writers, broadcasters who dictate the long-term intellectual thinking of the nation'. Along with Oliver Smedley and J. S. Harding, the IEA was established as a charitable trust on 9 November 1955. Fisher was determined that its work should not be party-political, hence the charitable status, which also allowed it to receive tax-free donations. In spite of the fact that its work touched directly on political issues, the IEA was careful to nurture and defend its non-party status over the years (Cockett, 1995, 131; Harris, 1974). It set out to influence opinion formers by organising lectures and seminars and publishing pamphlets and articles in the press. By 2005 it had an advisory board studded with eminent economists and a list of Honorary Fellows which included R. H. Coase, Alan Peacock and Samuel Brittan, all of whom had by then played a pivotal role in the evolution of thinking and policy around broadcasting in the UK (Booth, 2005:301).[7]

In 1956 Ralph Harris was appointed Director and in 1957 Arthur Seldon became Editorial Director. The IEA's publication programme sought to show 'the efficiency of economic liberalism and to apply the principles of the free market to all areas of economic activity' (Cockett, 1995:142) including, as will be shown later, broadcasting. It set out to influence opinion and policy, and it did.

Among the British politicians who had links with the IEA in the 1960s were the Conservatives, Geoffrey Howe, Enoch Powell, John Biffen, Keith Joseph and Margaret Thatcher, all of whom save Powell were to become pivotal figures in the Conservative governments of

1979–90. In 1967, Douglas Houghton, who had just completed a period as a minister in Harold Wilson's Labour government, published an IEA occasional paper on *Paying for Social Services*. He argued that the country could not afford to continue spending ever-increasing amounts on social services and concluded that people should be encouraged to spend more on social expenditure themselves. In 1970 the future Labour Prime Minister James Callaghan attended an IEA-organised lecture by the liberal economist and monetarist Milton Friedman.[8] By the mid-1970s, especially under the weight of the problems of inflation and rising unemployment, the leadership of both the main parties, the Conservatives more so than Labour, were receptive to critiques of Keynesianism. For example, while working as Chief Economic Adviser to the Department of Industry, Alan Peacock wrote to Arthur Seldon on 15 July 1975 about the reception of the IEA publication by Milton Friedman on *Unemployment versus Inflation* among some ministers in the Labour government under Harold Wilson (1974–6):

> Not surprisingly the . . . pamphlet excited considerable interest in Government circles and you will have received acknowledgement from some of our Ministers that it will receive attention.
>
> (Cockett, 1995:118, 144, 154, 156, 172, 174;
> Harris, 2005a:254; Thompson, 1996)

Shifts in ideas among political elites in this area cannot be attributed solely to the influence of a single pressure group, especially as the changes in economic policy during the 1970s and early 1980s were complex (Coopey and Woodward, 1996a). Indeed Keynesianism, it has been argued, did not die in the 1970s, but survived 'if somewhat mutated' into the twenty-first century (Tomlinson, 2007:429). Nonetheless it is clear that the IEA played a key role in sustaining and disseminating ideas associated with economic liberalism during the 1950s, 1960s and 1970s. In doing this they were aided by supporters in the press.

Arthur Seldon and Ralph Harris put considerable effort in the early years into gaining allies in the press who would notice or review IEA publications. In time these contacts included journalists on the *Financial Times, The Times, The News Chronicle, The Manchester Guardian, The Daily Mail* and *The Daily Telegraph* (Harris, 2005:244; Cockett, 1995, 182–3). In the context of the history of broadcasting and the ideas developed by the Peacock Committee, the most influential figures to align themselves with some of the ideas disseminated by the IEA were Peter Jay of *The Times* and Samuel Brittan of the *Financial Times*.

Peter Jay had worked at the Treasury from 1961 to 1967 where he had been a standard Keynesian economist. During his time as Economics editor on *The Times* (1967–77) he became convinced of the arguments in favour of monetarism, without embracing either Conservatism or Thatcherism, and tried to fit these ideas into a specifically Labour political context. He received IEA publications, attended IEA symposia and, in 1975, gave the IEA Wincott Lecture on 'A General Hypothesis of Employment, Inflation and Politics'. In the 1970s *The Times*, under Jay's influence, became a leading advocate of monetarism (Cockett, 1995:62, 185–8). In spite of being convinced of the arguments for controlling the money supply, Jay has since insisted that his engagement in these debates was not because of a general acceptance of all that the IEA promoted, but was based on a pragmatic approach to economic problems:

> I would certainly have regarded myself as a collectivist in the sense that I would have taken it as axiomatic that there are things which governments must and need to do, and that the distinction between the things they should do and the things they should not do does not rest on some absolute black and white view as to whether or not collective action is of its nature a legitimate or acceptable form of behaviour, but on a view of what the characteristics of the activity in question were.
>
> (Conference Transcripts, 2005: Opening Plenary)

Nonetheless it was via *The Times* that a key plank of IEA thinking garnered support and influence during the 1970s.

Samuel Brittan had studied economics and been taught, briefly, by Milton Friedman. After a stint at the Treasury he became the main economics commentator on the *Financial Times* where he was, for much of the 1960s, a Keynesian. By the late 1960s and, in part, as a result of attending an IEA lecture delivered in 1967 by Friedman, he became converted to a 'broadly monetarist position', and during the 1970s his work on the *Financial Times* 'crystallised much of the monetarist thinking of the period'. Like Jay he retained his independence from, while critically engaging with the work of the IEA (Cockett, 1995:184–5). Brittan has argued that in the middle years of the 1970s he and Jay were 'regarded as two terrible monetarist twins' and indeed together they did much to publicise to the elite readerships of their two papers the work that the IEA promoted on economic policy (Brittan, 1996:14, 20).

The contribution of the press was therefore 'crucial to the transformation in the intellectual climate during the mid-1970s'. This transformation involved a reassertion in policy circles of classical economic liberalism, a reassertion that took many forms, but which the IEA did much to promote. Alan Peacock, Samuel Brittan and Peter Jay were distinguished, independently minded professionals, but they also played their part in promoting this transformation. The IEA provided an important network of contacts, in which all three were involved. The IEA also influenced the establishment of other pressure groups, notably the Adam Smith Institute (ASI), that were to play a role in influencing government policy in the early- and mid-1980s (Cockett, 1995:276, 280, 285, 302). In 1984 the ASI published a report on the communications industry in which it developed liberal approaches to the financing and organisation of broadcasting (Adam Smith Institute, 1984; O'Malley, 1994:19–21).

By the mid-1970s the intellectual and political retreat of collectivist ideas was underway. The work of economists at the LSE and elsewhere in the UK and the USA, plus that of organisations like the IEA had, through argument and publicity, helped create this change. The economic crises of the 1960s and 1970s and the failure of successive Tory and Labour governments to tackle them successfully had provided fertile ground for the revival of classical liberal economics, even if the change did not happen on a large scale until the election of the Conservatives under Margaret Thatcher in 1979 (Thompson, 1996). The general economic ideas that were to underpin the Peacock Report, and key personnel involved in shaping the report (Peacock, Brittan and Jay) operated within this context, as did a post-war tradition of market-orientated criticism of public sector broadcasting that, subsequently, influenced the details in the Peacock Report. This tradition forms the subject of the next two chapters.

Notes

1. The governments of the UK since 1979 have been Conservative, under Margaret Thatcher (1979–83, 1983–7, 1987–90) and John Major (1990–2, 1992–7); New Labour, under Tony Blair (1997–2001, 2001–5, 2005–7) and Gordon Brown (2007–). All were committed to versions of economic liberalism.
2. When the issue of the relationship between the ideas sketched here and the Peacock Report was raised at the Peacock Legacy Conference in 2005, Sir David Nicholas, formerly of Independent Television News, pointed out that these concepts 'never came anywhere near our concerns at all. We were far more rooted in the bread-and-butter business of survival for our various

organisations . . . but certainly this wide canvass . . . [was] nowhere near our concerns' (Conference Transcripts, 2005: Opening Plenary). The truth of this comment does not detract from the fact that the politics driving the policy context to which ITV and ITN were reacting in the 1980s and 1990s were directly influenced by the ideas outlined here. Richard Collins emphasises different aspects of the intellectual heritage from which the Report drew in his contribution to this collection, but not to the extent of undermining the argument put here for recognising the history of ideas that influenced the Peacock Report.

3. George Orwell's *Animal Farm* (1945) and *Nineteen Eighty-Four* (1949) were literary expressions of this concern, from the perspective of a socialist. See Crick (1980).
4. An early reader of Hayek's book was Margaret Roberts, then an undergraduate and, later, as Mrs Thatcher, Prime Minister 1979–90 (Cockett, 1995:99).
5. The idea that collectivism, even if founded in the best of motives, will tend towards the restriction of individual, and consequently general, freedom was the recurring theme of writers, such as Orwell and Hayek in the 1940s and 1950s and found its most celebrated exponent in the work of the philosopher and historian of ideas Isaiah Berlin (see Ignatieff, 2000).
6. The article on wire broadcasting was by Coase (1948). The quotation can also be found in Chapter 12 of this book.
7. Booth (2005) contains a further detailed account by Ralph Harris about the early years of the IEA.
8. Callaghan's government 1976–9 gave serious thought to the policy of monetarism as a tool for curbing inflation (see Callaghan, 1987: 475–7). Yet the IEA's influence on the Labour government was partial and one ingredient in a turbulent period for policy development, see Thompson (1996).

2
Liberalism and Broadcasting Policy from the 1920s to the 1960s

Tom O'Malley

The Peacock Report drew on ideas about broadcasting that had been in circulation from at least the 1920s. This chapter traces some of these ideas across two phases. The first relates, largely, to the pre-television period, from 1922 until 1951; the second looks at how these ideas developed between 1951, the date of the publication of the Beveridge Report (Report, 1951) and 1962, the date of the publication of the Pilkington Report on broadcasting (Report, 1962). A third phase, which traces their presence in the period from 1962 until 1984, the period in which the broadcasting duopoly of the BBC and Independent Television (ITV) matured, is the subject of Chapter 3. In a sense the Peacock Report revived, re-articulated and supplemented an important, but until the 1980s, relatively neglected strand of thinking about broadcasting.[1]

1922–51

Ronald Coase taught economics at the London School of Economics (LSE) from 1934 until 1951 and, subsequently, held chairs in economics at the Universities of Buffalo (1951–8), Virginia (1958–64) and Chicago (1964–81). During World War II (1939–45) he worked in the UK's Central Statistical Office, an experience which did not convince him, or some of his contemporaries at the LSE, of the value of collectivist approaches to the economy. At the outset of a long career, which led to the award of the Nobel Prize in Economic Sciences in 1991 (Ronald Coase Institute, 2007), he published some key works on the BBC's monopoly of broadcasting. (Coase, 1947, 1948, 1950, 1954). These accounts of early broadcasting history preceded Asa Briggs' important study of the origins of the BBC (1961), applied a liberal economic critique to the industry and compiled a history of critical thinking about broadcasting from the 1920s to the 1950s in order to make his case. In his critique of the BBC's monopoly he concluded by making a direct link between political support for a monopoly and the general ideas circulating in society:

> this support for the monopoly also reflects the spirit of the age. According to our temperament, we welcome or acquiesce in the extensions of central planning, even it would appear, when it relates to a source of news and opinion. A monopoly is still regarded with disquiet; but only if it is a private monopoly. A monopoly held by a public authority, as in the case of British Broadcasting, is considered to be free from the vices of private monopolies and to possess virtues of its own.
>
> (Coase, 1950:195–6)

Although, in the period of the BBC's first Charter (1926–36) 'support for the monopoly went almost unchallenged:'

> Criticism of the monopoly was largely based on the threat to freedom of speech and expression which was thought to be implicit in the monopoly; the value of competition as a means of improving programmes was not ignored, but it was a secondary matter compared with the maintenance of free speech.
>
> In addition the advocates of commercial or sponsored broadcasting generally thought of this in terms of maintaining the BBC's monopoly and those in favour of competitive broadcasting thought in terms of non-commercial broadcasting 'or, at least, a large area of non-commercial broadcasting.
>
> (Coase, 1950:141–2)

On 15 November 1926, the Liberal MP, E. A. Harvey claimed in Parliament that 'There is not a single argument that can be used in favour of the liberty of the Press that is not equally applicable to the liberty of the wireless.' In 1934, in a similar vein E. A. Caitlin attacked the monopoly in an article in *The Fortnightly Review*:

> For three hundred years the English people have fought to establish, and have prided themselves in having established, freedom of speech and the Press. In a little more than ten years they have, in principle,

thrown that freedom away. In the case of the most important of all media for disseminating news and opinion, broadcasting, they merely retain the right to say such things as a censor, appointed by a government monopoly, approves beforehand.

(Coase, 1950:134–5, 137)

Neither the Selsdon Committee, set up in 1934 to examine the fledgling TV service, nor the Ullswater Committee's Report on the BBC published in 1936 found against the BBC's monopoly for, according to Coase, the 'thirties were the heyday of the broadcasting monopoly and the proposal that the television services should be placed in the hands of the BBC was hailed by the Press with enthusiasm' (Coase, 1950a). But unease about the monopoly and its implications continued to co-exist in the 1930s and 1940s with the dominant political consensus in favour of the BBC. On 16 January 1935, J. B. Priestley published an article in *The Star* arguing that the Corporation should be divided into two parts with one, the cultural part, under the BBC and another part, devoted to entertainment, organised on commercial lines. An article in the *Economist* on 22 August 1936 advocated splitting the licence fee between two corporations and giving listeners an element of choice by allowing them to distribute a small part of the fee to the one they favoured most (Coase, 1950:136, 141).

The issue of listener choice arose again when, in 1938, a joint committee of the Incorporated Society of British Advertisers and the Institute of Practitioners in Advertising under the chairmanship of Professor Arnold Plant of the LSE produced a 'Survey of Listening to Sponsored Radio Programmes'. This showed that the commercial rivals of the BBC broadcasting from France and Luxembourg, the most famous of which were Radio Normandie and Radio Luxembourg, had audiences on Sundays for some of their programmes that ran into millions. They were funded by advertisements targeted at the UK and by 1934 over ninety companies were placing adverts with the stations. (Thomas, 1966:5; Crissell, 2002:50–1)

As war approached, the issue of the relationship between the organisation of broadcasting and freedom of speech, which was to figure so prominently in the Peacock Report, was reiterated. Kingsley Martin, the socialist and editor of the *New Statesman*, thought competition a way of improving the content of news. In an article on 'Public Opinion and the Wireless', published in the *Political Quarterly* in April 1939, he argued that the BBC monopoly is a mistake. I believe that American wireless, urged by competition, gives a better and less nationalistic service than the British.... It may be that the Canadian method by which a government wireless must compete with those of private companies may be the right solution.

During the war, 1939–45, a series of books and pamphlets were published in which 'emphasis was laid on the threat to free speech which was involved in the maintenance of the monopoly'[2] (Coase, 1950:147).

In 1944 a series of articles appeared in the *Economist* under the title 'A Plan for Broadcasting'. They made the parallel with printing, querying what would have happened had control of the press been monopolised by a public corporation. The choice, the articles argued, was not limited to state monopoly or commercial broadcasting. Use of the then novel FM waveband and wire broadcasting would make it possible to develop a network of local stations. Three corporations could be established; one co-operative, one commercial and one like the BBC, each receiving a fixed proportion of the licence fee. Listeners, on paying the fee, could nominate one of the three to receive the final proportion. This would give the listener a greater choice of programmes and the organisations an incentive to please its listeners more than its rivals (Coase, 1950:148–51).

The issue of freedom of speech, so pertinent during and immediately after the War, when there had been domestic controls on information and when totalitarian regimes in Nazi Germany and the USSR practised ruthless suppression of media freedoms, was highly topical. In January 1946 the Labour government announced it would not establish another committee of inquiry prior to renewing the BBC's Charter, a decision which provoked a flurry of public debate. The controversy contributed to a change of policy and the establishment, in 1949, of a committee under Lord Beveridge to look into broadcasting (Sendall, 1982:4–5; Crissell, 2002:82). Sir Frederick Ogilvie, Director General of the BBC from 1938–42, contributed to this debate in a letter published in *The Times* on 26 June 1946. In a much-quoted passage he argued that

What is at stake is not a matter of politics, but of freedom. Is monopoly of broadcasting to be fastened on us for a further term? Is the future of this great public service to be settled without public inquiry, by Royal Commission or otherwise into the many technical and other changes which have taken place in the last 10 years? Freedom is choice. And monopoly of broadcasting is inevitably the negation of freedom, no matter how efficiently it is run, or how wise and kindly the boards or committees in charge of it. It denies freedom of choice to listeners. It denies freedom of employment to speakers, musicians, writers, actors, and all who seek their chance on the air. The dangers of monopoly have long been recognised in the film industry and the Press and theatre, and active steps have been taken to prevent it. In tolerating monopoly of broadcasting we are alone among the democratic countries of the world.

(Ogilvie, 1946)

Ogilvie had summarised themes that were to recur throughout liberal critiques of public service broadcasting. The dangers posed by the broadcasting monopoly to freedom of speech, employment and listener and viewer choice were contrasted to practice in the press. In addition, the technical possibilities for change were alluded to as reasons for further inquiry. Technology was to become an increasingly important theme, especially in the 1970s, and played a major part in the Peacock Report.

R. H. Coase

The attack on monopoly was elaborated in detailed critiques of British broadcasting developed by Ronald Coase, between 1947 and 1950. In 1947 he published an article on the origins of the BBC's monopoly, which he concluded by arguing that the monopoly was devised for administrative reasons by the Post Office:

The Post Office did not itself wish to operate the broadcasting service. Consequently the only solution was to attempt to establish a single broadcasting company. But the problem to which monopoly was seen as a solution by the Post Office was one of Civil Service administration. The view that a monopoly in broadcasting was better for the listener was to come later.

(Coase, 1947:210)

He followed this up in 1948 with a study of wire broadcasting in Britain. This account surveyed the growth of services that relayed BBC programmes and other, non-BBC overseas services to listeners using wires, and the largely successful attempts by the BBC and the Post Office to limit the range of material offered, so as 'to discourage the expansion of relay exchanges'. He drew attention to the argument of a former BBC employee, P. P. Eckersley that wire services had the potential 'to distribute a large number of different programmes simultaneously', thereby overcoming the limitations of broadcasting over the air. But, he asserted:

> It is unnecessary to consider whether this picture of the broadcasting system of the future is well-founded or not. All that is relevant here is that the monopolistic organisation of broadcasting in Great Britain has made it more difficult of fulfilment.
>
> (Coase, 1948:219–22)

Coase repeated these accounts and arguments in *Broadcasting. A Study in Monopoly*, published in 1950. Pointing to the emergence of public criticisms of the BBC monopoly, he argued that there had been a change between the 1930s and the 1940s:

> there is no reason to suppose that those anxious for the abolition of the monopoly represented more than a small minority. The difference between the position in 1936 and that ten years later was that the monopoly was no longer taken for granted. The monopoly was something to be discussed and justified; but among informed opinion the dominant view was that it should be retained.
>
> (Coase, 1950:176)

In *A Study in Monopoly*, Coase covered many of the issues that were to recur frequently in subsequent decades. On technology he argued that there was no evidence that 'it played a positive role in bringing about support for monopoly,' but once the BBC had been established it had been used to 'reinforce an opinion which was already made upon other grounds'. Even though technological factors dictated that wavelengths be allocated centrally to avoid interference, it did not mean that the same authority should operate broadcasting station and produce programmes, for these were 'separate and separable functions'. The experience in the USA also suggested that you did not need a monopoly to do simultaneous broadcasting. For Coase, technology did not dictate the social form that broadcasting should take (Coase, 1950: 132, 181, 184).

The licence fee came in for criticism. Coase argued that alternatives to the licence fee were not confined to advertisements but included sponsorship which could be from municipalities or universities. The licence fee might also be split, as had been argued in the *Economist*, between different organisations. The idea that the BBC was the best broadcasting organisation in the world and that monopoly was an essential part of this success did not prove that another system, if introduced, would not be better. The view that monopoly was necessary to balance the diet of programmes rested on the questionable claim that a monopolist was justified in determining 'on behalf of the listener which broadcast material he should hear'. The idea that attempts to raise standards of taste in society would be undermined if other stations provided programmes 'which many listeners preferred but which did not contribute to the raising of their standards of taste' was flawed. This assumed that a central body could determine what was good and bad taste and would continue to do so even though tastes change over time. This 'argument would justify and may in fact require a monopoly in a far wider field than broadcasting if its purpose is to be fulfilled' (Coase, 1950:127, 182–3, 189–91).

He picked up and developed the theme of freedom of speech, which was to play such an important part in the argument of the Peacock Report. Coase made use of the fact that during the 1930s, the Tory politician, Winston Churchill, was prevented from expressing his opinions on foreign policy on air because they conflicted with those of the government of the day. This state of affairs would have been less likely if 'some other broadcasting system to which Mr Churchill could have appealed for facilities to broadcast' had existed (Coase, 1950:162, 188–9). Even the BBC's opposition to foreign commercial and wire broadcasting 'was to prevent British listeners from hearing programmes which did not conform to the programme policy of the British Broadcasting Corporation' (Coase, 1950:186). He went on to assert the link between competition and freedom of speech:

> others have emphasised not merely that the programmes may suffer from the absence of competition but that such a concentration of power imperils freedom of speech. To those who believe this to be so, the question whether it would be possible , without establishing a broadcasting monopoly, to secure the degree of control which may be needed over programme content is therefore a vital one.

> But these considerations do not appear to have troubled those supporting the monopoly of broadcasting because they do not seem to have thought that it constituted a threat to freedom of speech.

> (Coase, 1950:186–7)

Indeed the argument that

> a monopoly was required in order that there should be a unified
> programme policy... is powerful... Its main disadvantage is that to
> accept its assumptions it is necessary first to adopt a totalitarian phi-
> losophy or at any rate something verging on it.
>
> (Coase, 1950:191; see also, Coase, 1950a)

Coase's arguments echoed and developed criticisms of the monopoly that had been in circulation since the early days of the BBC. His
book was published while the Beveridge Committee was deliberating.
Beveridge, who also worked at the LSE, read Coase's work on broadcasting. In a letter of 4 October 1949, to the Director General of the BBC,
William Haley, Beveridge invited him to comment on a statement by
Coase about 'the insistence of programme monopoly involving, in the
last resort acceptance of a totalitarian philosophy'. Beveridge and his
fellow committee members 'were prepared to make use of R. H. Coase
and others against monopoly; indeed they gave Coase access to the
evidence they collected.' In the end, the majority on the Committee
came down in favour of monopoly on practical, rather than principled
grounds (Report, 1951; Briggs, 1979:299, 376).

Coase was not alone in pressing for a fundamental rethink of the
organisation of broadcasting. Members of a Liberal Research Group and
individuals from a research group of the socialist Fabian Society argued for
the break up of the monopoly. Others argued for more autonomy for television or for an independent television corporation: these included the
Radio Industry Council, the Radio and Television Retailers Association,
the British Actors Equity Association and the Musicians Union. The
Institute of Incorporated Practitioners in Advertising argued in favour
of commercial radio and the Incorporated Society of British Advertisers
argued that there might be an advantage 'in having a programme that
is not linked consciously or unconsciously in the public mind with the
authority of a semi-official service' (Coase, 1954:212; Briggs, 1979:363,
366–7). The evidence of Beveridge then reflected, in part, an established
body of criticism of the organisational and financial basis of broadcasting. Although the Committee decided in favour of retaining the BBC's
monopoly in radio and television, the arguments recorded in the report
against monopoly and Selwyn Lloyd's minority report in favour of commercial broadcasting contributed to the passage of the 1954 *Television
Act* which introduced advertising financed television to the UK (Briggs,
1979:344–420).

The idea that the BBC should be a monopoly dominated political thinking about broadcasting between 1922 and 1951, but it did not go unchallenged. As Coase's work demonstrated, there were those who criticised the way broadcasting was organised in terms that were to have continuing relevance; the absence of choice; the need for competition; the assumption that a monopoly could know what was best for listeners and viewers; the parallels between broadcasting and press regulation; the possibilities offered by technology; and the linked perspective that monopoly posed a threat to freedom of speech. These ideas drew not only on liberal economic arguments, such as those articulated by economists at the LSE, but also on the contemporary concerns about the threat of totalitarianism emanating from Germany and the USSR. They were to be repeated, supplemented and developed in the context of discussions about broadcasting in the 1950s.

1951–62

The years between 1951 and 1962 saw major changes in UK broadcasting. The Conservative government, elected in 1951, broke the BBC's monopoly. The 1954 *Television Act* established the Independent Television Authority (ITA) which was charged with overseeing the establishment of a network of regionally based television companies funded by advertising. During the 1950s the number of people watching television surpassed those listening to radio in the evenings and the TV moved from a minority pleasure in 1951 to the dominant form of mass entertainment in 1962. This fed directly into the public debate surrounding the establishment of the next major enquiry into broadcasting, known as the Pilkington Committee (1960–2) (Briggs, 1979; Sendall, 1982, 1983; Black, 2003; Sandbrook, 2005:378–408; O'Malley, 2007). After 1954 arguments continued to be put forward by those who wanted to see increased competition, more flexible use of technology and greater consumer choice. In this period, though, it was not only the BBC, but also the fledgling ITV system that came under attack from those who wanted a more market-orientated system of broadcasting.

The debates which preceded the establishment of ITV crossed party lines and reflected the uncertainty that existed in society about the purpose and possible impact of television.[3] Lord Bessborough argued in 1952 that 'the economics of television are very different from those of sound broadcasting, and it seems clear that it will not be possible to run an adequate television service on the licence system.' If *The Times* could be both commercial and of a high standard, why could not television be the same? His was a plea for competition: 'let us not prevent reputable private interests from providing a complementary or alternative television programme' (Bessborough, 1952). Bruce Belfrage, an ex-employee of the BBC, argued that the sponsorship which was at the time being spent on the BBC's foreign-based competitor, *Radio Luxembourg*, could be of use to the Corporation, for instance in the provision of programmes of minority interest. Choice was also an issue:

> The BBC, accepting sponsored programmes, could control time on the air and draw revenue from it for these purposes. The essential point is that anybody who did not like sponsored broadcasting would not have to listen to it.

> (Belfrage, 1952)

Even the 'moving spirit' (Sendall, 1982:19) behind the campaign to prevent advertising-funded television, the Labour MP Christopher Mayhew, was not enamoured of monopoly. He was prepared to see a rival public service broadcaster set up:

> if the national interest now allows more expenditure on TV, let it be British-style, public service TV and not the American-style commercialised kind.

> (Mayhew, 1953: no pagination)

In December 1953, Sir Arnold Plant,[4] who held a chair in commerce at the LSE from 1930 to 1965 and had taught R. H. Coase (Tribe, 2004), argued that television 'can barely afford to meet, from its present sources of revenue, the insatiable demands for services... as no upwards adjustment of the annual viewers' licence fee which is practical will provide the solution'. The licence fee was also 'inconvenient and inequitable'. It could not pay for services 'which very many sections of the public desire and which many would be prepared to pay for, if faced with the alternative that they must otherwise go without them'. The way to deal with problems of finance and choice was to use pay television:

> Technological developments have already indicated the way in which specially expensive programmes, and in particular, those which do not make an equally strong appeal all the time to all owners of broadcast receivers, can be made available through ordinary receivers only to those who are prepared to pay their estimated share of the costs involved.

This was now being done, experimentally, by exploiting the technology used for scrambling and unscrambling confidential telephone calls. TV programmes could be scrambled and released in return for a coin in the slot or a credit-based payments system. All that was needed was for the authorities to direct 'the appropriate technologists to concentrate their attention, as a matter of urgency' on developing devices that could be applied to broadcasting; thus

> If there were a competitive television broadcast service, the negotiation of fees for broadcast rights would be fixed in the market by the competition of rival suppliers and rival broadcasting stations, and the finance of an improved service, including the determination of the appropriate charge to receivers of the scrambled service, would be a normal business venture. It should not be beyond the capacity of a public monopoly to proceed on similar lines. It would be highly regrettable if, wherever broadcasting remained a public monopoly, the service provided lagged in quality and flexibility behind that which alternative systems now have it within their means to provide.
>
> (Plant, 1953:33–6; Anon, 1953)

Plant, a leading exponent of economic liberalism, was thus arguing the case for pay-per-view television and basing his case on changes in technology. This theme was to recur over the next three decades and become increasingly more important to discussion as the technical and political environment changed in the 1970s and the 1980s.

The arguments about the need for more competition in broadcasting did not cease after the establishment of ITV in 1954. In May 1956, Sir Robert Grimston MP, chair of the Backbench Broadcasting Committee of Conservative MPs, 'and others' favoured the further development of the ITV system so that there were a large number of commercial companies competing both with each other and the BBC. The idea that 'the system should be changed to encourage competition between commercial companies... was to dominate much Conservative thinking about the medium for several years' (Milland, 2005:36, 46). In its 1958–9 report on the ITA's *Report and Accounts'* for 1957–8, the Public Accounts Committee of the House of Commons pushed the idea further by advocating, as the Peacock Committee was to 27 years later, putting the contracts for the regional ITV companies out to tender. The Committee took the view that

In future contracts the rentals, representing the contractors' capacity to pay, should be arrived at by competition, provided that the Authority judge the highest bidder to be of standing and technically and financially competent to provide the service.

(Caine, 1968:37–8)

In 1958 Sir Arnold Plant returned to the theme of pay TV in a talk on the BBC's *Third* Programme, subsequently published in *The Listener*. The licence fee finances an 'essential minimum service', he asserted, but it 'cannot meet the cost of... programmes which many sections of the public... would be willing to pay for'. ITV companies were funded by advertising so

if they are to serve their customers, the advertisers . . . they . . . must take particular care that their programmes make a steady appeal to the greatest common factor of the viewing public, that is, the masses.

Thus, much that could be broadcast was too costly and there were insufficient programmes of an educational nature and ones that appealed to small groups of viewers. His suggestion was to establish a third 'additional optional' pay-per-view system, building on the work of companies like the Zenith Corporation of Chicago, which had been doing research and development on subscription radio and television since 1931. Plant had seen their 'pay as you view' system when visiting the USA. The BBC could run the new service as it had 'the expert staff'. Plant was careful to argue that pay television would be an extension of public service television, not a substitute. Nonetheless, as in his 1953 intervention, his approach rested on injecting more choice into the system by using technology to create a direct link between viewer choice and the programmes transmitted (Plant, 1958).

Plant's approach was paralleled in the work of R. H. Coase, who had moved to the USA in 1951. In 1959 he was working on the political economy of American broadcasting. He was interested in regulation and studied the body that licensed US broadcasters, the Federal Communications Commission (FCC). He criticised the very idea of an FCC having control over broadcasting, for if it were ever proposed that 'a commission appointed by a federal government had the task of selecting those who were to be allowed to publish newspapers and periodicals' it 'would, of course, be rejected out of hand as inconsistent with the doctrine of freedom of the press':

Many of those who have acquiesced in this abridgement of freedom of the press in broadcasting have done so reluctantly, the situation being accepted as a necessary, if unfortunate, consequence of the peculiar technology of the industry.

In 1951 Leo Herzel, writing in the *University of Chicago Law Review*, had proposed that the price mechanism be used to allocate frequencies. Coase advocated using the price mechanism along with the creation of property rights as a way of allocating 'scarce frequencies'. The idea that a 'private enterprise system cannot function properly unless property rights are created in resources' was based he pointed out, with more than a tinge of irony, on the

'novel theory' (novel with Adam Smith). . . that the allocation of resources should be determined by the forces of the market rather than as a result of government decisions.
(Coase, 1959:7, 12, 14, 17, 18)

On 11 December 1959, he urged the FCC to auction frequencies, selling or leasing them to the highest bidder, so as to avoid the time-consuming procedures involved in frequency allocation, to rule out the inefficient use of frequencies, to avoid the arbitrary enrichment of station owners in possession of FCC licences and 'to avoid the threat to freedom of the press in its widest sense which is inherent in the present procedures, weak though that threat may be at the moment'. He linked the argument about the price mechanism to the contemporary Cold War suspicion of socialism in the USA:

Much is made of the fact that with commercial television the service is free. The argument is essentially the same as that for socialism and the Welfare State. What is being attacked is the price mechanism. The factors of production used in television are not made available for nothing. They will be paid for by someone: the government, out of taxation, the advertiser, or the consumer. What is important is that the factors of production should be used where their output is most valuable, and this is most likely to happen if the use of factors of production is determined by what consumers are willing to pay.
(Coase, 1961:53, 56)

Coase's attacks on the nature of regulation, therefore, not only referred back to the contrast between press freedom and state regulation of broadcasting, but also vigorously asserted the primacy of the market, through the mechanisms of pricing and property rights in frequencies. Writing at the same time as Plant, his North American audience was much more at home with the principles of free enterprise. The latter was writing for an audience in a country with a Welfare State and with a successful, popular system of public service broadcasting, in which commercial television had just been established. Nonetheless, they were both cogent voices for change and their arguments left permanent impressions on future discussions.

The Pilkington Committee

The Conservative Party was re-elected to government in 1959 and was thereafter faced with the problem of making decisions about the continuance of both the BBC's Charter and the statutory arrangements for ITV. Dan Ingman of the American advertising agency, Young and Rubicam, spoke to Conservative MPs on 1st February 1960. He criticised ITV's monopoly of advertising, argued for a third advertising-funded channel and suggested that the BBC could be financed by advertising (Milland, 2005:43, 154). There were divisions within the party between paternalists, prepared to live with the post-1954 situation and those pressing for more competition. ITV's profitability, stemming from its monopoly of TV advertising, had provoked widespread concern and comment, which fed into public debate about the future of broadcasting. The government finally decided to deal with the issue by establishing a 'Committee on Broadcasting' chaired by the industrialist Sir Harry Pilkington.[5] The terms of reference were constructed so as to allow for the possibility of alternative forms of distribution and finance:

> To consider the future of broadcasting services in the United Kingdom, the dissemination by wire broadcasting and other programmes, and the possibility of television for public showing; to advise on the services which should in future be provided in the United Kingdom by the BBC and the ITA; to recommend whether additional services should be provided by any other organisation; and to propose what financial and other conditions should apply to the conduct of all these services.
>
> (Report, 1962:1)

The Report, when published in 1962, endorsed the BBC's practices but savaged ITV, not because it was a monopoly, but because in the judgement of the Committee it failed to match up to high standards of public service broadcasting, a failure rooted in its dependence on advertising revenue (Milland, 2005). This conclusion was reached in spite of pressure from a politically credible, well-financed industrial lobby which was pressing for more competition in television in the form of pay TV. Indeed, the BBC was very concerned about the pressure for subscription television. The Director General of the BBC, Hugh Greene, 'had decided' by 1960, 'that pay-television was likely to be recommended by Pilkington' (Milland, 2005:121–2). In the end Pilkington rejected the idea on the grounds of cost and because it was unlikely to 'significantly increase the range and quality of programmes' (Report, 1962:270–1).[6]

Yet the issue had been very firmly on the agenda. Companies like British Home Entertainment Ltd, Choiceview Ltd, Tolvision, Associated Rediffusion, the Rank Organisation, British Telemeter Home Viewing Ltd, Teleglobe Pay-TV System Inc and the Zenith Radio Corporation pushed for subscription services (Report, 1962:262–71, 326). Tolvision's argument invoked the idea of choice and the importance of linking what was produced with what viewers wanted:

> We would be governed by what the public wants to see, and, as we will be paid for our programmes, we will have to give them the programmes that we feel they would want to see and pay for because, whenever they look into our programmes, it is going to cost them money.

The subject generated discussion and comments from at least 33 other organisations, companies and individuals who submitted evidence.[7] One of them was Christopher Mayhew, who had been a leader of the campaign against the introduction of commercial television. He was highly critical of ITV and not only thought that pay TV had 'an extremely bright future' but gave personal evidence to the Committee in support of the idea (Report, 1962:261–71; Milland, 2005:53–4, 122–3).

The Treasury considered that the question of whether the BBC should be funded by advertising or subscription raised 'fundamental questions of broadcasting policy' which it declined to comment on prior to the publication of the Committee's report (Report, Appendix E, 1962:3). The government, however, did consider it a possibility as the BBC Chairman Sir Arthur Fforde learnt in a meeting with Reginald Bevins, the Post Master General on 25 July 1962 after the publication of the Report (Milland, 2005:176). Harry Pilkington, however, was against pay

TV and so the Cabinet could not support it (Conference Transcripts, 2005: Opening Plenary). The Treasury and the Post Office considered the issue of finance in a joint paper prepared in May 1962 for internal discussion by a ministerial committee on the future of broadcasting. The ideas floated in this document included a levy on ITV, which in the end was the preferred option. But, one idea it considered, which was reminiscent of Coase's arguments (1959, 1961), was 'that contracts are let to the highest bidder who could give a satisfactory service, excess revenue over ITA needs being siphoned off to the Exchequer'. Within days of the publication of the report in June 1962, Alan Wolsencraft, Director of Radio and Television Services at the Post Office, drew up a paper including a list of ways of extracting 'the true market value' of licence payments to the Exchequer. These included competitive tendering 'among suitably qualified applicants' (Milland, 2005:169, 182).

This focus on what to do about ITV had been given added impetus by Pilkington's negative verdict on commercial TV. The report recommended that 'so long as independent television is constituted and organised as at present, it should not provide additional services.' The ITA was to take over programme planning and the sale of advertising revenue from the contractors. Sponsored, pay and subscription TV were rejected (Report, 1962:290, 294). Among Tory MPs there was considerable feeling 'that "the strictures on ITV" were grossly exaggerated. Some members expressed the view that "the first essential was to break the advertising monopoly"' (Milland, 2005:151). Nonetheless others 'were declaring themselves wholly in favour not only of the specific recommendations, but of the principles and arguments that underlay them' (Political Correspondent, 1962). There was division in the ranks of the Conservative Party, as Jeffrey Milland has demonstrated, between paternalists and those wanting more competition, and, in the end, the government responded by rejecting the wholesale restructuring of ITV recommended by Pilkington. It did, however, impose requirements on the ITA to ensure higher quality programming, especially in peak viewing times, and agreed that the BBC could have the third channel. This became BBC2, which started in 1964 (Milland, 2005; Crissell, 2002).

In the aftermath of the publication of the report, the case for more competition and choice continued to be made. In July 1962, Geoffrey Crowther, former editor of *The Economist* (1938–56), reminded the readers of *The Times* that 'monopoly of broadcasting is obviously dangerous and undesirable' and that 'if one thing is quite clear from the ITV experiment, it is that competition has been very good indeed for the

BBC.' He advocated a system of three networks, each taking a quarter of the licence fee, with the final quarter being allocated by members of the public expressing a preference when paying the fee; each 'would also be permitted to sell a portion of its time, subject to stringent controls'. This was the plan he had printed in *The Economist* in 1944 and which he had submitted as evidence, along with Sir Robert Watson-Watt, to Beveridge. Its merit was 'competition without undue commercialism' (Crowther, 1962; Coase, 1950:148–51).

On 13 July 1962, the Chairman of British Home Entertainment, took up the cudgels, and advocated 'a Pay Television service providing "first class" programmes which intelligent viewers want and do not now get'. Simultaneously he raised the issue of computers and the possibility of linking developments in this area to national economic development and to pay TV:

> We are entering the computer age, and a keystone to prosperity in the second half of the twentieth century is going to be electronic communication... I have noted that though the Pilkington Committee's mandate included 'to consider... dissemination by wire of broadcasting...' the report *admits* that no proper study of this has in fact been made. Should not such an investigation now be undertaken by the Government before decisions on this aspect of the Pilkington report are taken?

In language foreshadowing discussions about electronic publishing and the economic benefits of a national fibre optic grid, which rose to prominence in the 1970s and 1980s, he asserted that:

> An 'electronic grid' used by commerce and industry would be a big stimulus to the productivity of the nation. It could also transmit an educational service and provide 'links' between schools, colleges and universities; it would facilitate the change over of line standards; and it could be used for police and defence purposes. These are but a few of the more obvious applications of the grid. Pay Television would be one of its many customers, paying its rent for the use of the grid.
>
> (Slim, 1962)

The IEA joined in the debate by republishing a pamphlet on *TV: From Monopoly to Competition – And Back?* (Altman et al., 1962). A copy of the first edition was sent, to Richard Hoggart, a key member of the

Pilkington Committee, in April 1962. Hoggart thought it 'a shabby piece of work' and that its pro-ITV position, 'might stiffen any sinews that needed stiffening' and increase anti-ITV feeling (Milland, 2005:93). Regardless of Hoggart's opinion, the pamphlet contained ideas that were to have, in time, as large an impact on the way broadcasting policy developed as Pilkington's recommendations had on the nature of ITV and the BBC in the 1960s and the 1970s.

Walter Altman was a freelance journalist who had published in *The Times, Financial Times, Guardian, Observer* and the business press, as well as working on business magazines. David Sawers had done some academic economics and worked as industrial correspondent on the *Economist*. Denis Thomas was deputy editor of Independent Television News, a former industrial journalist and *Daily Mail* television critic (Altman et al., 1962). As Arthur Seldon pointed out in the preface to the first edition, the themes of the pamphlet were classic territory for economic liberals – 'the economic theme of competition and monopoly and the related sociological theme of free choice and good choice' (Altman et al., 1962:3). Economics was not the strong point of the Report as David Sawers' damning verdict made abundantly clear:

> Its obsession with hackneyed complaints about the nature of television programmes, and especially their triviality, which it approvingly quotes as 'more dangerous to the soul than wickedness', its parading of gossip and hearsay as evidence, its exclusive pre-occupation with the weary choice between the BBC and ITA, and its inclinations towards paternalistic control to raise standards, gave an aura of auntieness to the Report that got most journalists' goat. The tedious and unconvincing argument of much of the Report blinded critics to the elements of good that lie buried beneath the bad... its most glaring omission was a study of the economic factors.
>
> (Sawers, 1962:71)[8]

Altman drew directly on Coase's *British Broadcasting. A Study in Monopoly*, which he described as a 'brilliantly clear analysis of the origins of the monopoly' that 'left disturbing doubts concerning the arguments of those who created and defended it'. He also cited Sir Frederick Ogilvie's letter to *The Times* of July 1946 about the dangers of monopoly, the anti-monopoly evidence submitted to Beveridge by the Fabian Research Group, the Liberal Research Group and Crowther and Watson-Watt and Selwyn Lloyd's minority report (Altman, 1962:11, 18, 28).

The related issue of choice was developed in the pamphlet. Pilkington was attacked for being 'paternalist' a position which Sawers considered fundamentally undemocratic. The Report was

> concerned that people should not be exposed to degrading influ-
> ences and that accordingly the organisation of broadcasting services
> should not be entrusted to competing suppliers who would tend
> to give them what they would like. Whatever may be said for this
> approach, it is difficult to fit it into the theory of democracy which
> places power in the hands of the people and accepts their decisions
> with the accompanying results and risks.
>
> (Sawers, 1962:74)

There was a fundamental denial of choice embodied in the Pilkington approach:

> Nowhere did the Committee consider means of allowing the viewer
> to exercise wider choice among television programmes as he does
> with every other form of entertainment (except radio) because it had
> convinced itself that the choice must be administered by approved
> broadcasters who cannot be drawn into giving the public the variety
> it is acknowledged to want.
>
> (Sawers, 1962:88–9)

Choice was an indispensable means of building responsibility in citizens, it was an 'educator' and, having cited John Stuart Mill on the importance of not allowing people to 'grow up mere children', he argued that

> People will not learn to choose better if they do not learn to discrimi-
> nate between good and bad. To teach them to improve their choice
> they need not a system which chooses for them but one which
> allows them to choose for themselves.
>
> (Sawers, 1962:90–1)

Consequently

> Even allowing for the Committee's prejudice against relying on
> advertising revenue, its efforts would have been better directed to
> devising methods of allowing the viewers' choices to affect directly
> the revenue of the programme suppliers than to recommending
> market research as a way of ascertaining his opinions. When it is

possible to do so directly by pay-TV and indirectly by other means, the neglect by the Committee suggests a luke-warm attitude to the ideal of giving democracy the challenge of fuller and freer choice.

(Sawers, 1962:90)

By the late 1980s, immediately after the publication of the Peacock Report, choice had become a recurring theme in the language used by the Tory government in policy documents on broadcasting.[9]

The pamphlet also raised the issue of freedom from state control. Sawers argued that public corporations, even if run by individuals who 'try to present a balanced picture', were vulnerable to pressure; for, 'if these bodies depend on the Government for finance, they cannot escape covert desires to avoid offence. Commercial and political control have their weaknesses but commercial power can be disciplined by competition.' In fact the Pilkington Committee had taken a step towards greater centralised control by creating 'an ambitious programme for social engineering that might equally apply to press, films, theatre, books – and all other means of communicating ideas'. The answer was less, not more, control. He suggested a revision of the 1954 *Television Act* to remove 'the requirement that the contractors present a proper balance of points of view on all controversial issues' (Sawers, 1962:73–5, 112).

Denis Thomas argued that competition was the principle which should guide policy. ITV had provided competition for the BBC and in turn ITV had to compete with the Corporation (Thomas, 1962:64). In addition, 'to some extent an element of competition exists between major contractors, and to a lesser extent the smaller regional contractors' (Altman, 1962:36). The suggestions made by Crowther and Watson-Watt to the Beveridge Committee seemed to 'provide the best means of allocating the licence revenue' as viewers would 'be able to say at the end of each year which service seemed to them most deserving of support'. Nonetheless

For television the sky should be the only limit. Governments ought to organise as much competition as can be crammed into present wavelengths, and welcome any technical developments in broadcasting or wire that may enlarge the scope for still more competition in future.

(Sawers, 1962:115, 119)

The stress on more competition involved a criticism of ITV's monopoly of advertising revenue and its network system. The latter involved the larger companies controlling the number, type and income from programmes transmitted simultaneously on all regional companies at peak time, a practice known as networking:

> Commercial television has undeniably done many stimulating things in its first six years. But it has become a monopoly- a collective monopoly, perhaps, but a monopoly just the same . . . The programme companies never encroach on each other's preserves. By reciprocal manipulation of the network system, they manage to show the same block of programmes simultaneously throughout the country. The less enterprising companies can make a good living out of this system indefinitely. Is that what the Television Act intended?
>
> (Thomas, 1962:65)

The way forward was to allow the ITV companies to run a new service for four hours each evening to serve 'a minority audience, which by its standard would attract a different kind of advertiser' (Thomas, 1962:65, 68). Another suggestion was that

> a third service should be started, subsidised by the profits of the ITA contractors, on which any organisation that wanted to produce a programme could appear and the BBC itself buy time. The ITA would provide studio accommodation that could be rented, and the broadcaster could sell advertising time on his programme.
>
> (Sawers, 1962:105)

The problem of insufficient competition and ITV's monopoly would ultimately be overcome by pay TV and advances in technology. Pay TV was 'a case study in the Pilkington Committee's cavalier treatment of viewers' choice'. Not only had it rejected pay TV it had also paid it insufficient attention. The fact, however, that mainstream audiences were well catered for by ITV and BBC suggested that pay TV would develop through economic necessity 'into providing precisely those programmes most lacking from the present services' (Sawers, 1962:91–2). The level of choice and competition that pay TV could offer was obviously linked to technology. Sawers thought 'there was no knowing where technical development may lead it in the next 10 or 20 years' (Sawers, 1962:74). Improvements in wire broadcasting of TV programmes looked likely in the next decade. For, at the International Television Conference held in May 1962, Dr R. C. C. Williams suggested

> that it might soon be possible to transmit 18 programmes over one cable; this development could provide an alternative to wire-less

broadcasting and offer an even wider potential range of programmes. He suggested that a 'national electronic grid' could be established to carry up to 100 television signals between the main centres of population, thereby providing a new means of communication for business and other purposes as well as carrying more television programmes. The means of transmitting television programmes thus seem potentially plentiful in the future.

(Sawers, 1962:103)

The arguments promoted by the IEA on monopoly, choice, competition and pay TV clearly had no immediate impact on policy. The outcome of the debates around Pilkington was that the BBC was given the third channel, and ITV the 1963 *Television Act*. The Postmaster General, Reginald Bevins, did not accept the structural reform of ITV proposed by Pilkington, but did accept 'the criticisms of ITV, and incorporated the substance of them in the 1963 Act, despite considerable opposition from inside the Cabinet, and from Tory backbenchers'. This was the outcome of a successful alliance between 'those who wished to restrain what they saw as the excesses of ITV, and the Treasury, anxious to increase its revenue' (Milland, 2005:22, 164). The ITA was given more authority to insist on higher standards in commercial programmes, and a tax in the form of a levy was raised on the contractors but, even so, they remained profitable businesses.

The period 1951–62 was one in which TV expanded dramatically and this expansion was accompanied by controversy (Black, 2003; O'Malley, 2007). One aspect of this public controversy was the development of the critique of broadcasting outlined here, which had its roots in economic liberalism. Many of the ideas, about monopoly, choice and freedom of speech, had been in circulation since the 1920s. In these years they were applied with vigour to TV. Ideas criticising ITV's monopoly over advertising, advocating auctioning franchises and utilising technical developments to push the idea of choice and competition through pay TV were articulated and developed drawing on technical and academic work in both the USA and the UK. The period from 1962 to 1984 witnessed the intensification of debate about broadcasting policy and the further elaboration of the ideas described in this chapter. The key differences were that by the mid-1970s the political tide had begun to turn and the solutions to questions of public policy offered by economic liberals were becoming politically acceptable within the leadership of the Conservative Party. In addition by the end of the 1970s, it was clear that technological change had moved on considerably and that it presented the opportunity for radical change in the structure, organisation and finance of broadcasting. It is to these issues that we turn in the next chapter.

Notes

1. This chapter does not explore the rich body of socialist and progressive thinking about broadcasting that co-existed and, at times, overlapped, with the ideas described here (see Curran, 1986; Briggs, 1995:782–8; Freedman, 2003; O'Malley, 2007).
2. These included, according to Coase, R. S. Lambert's *Ariel and all its Quality* (1940), P. P. Eckersley's *The Power Behind The Microphone* (1940), P. Bloomfield's *BBC* (1941) and pamphlets by Sir Ernest Benn, *BBC Monopoly* (1941), and A. C. Turner, *Broadcasting and Free Speech* (1943) (Coase, 1950:147).
3. Briggs (1979) remains the best summary of the debates preceding the establishment of ITV. But see also, Sendall (1982) and Wilson (1961).
4. Plant was a member of the pro-commercial TV pressure group, the Popular Television Association (Briggs, 1979:913).
5. For full accounts of the Pilkington debates, see Briggs (1995) and Milland (2005).
6. One economist who analysed the strengths and weaknesses of the duopoly, at the time, considered the principal danger of subscription was its potential 'to skim the cream from existing programmes and programme producers rather than enrich the mixture' (Steiner, 1961:128).
7. These included Associated Television; Association of Headmistresses, British Board of Film Censors, British Boxing Board of Control; BBC; British Film Producers Association; British Institute of Radio Engineers; British Lion Films; Cinematograph Exhibitors Association South Wales and Monmouthshire Branch; Commonwealth National Committee; Communist Party of Great Britain; Concert Artiste's Association; Independent Group of Conservatives; Professor Boris Ford; General Post Office; Granada TV Network Ltd; Incorporated Society of British Advertisers; Independent Television Authority; National Broadcasting Development Committee; New Left Review Ltd; Picturedome (Eastbourne) Ltd; Pye Ltd; Relay Services Association of Great Britain; Society of Film and Television Arts Ltd; Television and Screenwriters' Guild; Theatres' National Committee; Trades Union Congress; T. W. W. Ltd; Variety Artiste's Federation; Viewers and Listener's Association; Mr John Whitehead; Woodrow Wyatt (Report, 1962:299–33).
8. Baroness Wooton of Abinger also felt that 'Great disappointment, however, must be felt by all concerned with social investigation at the poor quality of the evidence on which their assessment of programmes appears to have been made, and at their failure to undertake any first hand research. A great opportunity for a really objective review has been missed' (Wooton, 1962). An economist writing on the report asserted that 'it was written as if there was no such thing as *social science*, as if discursive and not rigorous reasoning were man's only tools' (Wiles, 1963:183).
9. See Home Office (1987, 1988).

3
Technology, Politics and Economics, 1962–84

Tom O'Malley

This chapter surveys some of the key interventions in debates about broadcasting policy between 1962 and 1984, most, but not all of which, drew on a framework based on liberal economics. The period after the 1963 Television Act saw the consolidation of UK broadcasting around the duopoly of Independent Television (ITV) and the BBC. There was considerable controversy about individual programmes and policies, but there remained, until at least 1979, a dominant political consensus in favour of state-regulated public service broadcasting funded by the licence fee (BBC) and advertising (ITV, Independent Local Radio). This consensus allowed for competition for audiences, but not for income, on the grounds that such competition might lower the quality and restrict the range of programmes (Briggs, 1995; Sendall, 1983; Potter, 1989, 1990; Curran and Seaton, 2003). There was rapid development of socialist and left of centre criticism of broadcasting and, for a time in the 1970s, this trend took centre stage in debates about broadcasting (Briggs, 1995; Freedman, 2003). These were also the years in which economic liberals, academics, journalists and the Institute of Economic Affairs (IEA) regularly attacked the system. By the early 1980s, therefore, there existed a body of ideas drawing on liberal economic thinking which had developed since the 1920s and formed the intellectual tradition out of which the ideas in the Peacock Report grew. Many of these ideas were disseminated in publications produced by the IEA.

Radio and economic freedom

In 1964 pirate radio stations, broadcasting from just outside UK territorial waters, began to offer a popular, advertising-funded diet of chat and pop music to the British public. They were part of a long-standing attempt, dating back to the 1930s, to break the BBC's monopoly in radio and were supported by advertisers, entrepreneurs and Tory politicians. The activities of the pirates provoked fierce controversy. The Labour governments under Harold Wilson (1964–70) responded by outlawing them with the 1967 *Marine Broadcasting Act*. The BBC set up the pop-based channel Radio 1 in the same year, and simultaneously launched its local radio service (Local Radio Workshop, 1983:5–22; Chapman, 1992; Briggs, 1995; Rudin, 2007).

In 1966 Denis Thomas, in an IEA publication, *Competition in Radio*, pointed out that the potential for competition in radio existed in the form of '120 companies registered and waiting to enter local broadcasting'. He cited Sir Frederick Ogilvie's 1946 letter to *The Times* attacking monopoly and pointed to the 'weighty evidence against the BBC monopoly' submitted to Beveridge. He also used Ronald Coase's work to raise the issue of auctioning (Coase, 1959). Thomas argued that

> Some economists have refused to accept that broadcasting facilities should be kept out of the operation of the free market. Orthodox administrators take fright at the notion that non-commercial radio users such as the police and the armed forces should be required to bid for all the allocations of wavelengths against, for instance, taxi firms, business networks, oil companies and film-makers on location. Professor R. H. Coase, in his study of the political economy of broadcasting in America,[1] pointed out that because broadcasting companies have never had to pay for their licences, many of them have made fortunes by buying and selling franchises – the right to radio frequencies – worth millions of dollars. Should the allocation of a licence to broadcast – issued free by a government department – be the equivalent in radio of Lord Thomson's 'licence to print money'? . . . No one suggests that publishers and newspapers proprietors should be licensed by the state. They are free to buy and sell each other's businesses in pursuit of profit.
>
> (Thomas, 1966:11–12)

More specifically, Thomas attacked BBC2, which went on air in 1964. It was 'non-competitive' and had 'felt no need to establish a distinctive identity' as a result of which 'It must stand as the most graphic example in recent times of the impossibility of reconciling paternalistic planning with democratic wants' (Thomas, 1966:23–4). As far as he was concerned 'the notion that the BBC alone, has a moral or prescriptive right to set up a local radio system is baseless.' Pilkington's objections to 'the whole concept of commercial broadcasting' were not shared by 'Press or parliament' and

> The success and popularity of ITV have gone a long way towards over-coming prejudice, except in the minds of unregenerate paternalists who believe in the principle that direction by a central bureaucracy is 'better' for us than the operation of free choice.
>
> (Thomas, 1966:21)

He went on to attack opponents of commercial pirate radio. Their hostility was 'a reflex action by established interests to unwelcome competition'. The argument that the quality of pirate broadcasts was 'below acceptable standards' was dismissed as an attack on popular taste: the BBC itself knows well enough how capricious 'acceptable standards' can be. Contempt for popular pleasures is not a democratic reason for banning them' (Thomas, 1966:28). Popular choice was not only a matter of taste it was also about democracy – the right of the public to have a say in what they wanted to listen to:

> Freedom of the air means the right of people to listen to any broadcast of their choice, free from government dictation. To refuse people such freedom simply because unlicensed radio has knocked a hole in the fabric of state protectionism seems an abject denial of consumer wants – and voters' choice.
>
> (Thomas, 1966:28)[2]

The IEA returned to television policy in 1968 publishing Sir Sydney Caine's *Paying For TV?* (Caine, 1968). Caine had graduated in economics from the London School of Economics (LSE) in 1922. His career in the Civil Service focused on the economic governance of the British colonies, and in 1947 he became Assistant Under-Secretary of State for the colonies. From 1957 until his retirement in 1967, he was Director of the LSE, and a member of the Independent Television Authority (ITA) from 1960 to 1967. He believed that governments exercised too much control over universities and so, in 1973, chaired the planning board for the UK's first independent university, the University of Buckingham, where Alan Peacock was the first Vice-Chancellor (1978–84) (Veljanovski, 1989:261; Pugh, 2004). Linked to the LSE, the IEA and the ITA it is not surprising that his pamphlet reflected the economic liberalism of the first two organisations and the experience of having been at the centre of the regulation of commercial TV.

ITV was 'viewed to some extent by a large majority of the population' and in 'economic terms there can be no question that a want has been met and a satisfaction provided'. Nonetheless there were problems. One was that the system, being based on advertising, lacked a direct link between the service provider and viewers because

> the income is not derived from the users of the service which it is the primary purpose of the system to supply, but from the users of an incidental or supplementary service (advertising).

In addition the system was 'a series of local monopolies without any of the ordinary safeguards against monopoly profits' (Caine, 1968:1–12, 23).

Another problem was the opaqueness of the method used by the ITA to award franchises to run the ITV regions. The ITA had never indicated 'in detail' the criteria it used to award these and in the 1967 round of awards 'there was a good deal of understandable concern about the whole procedure; and discussion in the press and in Parliament on whether an alternative method could be devised' (Caine, 1968:17, 32). Echoing Coase (1959) and the discussions in government about auctioning during the Pilkington process (Milland, 2005:169, 182), Caine thought that 'the balance of advantage has shifted towards the competitive tender:'

> The merits of a tender system lie not in any competitive element which it would introduce but in its effectiveness in diverting to the public coffers part of the 'surplus' income generated by commercial television, in relieving the ITA from the invidious task of arbitrarily selecting the prize winners in the periodic contract-awarding exercises and in assuring the public of the impartiality of such awards. Its dangers lie in the possible reduction of the effectiveness of the public authority in controlling the actual operations of the monopolist.
>
> (Caine, 1968:39)

In addressing the question of how to finance television, Caine's cautious approach pointed to some of the problems which the Peacock Committee dealt with when considering the possibility of putting advertising on the BBC:

> Extension of advertising – financing to the two BBC channels would have different financial effects. It would be a real extension of the viewing audience open to the advertiser; it would indeed come near

to doubling it. Viewer-time available for sale would thus show a real increase. Whether advertising income would increase proportionately is more doubtful; that must depend on the elasticity of the demand for television time by advertisers at current rates. There could be a reasonable chance that enough additional advertising income would be generated to cover the cost of two BBC channels as well as two commercial channels, but the chances of there being any large surplus over the costs of operation would be much reduced; and there might be a deficiency.

(Caine, 1968:47)

Pay-TV could make a major contribution towards solving the problem of financing broadcasting[3] as neither the licence fee nor advertising gave 'any assurance that the amount of resources directed to television corresponds at all closely with viewers' preferences'. Under pay-TV, however, 'the resources made available are determined by what viewers think it worth paying.' Pay-TV 'would establish a direct relationship between costs and consumer satisfactions because the income of the providers of pay-TV would be directly dependent on the amount of viewing'. If a system of pay-TV companies competing with one another were established, 'there would for the first time be something like a market in television.' The technical problems were not 'insuperable' (Caine, 1968:5, 35, 50).

Pay-TV would 'establish for television a system of financing which has for centuries been accepted as normal for the press'. To do this the widespread assumption held by British governments 'since radio first emerged, that it is somehow out of the question to put broadcasting in the state of freedom which is universally believed essential for the press' would have to be abandoned. Ultimately pay-TV and advertising should finance all broadcasting. That meant the end of the licence fee:

In my view the ideal future system would be one in which all television services, whether provided by the BBC or by commercial contractors, were provided through pay-television receivers and financed by a combination of payment by viewers on the basis of time spent in viewing and the sale of advertising time. The television licence fee would be abolished. All providers of programmes would be under common obligations as regards programme balance and other controls . . . so that there would be equal competition between them both for audience and for advertising.

(Caine, 1968:53, 57)

Caine had therefore taken ideas about freedom of expression, competition and choice and, using the ideas about pay-TV that had been mooted by Arnold Plant, produced a synthesis. These ideas, as well as those he discussed on auctioning, advertising and consumer satisfactions all found a place in the Peacock Report.

The BBC and ITV – public scrutiny and efficiency

Discussion about the financing of broadcasting was not limited to the question of pay-TV, nor did they have to await the stimulus given by the appointment of the Peacock Committee in 1985. The economics of the BBC and ITV was an ongoing subject of discussion and scrutiny in the 1960s and 1970s. In 1966 Hugh Greene, the Director General of the BBC, stated that 'whether we like it or not, money is, for the BBC as for other public broadcasting organisations, the basis of their programme policy.' For Greene the British public had 'accumulated an investment in the BBC' even though 'Enjoyment is not a matter which can be shown on the balance sheet.' Broadcasters needed 'a determination . . . to look to the long-term economy of their operation' (Greene, 1967:3, 15).

Indeed the BBC maintained that it kept a tight watch over its resources. In 1969, Greene's successor as Director General, Charles Curran addressed the Institute of Cost Works Accountants about BBC finances. He pointed out that when outside consultants, McKinsey, were brought in to study the BBC's practices, the Corporation's Finance Division provided them with

> papers covering an enormous range of subjects . . . for example . . . an analysis of the cost of all television output by departments, showing separately live performances, repeats and distinguishing programmes bought from other producing organisations over a number of years.
>
> (Curran, 1969:6–7)

The BBC felt the need to defend its financial record in public at a time of rising costs, which were putting the licence fee under pressure and scrutiny. In 1970 the Controller of Finance at the BBC, Barry Thorne, argued that the forthcoming decade held out 'uncertainty about our immediate income in the future' when the 'calls for restraint, the state of the economy, the political situation' were all 'inevitably part of the background' and would remain so until 'some device is found to remove the decision' over the licence fee 'from the purely political field'. Nonetheless the BBC was used to having its affairs 'kept under fairly constant scrutiny' by outside bodies such as the Public Accounts Committee, the Estimates Committee of the House of Commons, the Post Office, the Treasury and official committees such as Beveridge and Pilkington (Thorne, 1970:5, 17). Although the BBC was familiar with the external scrutiny of its financial affairs, it was, however, a scrutiny which focused on questions of adequate funding, efficient use of resources and proper forward planning, within a political context that did not seriously challenge the licence fee.

The ITV system was subject to similar pressures and scrutiny. By 1970, the possibility of its monopoly over advertising being eroded by technical change was being openly discussed. The 1963 *Television Act* had imposed a levy on the gross advertising revenue earned by contractors, which was 'designed to reflect the fact that the state had conferred upon them the sole right to operate a commercial television service'. By 1969 the levy had raised £29 million, but this was reduced in March 1970 to £23 million after representations from the industry about the worsening financial situation. On 31 March 1970 the Labour government asked the National Board for Prices and Incomes to examine 'particularly in the light of the introduction of colour television, the costs (including labour costs) and revenues of programme contractors' (National Board, 1970: p. iv, paras 1, 101).

Much of what it found pre-figured the criticisms of ITV that circulated in the 1980s. ITV lacked 'any established performance indices' that could be used to measure the efficiency of various parts of programme production. The Board concluded that 'at present production resources in the industry – i.e. both studios and men – are being used only to 65 to 70 per cent of capacity.' It argued for a 'more flexible use of labour and the control of the rate of increase in earnings'. The industry needed restructuring and this 'would require the acquiescence of the ITA in mergers of contractors'. It also asserted that ITV's reliance on advertising revenue could 'discourage the showing of programmes designed for minority or changing tastes' and suggested 'that to secure balanced programming the ITA needs to exercise more fully the formal power which it has' (National Board, 1970: paras, 106, 110, 119, 151, 157).

The Board also touched on another recurring theme in debates about broadcasting, technology and its impact on the industry. The levy, based as it was on the idea that it was a tax on the exclusive right to run commercial TV, 'could conceivably change with changing technology' (National Board, 1970: para. 5). In a passage that pointed forward to both Jay and Peacock's arguments, the Board mapped out a future in which the position of ITV would be radically undermined:

> The monopolistic character of these franchises, however, may be eroded and their value reduced by changing technology. New ways of transmission now being opened up could, subject to Government decisions, make it feasible for the viewer to have a wider range of choices. For example, a picture can be transmitted by cable, thus avoiding the use of radio frequencies and making it possible to transmit a greater number of different programmes.... It may also be possible to transmit back along the same cable a consumer's wish to purchase a service or product advertised, a call for emergency help, etc.... Yet again, it is becoming possible for a station on the ground to receive signals from a satellite and re-transmit them along a cable, with the same implication for the concept of a monopoly. Finally, in the remoter future signals could conceivably be sent straight from satellite to household without any intermediary on the ground, in which case it is doubtful whether there could be any monopoly at all.
>
> (National Board, 1970: para. 144)

Peter Jay and electronic publishing

Discussion, therefore, about the financing of broadcasting in the 1960s encompassed many of the issues that resurfaced with such impact in the 1970s and 1980s. These issues occupied people within and without the industry, including those who supported the duopoly and those, from the tradition of liberal economic thinking about broadcasting outlined in these pages, who wanted to see the system opened up to more competition. It was during the 1970s that many of these issues began to gather fresh impetus as a result of developments in technology. It was Peter Jay who, among others, saw the implications of the technological changes. In 1970 Jay was the Economics Editor of *The Times* and the son-in-law of the Labour minister, Jim Callaghan. This gave him a public profile, which allowed his opinions on the implications of technological change for the structure and finance of communications to gain a wider hearing and, ultimately, play a significant part in the thinking of the Peacock Committee.

Jay may have been persuaded by economists associated with the IEA of the case for monetarism, but his support for this doctrine 'was purely a thing about macroeconomics and nothing to do with ideology' (Jay, 2003). He 'regularly received' IEA publications:

> because they were very efficient at making sure stuff actually arrived on the desks of the journalists they wanted to be aware of it. Sometimes I looked at it, sometimes I reviewed it . . . I regarded it as a totally arms length relationship. It wasn't a meeting of soul mates. I regarded them as being a slightly suspect, rather to the right, organisation.
>
> (Jay, 2004)

His approach to economics was grounded in liberalism but was also influenced by his close association with Labour Party politics. His spiritual mentors in this area were the economists Evan Durbin (1906–48) and James Meade (1907–95)[4] who

> were strongly redistributionist and egalitarian and in favour of nationalisation of natural monopolies and all the rest of it. But, at the same time they had strongly argued that where . . . market[s] can work, as they are an immensely democratising instrument, they put the power and control into the hands of people, which is the only ultimate legitimacy for anything. That was something that I . . . applied to the broadcasting area.
>
> (Jay, 2003)

In approaching broadcasting from within this tradition, he had not come across the work of R. H. Coase or D. Sawers (Jay, 2004).

He had, however, attended broadcasting conferences 'in which there seemed to be a lot of self-interested people in effect covering their own nests and making all sorts of speeches arguing for a system that was wrong and I was emotionally repelled by this' (Jay, 2003). One such conference, however, had galvanised his thinking. This was the Symposium on 'Determinants of Broadcasting Policy', organised by the Department of Extra-Mural Studies of the University of Manchester in November 1970. There, Jay listened to a series of presentations from engineers about developments in communications technology.

J. S. Whyte, the Deputy Director of Engineering in the Long Range Division of the Post Office, discussed new developments in coaxial cable and digital technology, in which 'a new system having 5 times the bandwidth will soon start its trials'. Research was underway which aimed at providing even larger capacity systems at lower cost . . . based upon the use of special glass . . . drawn into the form of fine optical fibres along which light beams may be transmitted with low loss . . .

Fibre optics offered the possibility of 'a market arising for several broadband channels into the home to be in simultaneous use, not only for the concurrent reception of more than one entertainment programme but also for other purposes such as information services and education'. The new technologies were 'expanding more rapidly than ever before and with it our ability to serve our customers with a wider choice of entertainment and information services with greater reliability and lower cost is growing in proportion' (Whyte, 1970).

R. P. Gabriel, Director of Engineering at Rediffusion Ltd, described a technical system which allowed individuals to dial up programmes from 'a central distribution point or programme exchange' and to subscribe to 'particular channels . . . catering for special interests'. With 'additional apparatus' the system allowed networking between individuals of 'a viewphone type of service . . . or very high speed data to or from a computer, and so the system provides a basis on which to build a universal network covering all foreseeable needs for communication by sight, sound or data' (Gabriel, 1970). The Symposium also heard a presentation on the emerging technology of video recording which at the time was being developed by Phillips, Ampex and Japanese companies (Rogers, 1970).

On the following day Jay indicated that listening to these presentations had had a profound impact on his thinking:

> I start from what has already been said by some people . . . that one ought to take full account of what was said last night by the technologists. What they said has transformed my thinking about the social and ethical implications of television policy. I realised last night that the assumption which I previously made about the technical telecommunication parameters were static and obsolescent. Because of the technological changes which are in fact in prospect it is really necessary to think about the economic determinants and other problems of television choice in an entirely new way. I do think – and today's discussions have confirmed this – that we in this country are the victims of a framework of thought in regulating broadcasting which is an historical relic of a different technology.
>
> (Jay, 1970:68)

He was worried, therefore, about the relationship between broadcasting and society:

> My worry is that a lot of people are basically happy with the present oligarchic system because they are chiefly concerned, not with what they want to watch, but with what they want other people to not to watch. This is something against which a Liberal must struggle all the time.
>
> (Jay, 1970:68)

In echoing long-standing liberal critiques of the structure of broadcasting in the UK (Ogilvie, 1946; Coase, 1950), he saw a future beyond debates about censorship. Mrs Mary Whitehouse had established herself as a trenchant critic of what she and others thought of as the immorality of much television programming, and as a result had helped found the National Viewers and Listeners' Association in 1965 (Sandbrook, 2006:575–80). The new technologies, according to Jay, could be one way of accommodating the concerns she and others expressed about broadcasting:

> If . . . she is genuinely concerned with insuring positively that certain kinds of programmes which please the people whom she represents are shown, then in the context of the new technology with an indefinitely large number of alternative channels operating simultaneously the problem of the clash between her viewing tastes and mine disappears. It disappears not only for us, but also for the broadcasting authorities and the State – subject to any overriding laws of libel, pornography etc., which apply equally to books, films, theatre, newspapers, periodicals and television.
>
> (Jay, 1970:68–9)

The new technologies offered the possibility of real choice and removed the need for the State to regulate broadcasting in the way that it always had. The critique of the state-sanctioned monopoly in communications, based as it was on parallels with the press and echoing arguments that went back to the 1930s, found fresh support in Jay's grasp of the possibilities offered by what he had listened to. He saw a future in which there could be a market in communications, with freedom of entry for suppliers:

> I am not advocating faith in the market place as an automatically right way of allocating resources. In many ways it is extremely imperfect

and leads to all manner of side-effects which can be most damaging. Nonetheless, I think that, if we really take seriously what was being said last night, we can envisage a world in which there could be an indefinite number of channels from an indefinite number of sources. Consumers – viewers – would be free to choose whichever programme they want and to pay for it, perhaps by direct charging of the kind used in telephone tariffs (using the system about which Mr Gabriel was talking last night) ... if a radical change could be made to a situation in which anybody who wishes could become a supplier – like authors and publishers of books – originated and received as telephone calls (an indefinitely large number) and in which anybody could choose to dial and pay for any programme he liked, there would be an enormous gain in freedom, both in real choice for viewers and in access to the screen for originators.

(Jay, 1970:69)

The new market 'would be a market in what should be regarded not in the old sense as 'broadcasting', but in a new sense 'as telecommunications publishing' (Jay, 1970:70).

Jay returned to the issue swiftly thereafter in an article in *The Times* where he pointed to the contrasting forms of regulation for the press and broadcasting, arguing that 'our restrictive attitude to electronic publishing is an anachronistic hangover from a rapidly obsolescent technical feature of broadcasting.' He then outlined the developments in 'coaxial television cables . . . wave guides, glass cables and – to a lesser extent, satellites' that had been discussed at the Symposium. One way of developing the potential of these technologies was to have a system of meter charging for individual programmes, this being 'a decisively superior method of financing broadcasting than either licences or advertising'. Moreover if it 'opened the way to a progressive liberalisation over the last 20 years of the century of electronic publishing to match the present freedom of print publishing, it would be doubly justified'. He then attacked the licence fee in terms which were both reminiscent of the critiques surveyed earlier and which looked forward to the issues that arose during the Peacock exercise. Licence revenue was only buoyant when a new service like colour was introduced, bearing no 'automatic relationship to the trend of the B.B.C.'s expenditure'. The fee was 'highly regressive, being unrelated not merely to income, but even to expenditure'. It placed the BBC 'in recurring political jeopardy' whenever it needed an increase in the fee. Finally 'the licence method generates no useful data about the strength and direction of viewers' preferences and therefore yields no basis for future investment decisions.' Advertising 'shares most of the same defects . . . uses up and disfigures a significant proportion of the medium . . . is also extremely expensive in resources and therefore inefficient as a means of finance for broadcasting'. There needed to be, for both the BBC and ITV, 'a new buoyant and independent source of permanent revenue' (Jay, 1970a; see also, Jay, 1975).

By 1973 Samuel Brittan had read and absorbed Jay's arguments as published in the proceedings of the Manchester Broadcasting Symposium. Citing the proceedings of the Symposium, he argued that

> Technological changes are in prospect which should eventually make possible a much more extensive introduction of competition into both television and radio. There may in future no longer be any physical need to limit broadcasting to a small number of channels. Instead there could be an indefinite number of services, among which consumers could select and pay directly. The distinction between publishing and broadcasting would then largely disappear, with a consequent extension of cultural diversity and freedom. But there are so many institutional interests involved in present restrictions and such passionate feelings exist about what other people should be prevented from watching, that a strong rearguard action is likely to prevent any new technological opportunities from being fully utilised.
>
> (Brittan, 1973:258)

Jay's opinions on the new market-driven future for broadcasting therefore acted as an important statement of the possibilities opening up with the development of new technologies in the 1970s, one which influenced Samuel Brittan's approach to broadcasting policy.

Jay's most developed argument in this area was placed before the *Committee on the Future of Broadcasting* (Report, 1977) chaired by Lord Annan. The Committee sat between 1974 and 1977 and Jay submitted evidence in November 1975 (Jay, 1975a[5]). He posed the issue in terms of general principle: 'what in a free society should in principle determine the kind of broadcast services which are produced, to whom they are distributed and how they are paid for' [1], offering 'to illustrate the terms in which these questions need to be approached' [2].

He raised the issue of consumer sovereignty and the lack of fit between the regulation of broadcasting and the press, admitting to a

> bias against paternalism and corporatism, as now practiced by Governments of all hues . . . and the general disposition to replace

the sovereignty of the consumer in many walks of life by the fatherly dispositions of the benevolent.

[5]

Broadcasters did not 'exercise any very restrictive censorship over what is broadcast' but 'they could if they judged the public mood to favour such restrictions. There is no comparably placed authorities monitoring the publication of the printed word' [6]. He attributed the present systems of control to the 'physical scarcity of spectrum' and the widespread belief that broadcasting 'exercises over the public some extraordinary, almost hypnotic power' [10].

The case he then put was based on the twin pillars of technological change and the assumed benefits of markets:

rather before the end of the century it will be feasible at a very large initial cost to arrange that the nation's viewers can simultaneously watch as many different programmes as the nation's readers can read different books, magazines, newspapers etc.

[11]

Television or radio sets will become like a telephone and 'the number of channels becomes, if not infinite, at least indefinitely large' [12].

Then the market would take the lead role:

The rest of the conditions for a free electronic publishing market, with consumer choice and freedom of access, falls quickly into place. No general laws are required other than those which already govern publishing (libel, copyright, obscenity, common law etc), though there is nothing in the system to prevent Parliament making special laws for electronic publishing and some special laws may be needed to deal with copyright in a world of satellite transmissions and cassette copying.

[14]

Large and small publishers would be free to set up as well as individuals [15].

The State could subsidise 'particular categories of electronic publishing which are considered virtuous or in the public interest' [16]. The BBC and ITV could act as 'major publishers' and 'need not reflect any general policy for broadcasting' [17]. Advertising could continue but 'viewers would be free to decide whether they thought this nuisance worth the saving in charges or not' [20].

Pressing forward and pre-figuring an argument in Peacock, he asserted that there was a role for public intervention – 'so long as electronic publishing is confined to a limited number of channels, there is a plausible argument that consumer choice is maximised by giving one authority the duty to provide choice rather than forcing a small number of rival organisations to vie with each other for a limited mass audience' [22]. Nonetheless, in the future, a system based on direct payments by the public would be beneficial because it would generate 'invaluable information about the effective demand for broadcast material and therefore about the scale of resources which it is right to invest in supplying that material' [30].

Jay then considered the question of whether, given the nature of the technological change he predicted, broadcasting should remain under 'the degree of statutory supervision' exercised by the BBC and the Independent Broadcasting Authority (IBA). The answer to this question was normative: 'People will answer this question according to their different political and social philosophies' [38]. He selected three propositions which had to be held by someone who wished in an age where there need be 'no limit to what can be published electronically . . . to prevent the publication of lawful material which the public would choose and pay for' [39]. The first was that 'a man or woman does not always know what is best for him or her to receive' [39]. This he dismissed as 'a complete rejection of the philosophy of the primacy of the individual and of his liberty' [40].

The second was that free electronic publishing 'would in practice lead to a narrowing of choice' so that by preventing the publication of 'too many similar programmes of little "worth" resources can be kept free . . . for more worthwhile or varied productions' [39]. Under electronic publishing, he countered, 'it will pay entrepreneurs . . . to provide studio facilities . . . Small publishers and go-it-alone authors will rent what they need' [42]. No one, he asserted, 'has a God-given right to use whatever resources they want'. One has to pay for resources, or persuade a patron or financier to do so [42]. The third argument was that broadcasting exists 'primarily or exclusively for the benefit of those who work' in it, 'rather than for those who use their output' [39]. In principle this depended

on making a general rule of workers' sovereignty or on a special case for adding broadcasting to the list of exceptions to the rule of consumer sovereignty. The general rule leads quickly to absurdity; and it seems hard to think of a less appropriate or deserving exception to the more practical rule of consumer sovereignty in economic affairs.
[45]

It followed then that in the new world of electronic publishing 'there is no compelling need for continued monolithic (or indeed duo-, or oligo-lithic) broadcasting franchises' [46]. If there was no need to allocate scarce broadcasting resources between competing interests 'most of the problems which preoccupy public debate about the future of broadcasting disappear' [47]. But, this situation was not imminent and interim measures based on the principles of 'power to the individual viewer' and 'opportunity to the producer' needed to be implemented [55]. This meant that

> the highest priority should be given to introducing a system of direct payment for broadcasting services approximating as closely as possible to the metering and quarterly billing system used for telephones [59].

Simply increasing the number of channels would not suffice. That, he argued, was 'probably the worst of all possible arrangements, as American experience seems to confirm, whether consumer satisfaction or diversity of choice are taken as the criteria for judging a system' [53]. It might be possible to have competing channels 'under conditions of direct payment and differential pricing' and 'if channel franchises were auctioned . . . in conjunction with direct payment for programmes, the system of competing channels would work much better' [64]. But this might lead to 'a high degree of duplication' and 'limitations of choice' under conditions of spectrum scarcity' [65].

There should, therefore, be 'a single broadcasting "authority" charged with integrated scheduling of all available channels with a view to ensuring diversity of consumer choice and maximising consumer satisfaction as reflected in consumer preferences under a direct payment system' [66]. There should be multiple big publishers supplying programmes, but there should also be

> access to the schedules for an indefinite number of 'small' publishers . . . under a general rule of thumb that a minimum of, say, 20 percent of all general transmissions . . . must be drawn from such 'small' publishers.
>
> [66]

Jay's evidence mapped a general perspective on the future as well as providing interim proposals. His thoughts, rooted in conventional liberal economic thinking, and consonant with the tradition articulated since the 1940s by Coase and his successors, were not accepted by the Annan Committee. The Committee recommended that the BBC and ITV remain intact, that the licence fee and advertising should remain the main sources of finance, that a fourth television channel be established and that pay-TV on cable should not be authorised. The BBC and ITV were urged to show more willingness to buy programmes from independent producers (Report, 1977:474–90). The liberal tradition of thinking about broadcasting policy, articulated by Jay in his evidence, had to wait for the arrival of a more sympathetic Conservative government after 1979 before it gained wider acceptance among politicians, civil servants and policy makers.

For Jay, reflecting in 2004, 'Annan was the high tide of what I would still call the paternalist tradition' in which 'the guardians of society' decided 'what would be good and right and best for the children'. In addition it was not troubled by the kind of questions about the legitimacy of the system that concerned him as an economist (Jay, 2004). When Lord Annan met the Committee he was, as Alan Peacock has suggested, aware of the weakness of the economic dimensions of his report:

> Lord Annan came and talked to the Committee and emphasised (and this is my own account of what happened) why issues we faced required careful attention to the economics of broadcasting. And he said at the time that perhaps they had not paid enough attention to these issues.
>
> (Conference Transcripts, 2005: Establishing Peacock)[6]

Although Annan may not have focussed sufficiently on economics, the report did touch on the issues of cable and satellite, topics which thereafter occupied an increasingly important place in government considerations (Hollins, 1984). In July 1978 the Labour government issued a White Paper on broadcasting (Home Office, 1978[7]). The government recognised that new technologies would 'have a profound impact on broadcasting' [6] and rejected Annan's view that there should be no pay-TV cable services. It committed to establishing 'pilot schemes of pay-TV to be authorised subject to careful regulation to guard against the possibly damaging effects which pay-TV might have on television as a whole' [175, 178]. Cable was to be supervised by the IBA using 'broadly the rules and requirement which govern independent broadcasting' [181]. Satellite services were possible, but the government was cautious, considering it 'premature to reach any firm conclusions in the allocation of responsibility for satellite' [203]. So, the technical possibilities thrown up by cable and satellite were recognised, but the approach to policy in the White Paper was firmly within a gradualist tradition of incremental change, making no concessions to the liberal critique of broadcasting policy.

The election in May 1979 of the Conservative Party shifted the political landscape. Margaret Thatcher and many of her senior colleagues were influenced by the revival of economic liberalism that had characterised the 1960s and 1970s. They were therefore disposed to countenance the ideas about broadcasting developed by figures like Coase, Plant, Herzel and Jay. Thereafter, ideas about the need to extend market forces into broadcasting became common. Jay returned to the subject in his 1981 lecture on 'Electronic Publishing' delivered to the assembled ranks of TV executives, of which by that time he was a member, at the Edinburgh Television Festival. He used the argument that 'fibre-optic technology' could 'create a grid connecting every household in the country' to support his case for electronic publishing. He repeated the arguments in the evidence to Annan, and asserted, this time with more rhetorical emphasis, the principles which he thought were at stake:

> Second only, perhaps, to the right of individuals to think privately what thoughts they wish comes the right of individuals to communicate those thoughts with one another. The historic battles to establish this right after the invention of the printing press and the perception of the power and potentialities of what by the standards of those days may be called mass communication was, to be sure, long and bitter. But, for those who adhere to the libertarian and utilitarian tradition, it is not seen as a battle between two arguable propositions or legitimate interests, but rather as a simple struggle between a sound and fundamental ideal on the one hand and dark forces motivated by interest (or occasionally mistaken bigotry) on the other. We now regard it as axiomatic that mass communication of the printed word should be a free activity which does not require any general framework of government regulation or sponsorship, although according to our varying different individual points of view we may be more or less inclined to accept certain general marginal constraints on this freedom for such reasons as sedition, blasphemy, libel, race relations and national security.
>
> (Jay, 1981:221–2)

He issued a rallying cry for freedom against the impositions of vested interest, a cry that chimed well with prevailing sentiment among influential sections of the Tory leadership:

> Finally, however, those who care passionately for freedom in communication and publishing, whether electronic, print or simply oral, need now to gird themselves for a prolonged struggle against old habits and vested interests in order to ensure that the new freedoms, which the new technology will make technically possible, are in fact translated into real freedoms for both producers and consumers under law.
>
> (Jay, 1981:235–6)

Jay's approach to the economics of broadcasting and his attack on vested interests, plus the implications this had for the continuation of state-sponsored public service broadcasting tallied well with the approach of the Conservative leadership in the early 1980s. As part of its commitment to freedom the Conservatives, in 1983, promised the 'launch of new cable networks to bring wider choice to consumers, not just for entertainment, but of the whole new world of teleshopping and telebanking'. It boasted of having promoted competition in telecommunications and promised to sell 51 per cent of government shares in British Telecom (Conservative Party, 1983:6, 16, 20).

The intellectual foundations therefore for the changes that were to take root after Peacock were laid by the late 1970s. The IEA and the cluster of liberal economists and individuals who had attended to issues of broadcasting policy since the 1930s had laid an important foundation for the discussions around Peacock in the 1980s. This is illustrated by the roll call of influences in the 1983 IEA publication, *Choice by Cable*. Professors R. H. Coase and Alan Peacock were listed as members of its advisory council. In arguing for the minimal regulation of cable, the break up of British Telecom, competition between cable and telephone providers and that 'the case for de-regulating broadcast TV should also be given serious consideration,' it cited the work of liberal economists as well as people who had written on the topic for the IEA. These included R. H. Coase, Denis Thomas, Wilfred Altman, David Sawers and Sydney Caine, all of whom along with Arnold Plant had contributed to the development and sustenance of a critique of broadcasting in the UK from the perspective of economic liberalism (Veljanovski and Bishop, 1983:52–3, 61, 111–13). Their ideas were to form the bedrock of the approaches developed by the Peacock Committee, supplemented by the more immediate and higher profile articulation of that position by Peter Jay. One of the editors of *Choice by Cable*, Cento Veljanovski, was commissioned to do a report on broadcasting in Australia for the Peacock Committee (Report, 1986, Appendix C).

Conclusion

During the 1950s, and especially the 1960s, ideas about the need for competition, the desirability of auctioning TV franchises and spectrum, the problems of paternalism in broadcasting, the need for consumer choice, the defects of the licence fee and advertising as measures of viewer preferences and as signals for the allocation of resources, the disparity between the regulation of the press and broadcasting, the value of pay and subscription TV, the importance of transparency and efficiency in the finances of the BBC and ITV and the likely impact of technological change on broadcasting policy had been developed and disseminated.

The critique of broadcasting outlined in these chapters was driven by the critique of collectivism outlined in Chapter 1 (Greenleaf, 1983:14–24). This is not to say that all those who contributed to the development of these ideas identified themselves always, wholly, or even in part with the assault on collectivism. Nonetheless, many of the writers who criticised the broadcasting system were explicitly aligned with the revival of economic liberalism as it developed in the UK after 1945.Thus, the attack on broadcasting was situated within broader sets of ideas about promoting markets and individual choice, the need for less government intervention in the economy and fears about the dangers posed by government to individual liberty. The critics of postwar broadcasting effectively rejected the idea that common goals, such as the provision of the widest possible range of high-quality cultural goods to the largest number of people at low cost, should be a concern of government policy.

Yet ideas by themselves do not effect political change. The election in 1979 of a Conservative government, led by individuals disposed to place economic liberalism at the centre of national policy, provided the context in which ideas that had been on the margins could move to the centre, in broadcasting as in other areas. It was party politics that effected this transition. So, although ideas critical of public service broadcasting had been developed over a number of decades, it was the change in the political balance of power at the end of the 1970s which was central to the way in which they took shape in debates about broadcasting in the 1980s, and to the establishment of the Committee on the Financing of the BBC in 1985.

Notes

1. Coase, 1959.
2. In the same year the IEA made another intervention into communications policy, this time attacking state intervention in communications. Michael Cane, a postgraduate student at the LSE, published *Telephones- Public or Private* where he argued that 'the weight of quantitative evidence plus the impediments virtually inevitable to government-owned enterprises suggest strongly that the telephone service would be better off divorced from the public sector'. Just as IEA-sponsored ideas about broadcasting were to gain a hearing in the 1980s, so Cane's intervention 'started the long debate on the telephone system, and British Telecom was, of course, the first of Mrs Thatcher's major privatisations in 1984' (Cockett, 1995:146).
3. Arthur Selden prefaced the pamphlet with the assertion that pay TV would 'attract extra revenues' for the 'expansion and improvement' of the television system and, drawing on work by Coase, that it would cost only between one and five pence per viewer per hour (Caine, 1968:5).
4. Both Durbin, before, and Meade, after the Second World War had worked at the LSE with Lionel Robbins (Ellis, 2004; Howson, 2004).
5. References to this document are to paragraphs and are given thus [1].
6. The quotation can also be found in Chapter 12 of this collection, p. 310.
7. References are to paragraphs in the White Paper, thus [1].

4

Twenty and Thirty and Forty Years On: A Personal Retrospect on Broadcasting Policy since 1967

Peter Jay

I left the Treasury and joined *The Times* as its Economics Editor in 1967, 40 years ago at this writing. Later that year Tony Smith, then the Editor of the BBC's *Twenty-Four Hours*, a kind of proto-*Newsnight*, later the creative genius behind Channel 4, began inviting me to appear in items mainly about the economy. This led to my being invited to – and attending – conferences about broadcasting and, more particularly, about journalism as it was and should be practised on television.

Thus started a lifetime's interest in this deeply vexed topic in which I became variously involved as a practitioner, a theorist, a manager and finally, under the auspices of the University of Wales at Aberystwyth, an honorary academic. The purpose of this essay is to explore an aspect of this subject of which I was conscious from the very beginning, but which I have never before directly addressed, namely the differing and frequently opposed views of those who come to the subject with some training in economics and those who do not.

For the economist broadcasting was the purveying of a good or service to people who were its consumers and which therefore required some mechanism to decide what was produced, by whom, for whom and how it was to be paid for. To the non-economists, as I encountered and perceived them at least in caricature, it was more the celebration of a belief in a kind of grail where the activity was itself its own justification, where the viewers and listeners, though important, were not the central sovereign justification for the activity, but rather witnesses to what was, if properly done, a glorious cultural apotheosis, whether 'high' or 'popular', whose servants and guardians were by their own appointment those to whom the supreme truth had been sufficiently revealed and who in consequence were entitled to be supported so that they could fulfil this high calling without hampering financial or other constraints.

In other words it bore many of the hallmarks of a well-established and entrenched church . . . sustained by its infallible beliefs, served and in many cases managed and ruled by its own clerisy or priestly caste, entitled to substantial tithes from the working populace and only challenged by heretics too ignorant, vulgar or venal to acknowledge the overriding authority of divine purpose as manifested in the mission to generate a culture worthy of contemporary society, the details of which were most reliably interpreted by the elect class of programme-makers, best identified by their mutual recognition of one another. This links in a way to the question posed by Alan Peacock himself at The Peacock Legacy Conference that

> whether you shouldn't disestablish the BBC rather like you disestab-lish the church, because anybody who has anything to do with the BBC over a long period of time, as I have, notes that it has all the characteristics of a church. It sees its position vis á vis the govern-ment in the same way as the Church of England; remember the Church of Scotland, nor the Church of Wales, is a part of this estab-lishment area.
>
> (Conference Transcripts, 2005: Closing Plenary)[1]

It may seem that I am unsympathetic to this ecclesiastical outlook; and that is so. But in many ways I might have been expected to identify with it.

My political background was on the broad non-Marxist left; and I was reared in a tradition that was self-consciously high-minded, cultivated, self-persuaded that its privileges and élite advantages conferred upon it a duty, as well as a right, to promote these standards more widely for the edification and improvement of those less fortunate than themselves. The mission of the philosopher king – or the economist-statesman – was never far from the Wykehamical mind[2]; and the idea that high cultural standards were self-evident to the educated mind and that the height of those standards itself justified their promotion as a matter of public policy – and at public expense – slipped down the Wykehamical throat with scarcely a swallow.

Unquestioningly those raised in this tradition thought of government and collective social action in the first person plural – we, us – while business was in the third person, what they do. Indeed, I suspect that many of us secretly, like the lady in Trollope, 'had but a confused idea of any difference between commerce and fraud' (Trollope, 1951:99–100). At the very least business was not nice. We remembered the wartime and early post-war spivs; and we were not sure that trade is a suitable occupation for gentlemen, whereas broadcasting was manifestly a profession, especially if it was 'public service' broadcasting. Naturally therefore 'they' could not be relied upon to recognise, still less to seek, the public good, unless so constrained by some hand, whether visible or invisible; whereas 'we' who acted on behalf of society, whether through government or otherwise, would of course and unfailingly promote the general welfare, because that was why we wanted to do it.

Moreover, a good part of my working life was given to the theory and practice of broadcast journalism at the so called 'upper' end of its supposed spectrum between the 'enlightening', at one end, and the 'dumbed down', at the other. From *Twenty-Four Hours*[3] through *Weekend World*,[4] *The Times* articles (with John Birt) on *'The Bias Against Understanding'* (Jay, 1984:191–218), TV-am's 'mission to explain',[5] Channel 4's *A Week in Politics*,[6] to a final decade as the BBC's economics editor I both enjoyed the privileged opportunities which the public service broadcasting tradition afforded and expounded the case for what I regarded as a better standard of broadcast journalism, a notion whose epistemological and ethical foundations were more fully explored in my 1982 Royal Society of Arts Lecture *What is News ?* (Jay, 1984:237–65).

No quarter was given in any of this to 'vulgar populism' or 'ratings-chasing', still less to the tinsel trash of 'reality' and 'celebrity', which had mercifully not yet been concocted. Picture-led news programmes were anathematised; and the values of both the movie industry and the local newspaper newsroom were pronounced to be false models for an authentic television journalism standing on its own professional feet.

The breakfast television franchise was indeed won[7] on a prospectus that promised 'popular intelligent journalism in all of its aspects from the front page to the back', which certainly intended its journalism to be entertaining, but not entertainment, and which, whatever celebrity its protagonists evinced, embraced the 'OIC ideal' of a journalism which elicits from its audience that magical moment when he and she exclaim, 'Oh, I see*eee* !' For me the BBC's star reporter Charles Wheeler and the cricketer and commentator Richie Benaud were the great exemplars of this art, later followed by the tennis expert John McEnroe.

So, why also then have I been associated with the seemingly contrary notion that broadcasters were essentially in the publishing business and that an electronic publishing market was a framework devoutly to be wished for?

For a start much depends on what role one is playing. As a journalist it is desirable, natural and perhaps obligatory to have a set of professional ideals which define goals and standards for the work which one is trying to do, rather – without being too pompous about so modest a trade as reporting – as a medical man has his professional ethics and clinical standards. In that context the generation and practice of a mission to explain, for example, may well be a legitimate personal and professional ideal; and a regime based on the concept of public service broadcasting may well provide welcome and congenial opportunities to fulfil such an ideal.

But as a system-builder or policy-maker or contributor to debates on the organisation of society, its culture and economy, one needs quite other criteria. The question no longer is what kind of journalism do I as a journalist wish to practise and believe to be of the highest intellectual or cultural value, but instead becomes what structures and rules will best serve most people most of the time.

Only if the general interest is defined to coincide with the fulfilment of the professional ideals of the journalist will there be any necessary coincidence between what I as a journalist aspire to achieve and what I as a citizen recommend as a general regime for, say, news and broadcasting. A soldier may honourably recommend and aspire to practise high ideals of military science and courage while also honourably arguing for peace and demilitarisation.

The belief that soldiers should be good soldiers does not logically entail any belief that society should be organised so as to afford the widest possible opportunities to practise good soldiery, for example, by plunging it into general warfare. No more is the good apple-farmer justified in wanting to cover the face of the earth with apple orchards, though his spokesmen probably will. The word good here is being used in the sense of 'professionally excellent' and should not be confused with either moral or 'up-market/down-market' issues. Whether or not there is a market for professional excellence in any particular field is an open question, to be answered by consumers, usually by paying for it, not by those who wish to supply it, usually at someone else's expense.

Indeed, the logical slide from the belief that 'good' broadcasting is a high ideal for broadcasters to the belief that society should be organised so as in general to foster good broadcasting (to say nothing of good incomes for 'good' broadcasters), whether or not that coincides with the wishes or interest of the general public, is fundamental to the fallacy that high broadcasting standards should be objects not just of those who work in the field, but also of public policy, public spending and public regulation as well.

That is not to say that there may not be good reasons for public policy to support public service broadcasting if, for example, the best available market fails to deliver what the general public wants or needs; but that has to be shown to be so independent of the natural but unwarranted conviction of all producers of goods and services that the public ought to want what they supply.

For all of which reasons I make no apology for seizing the opportunities available at the BBC, Independent Television (ITV), the breakfast time franchise, Channel 4 and then the BBC again to try to practise the kind of broadcast journalism I believed in, while also pressing the case for an electronic publishing market in *The Times*, in my 1981 McTaggart lecture *Electronic Publishing* (Jay, 1981) and in evidence to the Peacock Committee (where I argued that the existing market for books and magazines, embracing great popular publishers like Penguin as well as more specialist publishers, provided the best long-term model for the organisation of publishing by electronic means).

That idea reached its first full expression in the McTaggart Lecture. But it began on 13 June 1975, when I met Dr Alex Reid of the future technology department of the Post Office. Dr Reid told me about fibre optic cables; and, as we talked, the idea of a functioning electronic publishing market, embracing what we then thought of as broadcast materials, began to form in my mind.

For, if fibre optic cables could deliver the breadth of spectrum described by Dr Reid, two consequences seemed to follow. First, the possible end of spectrum scarcity – or at last of acute spectrum scarcity – undermined the classic necessity for a spectrum policeman, that is, the government, as in the nineteenth century Wireless Telegraphy Acts leading up to the 1904 Act, which was the fulcrum on which almost all subsequent statutory regulation of broadcasting had been levered. Secondly, it enabled the reception of broadcast signals to be monitored – and therefore to be charged for – rather in the way that the telephone company recorded and charged for telephone calls, thus opening the door to commercially practical electronic publishing.

Thirty years after my lunch with Dr Reid and a quarter of a century after the McTaggart lecture, I was pleased to hear Professor Kevin Williams say at Gregynog:

> it is interesting how a lot of aspects of Peacock started to seep their
> way into the Labour Party documents and discussions about the

future of broadcasting. Particularly Subscription, Stage Two and Stage Three, discussions of electronic publishing; these started to slip in. I would say that, looking back on it, Peacock was twenty years ahead of its time.... I think it is important to emphasise this, that in some senses Peacock coincided with the start of the Labour Party's long march back to the market.

(Conference Transcripts, 2005: Influence)

This new technology, I could see, opened a doorway to an electronic publishing market, with the BBC in a role like Penguin Books in their heyday, what I called at The Peacock Legacy Conference 'perhaps the biggest, certainly one of the biggest and most active publishers in this electronic publishing market' (Conference Transcripts, 2005: Influence). This possibility appealed strongly to me because as a person trained in economics I wanted to be able to ask the question, without being knocked down by some engineering objection, why should broadcast products – programmes – not be created and purveyed to those who wanted them in the same way as books and magazines. I was correspondingly happy to hear Tony Lennon say at The Peacock Legacy Conference:

> More significantly, there was this concept of the electronic publisher and the BBC, as a publisher. I think that really gave legs to an argument that people like John Birt went on to use in the 1990s, in a way that preserved and protected the position of the BBC, in a manner which even people like me didn't fully twig at the time . . . Actually, the Committee was unbelievably prescient in one or two respects . . . , we were absolutely with you, . . . there is this wonderful quote in Paragraph 115, which essentially was: British Telecom and the market should be left to get on with obvious thing, which was in fact to put a fibre optic link into everybody's home.
>
> (Conference Transcripts, 2005: Influence)

This was exactly what I had argued in the McTaggart lecture and in my evidence to Peacock. And there were anyway, it seemed to me, obvious a priori reasons for regarding that market as a relevant and potentially attractive model. In a very straightforward way it embodied the basic freedoms of thought and expression, which our society purported to regard as fundamental. You could write what you liked and read what you liked, once the eighteenth and nineteenth century heroes of those battles had won the necessary immunities from most of the earlier oppressive taxes and other laws circumscribing freedom of speech.

Of course these elementary negative freedoms (though one must doubt whether John Wilkes regarded them as either elementary or negative) were open to the complaint that they were only available to those who got published and/or who could afford to buy the books and magazines in question. But I had long ago decided that this objection to the negative freedoms proved too much, throwing out the baby of the free competitive market place with the bathwater of inequality.

Yes, equality mattered and needed to be addressed through redistributive tax-and-spend mechanisms; but it was crazy – disproportionate and counter-productive – to make it a reason for rejecting the near-magical ability of properly functioning markets to match resources to the infinitely various and infinitely varying wants and preferences of people as consumers and to motivate others to apply their skills, energies and savings to supply those choices.

This does perhaps bring us close to the heart of that great divide among the theorists of broadcasting between, crudely, the 'economists' and the 'non-economists', though sometimes it also corresponds to a left – right disagreement about both ends and means. The terms 'economists' and the 'non-economists' are of course caricatures; and there are of course plenty of well-qualified economists who may not subscribe to the views so labelled here – and vice versa.

Nonetheless, the distinction may be useful. The economist tends to see in a properly functioning market a mechanism which at least starts with a number of attractive features going for it. In principle it looks capable of reconciling many of the issues which arise when people move beyond supplying all their own wants and begin to specialise and exchange, though it is equally well known that in detail there may be abuses and failures which impair or wreck the otherwise benign outcomes to be presumed from the model of the pure market.

The non-economist is much less likely to buy into this starting presumption, seeing instead a simpler and nastier march of commercial greed and financial power, un-channelled by any hidden hand towards useful, just or democratic outcomes. To him the sovereignty of the consumer is not apparent; and the might of the corporation, especially if it be 'multi-national', is all encompassing.

There are of course right-wing non-economists who, though equally oblivious of how markets can and should work, see nothing wrong – at least for them – with the outcomes so vilified by other economic laymen. And there are many, very many, economists on or inclining to the left for whom the failures of markets to deliver their theoretical benefits are far more numerous than their successes. But, even so, the economists and the non-economists will tend, among themselves, to argue these matters in noticeably different ways; and when the economists argue with the non-economists, whether of leftish or rightish views, the result all too often is a dialogue of the deaf in which the opposing views pass each other like rival fleets in thick fog.

For example, to the non-economists an electronic publishing market, which they barely or only dimly distinguish from laissez-faire jungle-warfare, is just an opportunity for the likes of Rupert Murdoch to get rich by broadcasting trash, whereas to the economists it can and should subject such entrepreneurs, under strict laws (legal laws and economic laws), to the sovereign democratic choices of free citizens acting as consumers. To the non-economists the remedy in part is to appoint non-commercial 'great and good' guardians of 'public service broadcasting' to deliver non-trash.

To the economists it may be equally important to subject these very same guardians, who all too easily may become the captives and the representatives of the vested producer interests in this industry, to the same democratic accountability. To the non-economists, markets are dominated by business and therefore merely concentrate power. To the economists, so long as the markets are competitive and open to all, they can diffuse and democratise power.

An economist wanting to make the case for public service broadcasting or at least for continued financial support from public funds for the BBC will acknowledge an intellectual obligation to demonstrate the market failure which he proposes thereby to remedy (see Graham and Davies, 1997). He will in particular recognise the critical importance of the Peacock Committee's findings that the part of broadcasting in Britain which was financed mainly from advertising was engaged in selling audiences to advertisers, not programmes to consumers, and selling them in what were state-sponsored regional monopolies.

To the non-economist's eye, the ITV companies may have appeared just as 'commercial', 'free enterprise', 'capitalist', etc. as any other private sector business; but to the economist's eye they exhibited few of the benefits of a liberal market regime: the consumers of programmes could express no preference between products by their buying decisions since all viewers and listeners in a given social-economic class counted equally to the programme-maker; and no new entrant into the market could offer the advertisers access to the same potential customers on better terms.

This was a critically important reason why the Peacock Committee, in which the economists played a notable role, rejected the 'commercial' (and political) pressure to equate advertising finance with market forces and instead laid out a programme for moving towards a true electronic publishing market in ways which were both less comfortable for ITV companies, who were in due course obliged to bid for their lucrative franchises, and more comfortable for the BBC, which was not obliged to accept advertising on its main channels. Peacock was economically literate, but never (e.g. the recommended auction of ITV franchises) 'business friendly', which is a very different thing. Indeed, trained economists tend to share Adam Smith's worldly view that

> People of the same trades seldom meet together even for merriment and diversion, but the conversation ends in a conspiracy against the public, or on some contrivance to raise prices.
>
> (Smith, 1812:116)

Another aspect of the dialogue-of-the-deaf characteristics of the economist/non-economist debate on broadcasting is the tendency of each side to regard the other as presumptuously pretending to the more Olympian overview while in fact offering but a partial and distorted glimpse of what is really a wider landscape better viewed from a loftier vantage point, such as their own. Jeremy Hardie at The Peacock Legacy Conference made the point that:

> if you are an economist you believe that economic analysis is generic, meaning that you can apply it to every problem, and I certainly came to it from that point of view.
>
> (Conference Transcripts, 2005: Establishing Peacock)

Sir Alan Peacock himself readily acknowledged that when he came to look at broadcasting, one of the things he immediately saw was what any trained economist familiar with the literature would see, namely not the great paternalist dispensations of Reith, Pilkington and Annan, but a classic – and cosy – duopoly. This then immediately poses the question whether broadcasting is, like the lighthouse in Adam Smith's analysis, a public good which needs to be provided by public authority, and at public cost, or whether thanks to technical change, it can be replaced by a true market, which must always be the preferred 'default' setting:

> I certainly had to scratch my head a bit . . . in trying to apply [the theory of duopoly] to the chapter on 'The Comfortable Duopoly'; but . . . the classic example of . . . public goods theory was always the lighthouse, and that's a classic case, you see, where technology

has changed the situation. Where a lighthouse was something where the beams could not be restricted to those ships willing to pay for them . . . now you can . . . create a market in a navigational aid of this kind. The result is most of the lighthouses are disappearing; . . . maybe technology will [also] alter the whole nature of the possibility of having a more direct relationship through, for example, subscription or pay-per-view, between the listener or viewer and the producers.

(Conference Transcripts, 2005: Establishing Peacock)[8]

Thus the economists may see the broadcasters as no better than farmers, lobbying for subsidies to support them in their chosen occupation without the painful necessity of earning their living in the market place. The non-economists retaliate by portraying the economists as purveyors of a narrow 'Gradgrind' materialist philosophy which takes no account of other and higher values, in short philistines, bores and bean-counters.

Not all of this is entirely edifying. And, in polite and sophisticated forms, we had some of it at The Peacock Legacy Conference. Jean Seaton knew the enemy when she saw them:

because actually ranged against, on the other side from us are a set of extremely articulate, very well-paid, very self-interested newspaper and commercial interests, all of which are paid very much more, very much better at lobbying, who have very, very particular interests in outcomes in this area.

(Conference Transcripts, 2005: Closing Plenary)

Professor Tom O'Malley is nothing if not a devout champion of using the power of broadcasting vested in the state to accomplish collectivised delivery of cultural goods equally and universally in order to promote wider social and cultural purposes; and he has struggled valiantly and sincerely to get his mind round the economists' way of thinking. But for him it remains something of an alien intrusion into a broader and, to him, more enlightened tradition:

Now it seems to me that an underlying motif of the Peacock Report is this belief in liberty, something implied, along with other things, in the concept of consumer sovereignty.... This drew, broadly, on Hayek's economic thinking . . . and found its most important home in the UK in the London School of Economics where I understand Sir Alan . . . spent the early part of his academic lecturing career.... This promotion of the market as the optimum mechanism for producing wealth and liberty, and its concommitant critique of state planning, has influenced successive cohorts of policy-makers, politicians and journalists from the 1960s and 70s onwards.

(Conference Transcripts, 2005: Opening Plenary)

Sir Samuel Brittan, a libertarian both as a philosopher and as an economist, was provoked by this to seek to restore economic thinking to the intellectual mainstream, observing

the ideas (consumer sovereignty and so on) which Alan Peacock brought were . . . not some outré doctrine from Austria. They were the application of what he regarded as normal economic analysis.

(Conference Transcripts, 2005: Opening Plenary)

Alan Peacock himself was keen to rescue economics from a different slur. While he acknowledged a professional bias as an economist, he rejected any implication in Tom O'Malley's reference to the market's capacity for producing wealth that his, Peacock's, approach to cultural goods was therefore tainted by base materialism:

One of the things I was very much concerned about in the writing of the Report was that this would be something which would be accepted, if critically, by fellow-economists in the widest sense . . . I don't mean by that . . . materialistic behaviour or behaviour in any kind of narrow sense. You are talking about the decisions which individuals have to make about the use of resources at their disposal, and that what they do in one direction is at the cost of what they do in another direction.

(Conference Transcripts, 2005: Closing Plenary)

A third response to Tom O'Malley's thesis was my own. I suggested that the division between the non-economists and the economists in some ways transcended even Tom O'Malley's big divide between the libertarians and collectivists. Collectivist economists talked differently from other collectivists and shared a specific reference framework with non-collectivist economists, viz.:

at the time of that debate, I would certainly have regarded myself as a collectivist in the sense that I would have taken it as axiomatic that there are things which governments must and need to do, and that the distinction between the things they should do and the things they should not do does not rest on some absolute black and white view as to whether or not collective action is of its nature a legitimate or acceptable form of behaviour, but on a view of what the characteristics of the activity in question were . . . As I recall it, conventional economics of that period would have said, 'We the economists have a way of distinguishing between those things which ought to be interfered with by public authority and those which ought not, and that is in terms of a thing called market failure.'

(Conference Transcripts, 2005: Opening Plenary)

This, I argued, united economists, whether or not they were 'collectivist', in a more profound way than that in which ideology united economist and non-economist collectivists.

Less complacently, Jeremy Hardie, a member of Peacock and a former economics don, drew attention to the tendency of economists to be united by the limitations of their vision as much as by their shared understanding:

it is very striking how Peacock is full of economics, orthodox economics.... I think that . . . economists . . . are not very good at institutions. Institutions are just sort of logical constructs in economics most of the time and I think that that is something about the way the Peacock Committee was operating. It was operating in a world in which economics was seen – particularly by the economists – as being the thing you brought to problems of this kind.

(Conference Transcripts, 2005: Opening Plenary)

For Samuel Brittan, the economist/non-economist schism did not fully capture the divisions within the Peacock Committee. He identified a three-way split on the Committee, none of which represented the alleged hankering of the Prime Minister, Margaret Thatcher, for a crude tilt towards greater commercialism by the BBC, a hankering which itself owed nothing to economics:

there were at least three groups of people within the Committee. There were . . . those, like Alan Peacock and myself, who had if you like a bias towards markets and a bias towards personal choice. There were two people the other end, unfortunately no longer alive, who were very devoted to the status quo and very afraid of a force they called 'Murdoch & Maxwell', and in between there were the reasonable English people like Jeremy who had to be won over.

(Conference Transcripts, 2005: Opening Plenary)

But Jeffrey Milland restored the role of economists to the centre of debate when he brought out very clearly the contrast in mindset with the earlier Pilkington Committee, which effectively assigned the third channel (now BBC2) to the BBC:

> Pilkington hardly discussed the question of Pay TV at all. It was raised very early on in their deliberations, and they agreed unanimously that it would be totally contrary to what they saw as the principles of public service broadcasting, and dismissed it . . . There were no economists at all on Pilkington's Committee; I don't think it occurred to any of the civil servants who were largely responsible for the appointment of that Committee to have an economist on it. But the unanimity of that Committee was extraordinary.
>
> (Conference Transcripts, 2005: Opening Plenary)

The civil servants never doubted then that the grown-ups, or at least the great and the good, could and should decide what forms of information and entertainment should be provided in the nursery. Its inhabitants could not be trusted to judge their own best interests. Still less should their choices prevail over their interests as assessed by their betters. With no economists in the room, the sovereignty of the consumer did not show its rude face.

Tom O'Malley picked up this contrast between the paternalistic presuppositions of the Pilkington debates and the absence of cultural dirigisme in the Peacock inquiry, again reflecting the absence or presence of economists:

> prior to Peacock, the discourse of public broadcasting policy was one which used words like 'public service', like 'education', which sought to have instruments for achieving those social goals which were state-centred in one form or another. The remarkable thing about Peacock – possibly because of the generational surge in economists, is that it didn't do that, and I think that Jeffery [Milland] has illustrated that there was some kind of shift going on there.
>
> (Conference Transcripts, 2005: Opening Plenary)

He then went on to crystallise the deeper philosophical opposition between libertarians and egalitarians in terms which transcend the special preoccupations of (conventionally educated) economists and which come close to Isaiah Berlin's distinction between negative and positive liberty (Berlin, 1998):

Popper says if it's a choice . . . I opt for freedom over equality . . . And it seems to me that the Popperian connection in that argument with Peacock is that in consumer sovereignty, in the stress upon the rights of individuals to make these kinds of free choices about goods, like it or not . . . there is [an] implicit rejection of a view that said broadcasting policy should be about promoting equality of access to cultural goods.

(Conference Transcripts, 2005: Opening Plenary)

At this point the economists qua economists may have little to say. In their presupposed and/or their recommended world all have full and equal 'access' to the market place, unless 'access' is defined to include the ability to pay any price demanded in that market place. If that is the problem which is denying access to some, then this is really an argument about inequalities of wealth and income, about which economists may have much to say, but about which economics has much less to say. It can perhaps address and investigate the possible effects of equality and inequality on incentives and economic performance and perhaps even measure inequality itself; but it has nothing definitive to say about the ethics of inequality or about efforts by governments to mitigate it.

Some libertarians may inspect sceptically the phrase 'equal access' and ask whether this may not on occasions be a euphemism for 'equal – or even the same – experience', thereby dispensing altogether with individual choice; and they will be met by the argument that choice may also be denied, in effect, even if not by government fiat, by highly commercialised environments which somehow constrain consumers towards outcomes pre-selected by large business interests. On whether or not that is possible and whether or not it happens, economists may have something to say. Insofar as that something is sceptical of the power of corporations to manipulate their markets, the economists may run into the Mandy Rice-Davies objection that, because of their affection for markets, 'they would say that, wouldn't they?'

In the end there may be irreducible trade-offs between freedoms and degrees of inequality or means of mitigating it. Economics may throw light on many aspects of such trade-offs; but it cannot arbitrate the dispute from a higher vantage point. Nonetheless it may perform a useful hygienic function in examining sceptically arguments advanced in the name of equality, or even in the name of equality of access, with a view to exposing the cases where such arguments coincide with the interests or prejudices, either as producers or as rulers, of narrow sections of society effectively accountable to the general public neither through the market place nor through the ballot-box.

But this sterilisation does not in the end dispose of that kernel of conviction that there is still something – even if it cannot be stated – about cultural goods which economics is missing. Tom O'Malley affirmed this with endearing modesty close to the end of the Peacock Legacy Conference:

> there is something about all this [freedom versus equality] that leaves . . . [one] feeling uncomfortable – but that's not your [Peacock's] fault! (Laughs) It's not a problem that you've generated; you've identified the problem of how you justify this in this context.... [But] there are things there, values about public service broadcasting, that I think are extremely important. If you asked me to justify them within a liberal theoretical perspective, I would have difficulty in doing it. But I hope some day it will happen.
>
> (Conference Transcripts, 2005: Closing Plenary)

The resolution of the apparent tension between concerns about liberty (of speech, of creation and of consumer choice) and concerns about cultural standards may depend, in part, on insisting upon the distinction between some measure of 'average' cultural standards and measures of the cultural peaks. A regime – such as a free publishing market with substantial patronage of admired writers and artists which produces Shakespeare, Milton and Dickens – may be judged benign without regard to how much trash lurks in the valleys and lowlands between these Olympians.

By parity of reasoning, attempts to engineer a higher average cultural level above, as it were, sea level, especially if they rely on the suppression of trash rather than enhancing opportunity for those who wish to reach for the sky, may be judged misguided and prejudicial to the freedoms of consumer choice and producer enterprise. This judgement grows more convincing the more access broadens from a handful of terrestrial TV channels to limitlessly large numbers of platforms and modes of publication and the less that market fails as the formally dominant sale of audiences to advertisers gradually yields to the sale of programmes to people.

'Fuzzies' may still cherish the dream of a wholesome popular culture sustained and propagated by creative idealists and by a regime of public service financing allied to some species of official discouragement of the trash which panders to the dumbest instincts. They may believe too that in this way they are somehow protecting the weak and the poor, the old and the young, from exploitation by ruthless commercial raptors and instead widening their access to a better and more liberating culture.

This, I fear, is the root error, the Pilkington–Annan fallacy. It is not just that suppression of the rubbish is most unlikely to succeed, but also that it would be wrong even if it did. The average cultural level of a society – highbrow or low, wholesome or crass – simply is not a legitimate goal of law and public finance in a free and democratic society, though patronage of the arts, improvement of education and correction of market failures may well be. It is not legitimate because it arrogates to self-appointed guardians of the culture the right to decide for their fellow citizens what should be their cultural tastes and choices; and this is unwarranted, however well meant.

Nor can the warrant be found in the obnoxiousness of those who supply and profit from the trash, however strong the British tradition of looking down on trade and sneering at spivs. It has always been, as Adam Smith taught, that:

> It is not from the benevolence of the butcher, the brewer, or the baker, that we expect our dinner, but from their regard to their own self-interest.
>
> (Smith, 1812:27)

Likewise must we expect our entertainment and information from labourers who are worthy of their hire, junk-merchants or otherwise?

A liking for *Dallas*, football and quiz shows – or even pop music – may be lowbrow; but its suppression or discouragement is not a proper object of public policy as though it were a cultural form of slum clearance, itself a policy with disastrous social consequences. What should matter to the guardians of culture are the freedom and opportunities for artists and writers to take their wares to market, or to suitably benevolent patrons, and the freedom of people to choose their works.

If that latter freedom is impaired by poverty it is to the relief of poverty at source – in deficient incomes – that the radical should chiefly look, not to gerrymandering and manipulation of the market for books and electronic publications or, indeed, of public transport systems. If the impairment lies in the shortcomings of education, then it is to better schooling that the reformer must turn.

Opportunities to create and to choose, not high – or even middle – brow outcomes, are the proper goals of those who would maximise the cultural vitality of their society. A free competitive electronic publishing market – augmented (as the Peacock Report contemplated with their

Arts Council of the Air idea) by public and private artistic patronage and by compensation for market failures where they occur – does just that, as well as promoting efficiency and setting proper rewards.

That, of course, is all still opinion and not yet universally accepted. My conclusion therefore is still the same as it was at the end of the Peacock Legacy Conference:

> the profound and fundamental chasm that has run through this Conference, as perceived by me, is the different way which essentially the economists and the rest (whether or not they are called Fuzzies) think about these things. For me, this is not a question that should just be left there as a subjective matter about which you shrug your shoulders and say 'you pays your money and you takes your choice and either you are an economist or you aren't and that's the end of it'. These two universes of discourse claim to be disciplined, intellectual processes, which have rules, which accept the overriding imperatives of logic and evidence and fact, and it seems to me that what is called for is a serious and incisive effort to investigate the apparent chasm between these two universes of discourse and to decide, to put it ruthlessly, . . . whether in some sense systematically one group has got it right and the other group has got it wrong. But what is clear to me is that it is a dialogue largely of the deaf . . . It should not be beyond the power of man, I would hope, to convene a conference of people of suitable higher skills – I think of philosophers as having a role to play in this – to investigate why there is this cultural chasm between these two things and what further can be said about it. I will conclude, in order to be totally biased, by recalling what Keynes said about two economists of his acquaintance. He said that the one carved in stone and the other knitted in wool.... That is my perception of the two sides of this debate. Whether I am right or wrong is something that the next conference organised by . . . perhaps the University of Wales should investigate, because I think it is an excellent area in which real progress should be able to be made.

(Conference Transcripts, 2005: Closing Plenary)

Notes

1. The quotation can also be found in Chapter 12 of this collection, p. 341.
2. The product of the school I attended, founded by William of Wykeham.
3. BBC nightly current affairs TV programme started in the 1960s.
4. London Weekend Television's Sunday morning current affairs TV programme on ITV from September 1972.

5. A phrase I originally used in improvised remarks to a public meeting in Croydon on 24 September 1980 convened by the Independent Broadcasting Authority to discuss the possible advent of breakfast television (see Jay, 1984:191). Much later it became associated with John Birt's policies at the BBC for broadcast journalism, though as far as I know he never used the expression. Its advocates meant by it reporting that helped viewers to understand what was happening and why, while its critics alleged that it replaced 'fact' with 'analysis' that was merely opinion. It is at best a professional ideal for a practitioner, not a public good to be promoted by public policy or law. It appears to conflict with consumer sovereignty only if it is wrongly construed as 'up-market' in a world where consumers have only base tastes. It applies as much to popular as to 'high-brow' journalism. The interplay of the professional ideal and the sovereignty of the consumer are best reconciled by competitive market forces.
6. Brook Productions, weekly current affairs TV programme on Channel 4 in the 1980s.
7. By TV-am on 28 December 1981.
8. The quotation can also be found in Chapter 12 of this collection, p. 305.

5
The 'Politics' of Investigating Broadcasting Finance[1]

Sir Alan Peacock

(The only time in my life that I found myself pursued by the media was when I was appointed to investigate broadcasting itself as Chairman of the Committee on the Financing of the BBC in March 1986. It was widely assumed that the Committee members were hired guns instructed to conclude that the BBC should cease to be publicly funded and should rely on advertising income, a view particularly associated with the then Prime Minister, Mrs Thatcher. Any hope that we would be allowed to get on with our investigations uninterrupted by media attention was soon dispelled, for too much appeared to be at stake if the government were to take our findings seriously. Various attempts were made to manufacture disagreement between our members, and I am told that a particular major consultancy employed someone to examine my career for flaws in my professional reputation and character that might be used to 'rubbish' our final Report! It followed that a strategy had to be developed which would create the conditions which would make it possible for the Committee to concentrate on the task before it. This involved negotiations with the government itself over terms of reference and resources available to conduct appropriate research, with the interest groups (including politicians) anxious to influence our findings, and with the public at large, whom the system is meant to benefit. As Chairman, therefore, I had to become a political animal, and it may be that my experiences may suggest that social scientists have much to learn by becoming, if only temporarily, part of their own subject-matter.)

Introduction

The Committee on Financing the BBC, of which I was Chairman, submitted its report in May 1986 and it was published in July of that year. Its recommendations received widespread publicity and produced a deluge of comment, particularly from those most likely to be affected by its conclusions – the broadcasting companies themselves. This article is not concerned in any detail with the Committee's analysis of the problem of financing television and radio and is certainly not a defence of the recommendations. It concentrates on a study of the process of carrying out an enquiry of this kind, in the belief that such a study may be both interesting and instructive. (The economic analysis underlying the Committee's work is presented in Peacock, 1986, Budd, 1986 and Brittan, 1987.) Nevertheless, it is worth a sentence or two to remind the reader of the main contents of the Report. It describes the existing system of broadcasting finance and how it evolved, and draws attention to the phenomenon of the 'comfortable duopoly', in which the broadcasting market is carved up between the BBC, largely financed by a compulsory levy – the licence fee – and the ITV companies who are protected by a franchise arrangement which allows them to dominate access to broadcasting time 'slots' for advertising. The Committee argued that this system is inherently unstable and will in any case be challenged by technological changes, notably cable and satellite transmission, which will offer consumers more choice. Furthermore the major objection to a subscription system for broadcasting or to charging for particular programmes (Pay TV) no longer holds given the growing sophistication in methods of encoding broadcasting signals. Its recommendations were designed to prepare the way for the development of a 'consumer-driven' system of broadcasting in which the individual viewer and listener would express choices by payment, and in which more freedom of entry of independent producers would be encouraged, while at the same time protecting the public interest in supporting programmes of an informative and instructive nature which would not survive commercially (see Report, 1986, Chapter 12).

The Committee's approach to the financial problems of broadcasting and its far-reaching conclusions came as a surprise. It was supposed to have been appointed to reach foregone conclusions. This was not the case. It was widely expected to recommend that the BBC should take advertising. It did not so recommend. It was believed that the terms of reference would so confine its activities that it would not be able to consider the wider aspects of broadcasting resources and how they should be financed. In fact, it offered revolutionary proposals designed to alter the whole system of broadcasting finance. A running commentary by the press made much of wide differences of opinion among members of the Committee on essential matters, yet the Report was unanimous, with notes of reservation offered in only two cases. (In one of these the disagreement was not about aims but about means.) The longer-term scenarios for facilitating the introduction of a consumer-driven system of broadcasting were accepted by all members of the Committee. It was forecast that the Committee would not make its deadline of reporting within a year. It did. It was suggested that in the time available, no empirical research worth the name could be provided. In fact, the commissioned research is generally recognised amongst experts as of very high standard. On its appearance, it was widely believed that the government would 'kick it into the long grass'. (Mr Robert Maxwell went so far as to warn me that the Committee has committed the terrible crime of having deprived the Prime Minister of an election issue!) It is early days yet to say how much attention the government will eventually pay to our findings. At the time of writing, it had set up a Cabinet Committee to consider its proposals in detail, chaired by the Prime Minister. In January 1987 two of the main short-term recommendations – no advertising on the BBC and indexing of the licence fee to the Retail Price Index – were accepted by the government. Those most affected by the proposals have declared their implacable opposition to the Report. That much is true but virtually no broadcasting pundit believes any more that the '*status quo*' remains an option. Some of them, such as Lord Thomson of Monifieth, Chairman of the IBA, have been gracious enough to state that the report provides the essential agenda for discussion of the future of broadcasting.

I cannot fully explain this remarkable disparity between the general expectations of those who take an interest in broadcasting – press, politicians and broadcasters themselves – and what our Committee has recommended, and the subsequent discussion of our findings. A partial explanation must lie in the intense emotions which the obtrusive medium of television seems to engender and the strong vested interests in its structure and mode of operation, both of which encourage rumour and speculation at the very mention of possible changes in the broadcasting system. Such an atmosphere, reminiscent of the soap operas which to many represent the very essence of television, hardly encourages the belief that a group of individuals with differing professional backgrounds and experience can sit down and agree on what the important issues are, and what information and analysis will throw light on them. Indeed, those who created such an atmosphere, or some of them, clearly intended that the Committee should be prevented from conducting its operations in the cast of mind which would encourage the cool look at the task before it, from being able to collect its evidence unhampered by premature claims that we were selecting that evidence and from being able to keep our counsel on matters of policy recommendations until we had carefully considered how far we could agree amongst ourselves.

This contribution is a personal account of how, as Chairman, I tried to fulfil the task set before the Committee. This is not an original idea. Lord Annan (1981), the Chairman of the previous enquiry into broadcasting, produced a most lucid and absorbing account of his experiences, which I cannot possibly emulate. I shall differentiate my product from his in a number of ways which are best explained by saying that I speak as an economist rather than, like Lord Annan, as a historian. But both accounts have this in common. The task of being Chairman of a Committee of Enquiry on a controversial issue has to be something more than that of producing answers to difficult questions in co-operation with colleagues. It must include the creation of the conditions which make it possible for the Committee to pursue its proper task. This involves the Chairman in activities which I shall broadly describe as political. I shall therefore concentrate on the negotiation and discussion with the outside world and not on the internal politics of the Committee, though clearly the internal and external politics will be inter-related. My aim is to describe and to analyse rather than to criticise the behaviour of those who took part in this political process.

Initial negotiations

The first area of negotiation concerned my own appointment, and what might be called the job specification.

Once having agreed in principle to be Chairman of a Committee, one might have expected that there could be an intense and concentrated period of negotiation between the Chairman, the relevant Secretary of State and his senior civil servants about the objects of the enquiry, the role of the Chairman and individual members, the choice of members themselves, and the resources to be provided and instructions on their use. Clearly a good deal could hang on such negotiations, including whether or not one should commit oneself finally to taking on the job.

I had no difficulty agreeing the terms of reference with Mr Leon Brittan, then Secretary of State for the Home Department, and this saved a lot of time because terms of reference are not negotiable, though a Secretary of State may be willing to discuss amendment and may even ask for advice (but not for a decision) on their scope. I was particularly pleased that the terms of reference covered a wide range of options for financing broadcasting, and that they recognised the close connections between the different parts of the broadcasting system and between that system and the Press. The one thing that I was concerned about was the question how far we should simply examine alternative systems of finance only or would be expected to make specific recommendations. There was a good chance that a Committee might agree on the effects of financial changes on the broadcasting system and on the welfare of viewers and listeners, but it seemed to me at the time that to go further might only offer us the opportunity of agreeing to disagree on the ranking of the options that we were to examine. I was assured that on this question the Committee could decide for itself. Subsequently, much was made of the narrowness of the terms of reference and a conspiratorial view was taken of them. Some very anxious TV personalities, for example, wrote to *The Times* complaining that our terms of reference did not permit us to discuss the merits of the *status quo*. My reply was the first of a continuous series of statements trying to reassure the public that the government was not committed to change, had said so, and that therefore the examination of the status quo as an option was essential, if only as a frame of reference which would facilitate comparison between alternative methods of financing broadcasting.

A remarkable feature of these initial negotiations with the Home Office was the lack of concern over what some would regard as important details in any job specification. Let me give a few examples. Firstly, I do not have in my possession an official letter of appointment, not because I have lost it, but because such a letter does not exist! A parliamentary statement of my appointment was taken as sufficient. Secondly, I was given no advice or instructions on the Chairman's function or on the conduct of business. Although I have served on government committees and on a Royal Commission before, and could claim some knowledge of the inner workings of government, I was not aware of the so-called 'Balfour Rules'[2] on the conduct of committees, and these were certainly not drawn to my attention. It suited my temperament to be left to get on with things, so I worked on the assumption that if I did anything totally outrageous or violated the Constitution, I would be duly admonished. A third example is more important. At no stage was any observation made or instruction offered by members of the government on what they would consider should be the Committee's conclusions. I made a particular point of finding out at an early stage what form official evidence would take. In the case of the Prime Minister's office, I was informed that no evidence would be offered. It was natural for the Home Office to provide us with what turned out to be an extremely useful survey of the broadcasting scene, but it contained no recommendations. We received much useful technical advice from other Departments, notably my old Department, Trade and Industry. We almost pleaded with some Departments, such as the Treasury, to give us their views, but they were not to be drawn.

I labour this last point because a deliberate attempt seems to have been made by politicians and others opposed to the Enquiry to claim that it was rigged in order to be sure that it would recommend that the BBC should be forced into the market place. The kindest words that I can find about such allegations is that they were naïve. If a government has made up its mind on a policy matter, then the obvious vehicle for the design of policy recommendations is an inter-departmental committee of officials with outsiders confined to the role of advisers, as with the recent committees set up to examine the future of the pensions system (on which I served). It hardly indicates confidence in a particular policy if an outside body had to be employed to whitewash it, and even if such a curious procedure were adopted, the government would have to choose a body of 'yes-men' ('yes-persons'?) to apply the solution. Such a description certainly did not fit our Committee, as its list of members[3] makes clear.

Why, then, will a government give so much of a free hand to a committee both in respect of the interpretation of its terms of reference, and of its procedures and practices? The answer lies, I believe, in the fact that the government had no obligations towards such a committee. It could dissolve it at any time, as has happened with a change of government. It is not bound to publish its findings. No constitutional procedure requires that its contents need to be reviewed and commented on by any administrative or legislative committee, or be the subject of parliamentary debate. The financial risks are very limited. Funds could be withdrawn at any time, and members are not normally remunerated, at least not in a form which could be the subject of a claim for redundancy payments.

Negotiating resources

The second area of negotiation concerned resources and their deployment. The first question which concerned me was the location of the secretariat. Living in Edinburgh as I do, it occurred to me that whatever might be the optimal location for Committee meetings and taking of evidence, valuable time might be saved all round and expenditure cut if the secretariat were centred in Auld Reekie. I lost this round with the Home Office who saw difficulties, as the sponsoring Department, in having staff of their own seconded to a 'foreign country' and beyond immediate face-to-face contact or, alternatively, in having to persuade the Scottish Office in Edinburgh to detach staff to serve us. Like all skilful negotiators, they offered me an option by asking me not to make up my mind until I had met the civil servant whom they wished to recommend as Secretary. I quickly realised that they were recommending an absolutely first class man, a highly trained physicist and OR expert for whom servicing the Committee, were he appointed its Secretary, would be his 'blooding' as an administrator. Bob Eagle might have to be anchored professionally and domestically in 'The Smoke', and has an understandable aversion to air travel, but he proved to have all the qualities necessary for a difficult assignment – quick on his feet, immense industry, unflappability and cheerfulness! The problem of running an office had no terrors for him and he sensed very quickly what would be the important 'inputs' which would require negotiation. An important example was his insistence that we had an in-office word processor with a full-time operator. The effect of this on the productivity of draft preparation and revision was quite dramatic and made the time-scale look much less forbidding.

The second concern was the budget. Being difficult to cost, the total budget allocation had to be fairly flexible and negotiations were more concerned with authorising forms of expenditure and the application of established civil service rules about making contracts, the scale of allowances to committee members and research staff and matters of this kind.

My previous experience on committees alerted me to the possibility that the Home Office might question the use of funds for research. Committees sometimes have access to research already undertaken in government departments, and in fact we were given full information on the present state of broadcasting technology and on the system of broadcasting regulation and useful impressions of broadcasting policy problems in other countries by the Foreign Office. Some Committees rely almost exclusively on those who present evidence to generate research, and certainly some of the evidence we received was backed by empirical research of high quality. However, I formed the impression very quickly that there could be no guarantee that the research already conducted or likely to be generated by the Committee's existence would necessarily address itself to the questions of direct interest to the Committee and, indeed, it would be difficult to forecast what some of those questions might be or where they might lead. We clearly needed a team of researchers offering tailor-made studies, who could turn their minds quickly to issues presented to them as we progressed and who could offer expert appraisal of statistical and economic evidence as it came before us. The Home Office raised no objection to this while rightly insisting that scales of remuneration had to be agreed with them and that outside contracts must follow their tendering rules. They also co-operated fully in achieving quick publication of the major research studies.

Committees of this kind, as I have indicated, are not remunerated, though I remember that Sir Roy Allen as Chairman of the Committee on the Impact of Rates some twenty odd years ago, of which I was a member, insisted that we should be paid a fee per meeting attended. The allowances for Committees of this kind are traditionally less than generous, and my Committee was no exception. Two matters nearly resulted in revolution. When I was temporarily a Deputy Secretary in the Department of Trade and Industry (DTI), I was obliged to take a taxi even for short distances if an official car was not available. As Chairman of the Committee I could not claim a taxi fare unless I signed a statement claiming that I had heavy baggage. (Shortly before becoming Chairman of the Committee I was approached about the possibility of becoming Chairman of a standing Advisory Committee for a Department of Government that I prefer not to name. The post was unpaid and the senior official who was asked to sound me out, when he heard that I was moving back to Scotland, actually had the temerity to observe that it might just be possible to pay my travel expenses to London meetings!) Gladstone said that the income tax had turned us into a nation of liars. That observation might well apply to expenses. There is a strong temptation to lie in order to be able to take the occasional taxi and I am fairly sure that had I claimed to be loaded to the gunwales with papers on coming to London my word would not have been questioned, though it might well have been doubted. The problem was solved and within the rules, by allowing me when under time pressure to hire a car from the government car pool and to charge it to our budget. The second matter concerned allowances when abroad. Four members of the Committee sat down for an evening meal in Rome – not a frugal but certainly a modest affair – and discovered on paying the bill that they had exhausted one whole day's allowance!

There is no satisfactory solution, I suspect, to this matter which must sound petty to some. There must be rules, and no one expects ever to be fully compensated for their expense in terms of both time and money. On the other hand, there is the lingering feeling that members of such Committees are being had for suckers and perceived their treatment as that of lesser beings than those of comparable experience and professional standing within the Civil Service.

Negotiating with interest groups

It might be thought that a Committee appointed to consider a radical change in the structure of broadcasting finance would not need to apply itself to the task of generating evidence. Interested parties would flood it with memoranda, taking the opportunity simultaneously to make their views public in a way which might influence those in power in their attitude to the eventual conclusions that the Committee might reach. The supply of evidence and the offer to give oral evidence would far outstrip the demand in terms of the time available for the Committee to digest the evidence and to question those supplying it. It is certainly true that there was no lack of evidence submitted – 843 individuals or organisations made submissions. However, whatever the volume of supply of evidence we were particularly concerned that it was not dominated by the large producer interest groups who, very understandably, would not wish to encourage competitive evidence from those who wished to enter and to share their market or who might claim that they did not provide good service.

To this end, the Committee first of all went further than most, I suspect, in disseminating information to the public about its view of the issues which would have to be resolved. Invitations to address meetings were readily accepted and serious queries about our activities answered. We were responsible for an innovation in holding a one-day conference on 28 November 1985 in Church House, London. The idea was to have the main interest groups present their views in public and to discuss them in front of the members of the public who were admitted on a first-come first-served basis. It was hoped that this public exposure would indicate that the issues that we were concerned with were not simply short-term ones but, given rapid changes in technology, concerned the whole future of broadcasting transmission and its effect on the ordinary household. I cannot claim that the meeting was a pronounced success. The actors in the public drama were not disposed to discuss with one another, but, by and large, further publicised their entrenched positions. The 'public' merely heard a repetition of what had become a dialogue of the deaf. Instead of acquiring a reputation for openness and receptivity, the Committee was attacked by those who had not been asked to present their views as having reduced them to the role of second-class citizens. Members of the observing public present resented not being able to participate, and this fact was exploited by one politician present, who, I believe, would be against the televising of Parliament. The television interviewers were able to make mincemeat out of me, and I thoroughly deserved it, having obviously made a naive forecast of how the meeting would go. It was a political error, but, I hope, an understandable one.

I shall not dwell long on the ways in which the Committee itself took a positive role in obtaining evidence, for the methods of doing so are familiar and do not enter into the realm of politics as I have defined it. I suppose it could be claimed that the Committee's wish to have independent sources of information and analysis was designed to strengthen its authority in later debate. Indeed, it was partly designed to steer the debate itself, and I believe it was a useful strategy to publish our research findings as far ahead of the main Report as possible, thus showing that the Committee would rest its conclusions on the weight of the evidence and not on *ex cathedra* utterances. Visits to television stations, meetings with the top brass of broadcasting authorities at home and abroad were clearly *de rigueur*. Each of us would have favourite stories to report of our travels. Those of us able to make it to Rome will remember for a long time the lunch given for us by the British Ambassador to Italy, Lord Bridges, at which he lectured us and his guests on the importance of maintaining broadcasting standards through pubic authorities, all in beautiful Italian! A more unusual feature of self-education was the video-cassette of 'prime time' programmes from several countries which included advertising which was a first introduction to some members into the mysteries of VCRs. I was supplied with a satellite dish to receive about eight European channels. This required me to obtain, with a little difficulty, a DTI licence and, with rather a long delay, planning permission from the Edinburgh District Council. This excited some press interest and my neighbours, far from objecting to a dish of 1.8 m diameter over the wall, asked to be cabled up to it. This news spurred the Director of the Cable Authority to write to me that cabling up my neighbours turned my house into a cable station. This would require two further licences, but, as the Edinburgh cable concession had already been allocated to another company, any application made by me would have to be refused! This was an interesting insight into the issues surrounding freedom of entry into the broadcasting business.

Negotiation in the assembly and hearing of evidence required me, advised by the Committee, to make sure that we had a clear understanding with the BBC about procedure. Before considering this aspect of politics, I should say something about the BBC's posture on matters of this kind. As we all know, it commands at home and abroad great respect as a pioneer of broadcasting, and its reputation within its peer group approaches the invincible when it comes to awards conferred by international broadcasters on one another. It is the owner of an enormous stock of programmes and archival material. It is justifiably proud of its innovations in transmission technology. It sponsors major research effort in listeners' and reviewers' reactions to programmes. It is a large music and book publishing house. Small wonder then that it impresses, indeed overawes, those who are appointed to investigate its functions. It is indeed a body 'on whom assurance sits as a silk hat on a Bradford millionaire' (Eliot, 1940, lines 233–4) and none the worse for that some might add.

In my first meeting with the Chairman of the BBC and senior executives, something of this patrician stance was conveyed and I remember that this was symbolised in two towering figures with menacing scowls who looked down on this stocky figure like the giants Fasolt and Fafner on the dwarf Alberich in *Das Rheingold*. According to a report in *The Times* I caused consternation by answering the Question 'what can we tell you?' by replying 'nothing' and by requesting that their evidence should be with the Committee in two months. As it was agreed on this occasion that we would make more progress if we had informal confidential meetings, the BBC started one down with us by babbling to the press. But nothing was to be gained by sticking to these preliminary postures and Stuart Young and I were easily able to agree to have a schedule of meetings with full opportunity for the presentation of supplementary evidence. Once the BBC had realised that we knew what questions to ask, they seemed only too willing to act as our guide, philosopher and friend through the labyrinthine structure of broadcasting, even to the extent of arranging our visits abroad. This offer had to be politely refused. It would have been wrong to have proceeded on the assumption that the BBC knew all that was to be known about broadcasting even if it were true. Indeed some of us suspected, and it turned out to be the case, that they were unfamiliar with the economic analysis of broadcasting for the simple reason that they have never had to concern themselves with major economic issues.

Although it is not my purpose here to comment on the evidence presented in any detail, I feel bound to add that the BBC missed a crucial opportunity to display its command of broadcasting issues in its presentations. Instead of taking the lead in a full discussion of the financing options available and how these might relate to criteria for policy, the BBC brushed aside any suggestion that change was necessary, other than some minor adjustments in the methods for raising the licence fee which might make the fee more acceptable to the public. It relied on the weight of its authority and its past experiences and not on a properly structured economic analysis which considered how far past experience would remain relevant. The attacks on the Committee's views on Subscription and Pay-TV made in their name, once the report had appeared, were embarrassing in the crudity of their language and speciousness of economic arguments.

Naturally enough, professional politicians were monitoring our activities and some were anxious to influence our approach to financing problems. Some of them submitted evidence in an individual capacity, notably the former Home Secretary, Mr Merlyn Rees. After the initial reactions in parliament to the setting up of the Committee I had expected to be taking shelter from the flak rather than be entering into negotiation with sceptics. The most active group demanding clarification of our approach was the Conservative Party Media Committee in the House of Commons, several of whose members had been or still were TV personalities or had been closely concerned with the regulation and administration of broadcasting. They tried very hard to draw me on what our conclusions were likely to be and how they would view them, but there was a notable lack of unanimity of view on broadcasting finance amongst its experienced members. I dare say that this lack of unanimity also characterises comparable opposition committees, but I was not asked to meet them. At his request, I willingly met Mr Clement Freud, the chairman of the Liberal Party committee, but hardly expected to be told in as many words that our journey through broadcasting finance was unnecessary and, even if a case for looking at broadcasting issues could be made, we were, he supposed, hired guns and therefore not to be trusted. As the Leader of his Party had publicly expressed confidence in my judgement, if also expressing doubt about my mission, and his predecessor, Lord Grimond, had agreed to chair our public meeting, I am afraid that I was unforgivably angry with and extremely rude to Mr Freud about this slur on our characters, all the more unforgivable because I rather enjoyed myself. Mr Freud was relieved, I believe, that he was not actually physically assaulted. Mr Norman Buchan of the Labour Party and I have come to know each other rather well as members of the travelling debating society created by the Committee's existence, so I was disappointed when he was not able to deliver his Labour comrades to me and me to them. Our easy passage, whilst in situ, with the professional politicians had probably nothing to do with skill in discussion and negotiations and is more likely to be a reflection of the opportunity cost of their time when issue after issue on which they are expected to pronounce is forced on their attention. Spasmodic eruption of interest in our doings is all that one should have expected and to have thought otherwise indicates how one can become obsessed with a public issue and greatly overestimate its importance and one's own.

Defending our findings

I come to the final stage which is perhaps the most fascinating of all for the participants, all eager to know how their creation will be received.

There is first of all an important personal decision to be taken. Once a Committee Report is received by the relevant Department, that Department, as I have explained, has no further obligation to the Committee though good manners requires the Secretary of State to thank its members by letter. I have served on some five committees and in all but one, the thank-you letter came from a different Minister than the one who had originally appointed the committee. Mr Hurd did more; he gave us an excellent dinner. It would be entirely understandable if committees returned to known fields and pastures old, thankful that it was all over and like Florestan in *Fidelio* consoling themselves with the words 'süsser Trost in meinem Herzen meine Pflicht hab' ich getan'.[4] The report could be left to make its own way into the world and obligations to it would be completed by good proofreading before publication.

Lord Annan stated in his splendid Ulster Television Lecture (Annan, 1981) that he regarded it as his duty to expound and defend his Report and he clearly did so with great skill. I was less sure about where my duty lay but I was concerned about the lack of champions to defend the interests of those for whom we agreed that the whole system of broadcasting was designed – the viewers and listeners – as were other members of the Committee. Moreover, having made recommendations which would clearly affect powerful producer interest groups in ways which they would perceive as adverse to their interests, there was no guarantee that the forthcoming debate would be conducted on impartial lines.

I did not view this task with relish when the Report was about to appear. There had been a set of unfortunate leaks, unfortunate because they took particular recommendations, such as the rejection of advertising by the BBC, out of context. The press was also unanimous in their view that members of the Cabinet were reacting most unfavourably to what they had been told about the Report's contents. Our child would be strangled at birth. The producer groups most affected by our recommendations controlled not only the channels of communication with the public, but also the professional bodies who had the best facilities for organising discussion and debate of broadcasting issues. They had immense resources for promoting and disseminating their views. The work of the Committee being over, I had no further claim on comparable facilities. I had my typewriter, access to typing and precious little else. What should be one's strategy?

I had little time to think out what to do before I was inundated with invitations to speak at conferences, write, lecture at home and abroad, take broadcast 'phone-ins' or radio and appear at short notice in television interviews. At least there was no difficulty about entry into the business of discussion, even though in some cases I was obviously being set up as a sitting target. I decided that at the outset I should accept as many invitations as possible in the early days in order to establish as clearly as possible what was correct and what was myth in the exposition and criticism of our findings and conclusions. I appeared on every kind of radio and television programme, ranging from a breakfast appearance to the late night news. I expounded our main thesis at all levels of discourse from the academic lecture to the popular newspaper article. I wrote at least six separate scripts adaptable for different occasions and which has to be kept in constant repair. I made appearances in places as distant from one another as Toronto and Stockholm, Edinburgh and Milan. I bombarded anyone who expressed interest in our work with manuscripts. I made contact with any public official who showed the least inclination to listen to me. Following Lord Annan's precedent I shall keep this up for a year, subject to avoiding exhaustion and divorce.

I shall only make two observations drawn so far from this feverish activity. The first concerns relations with government after publication. I have had only two short official meetings, one with all Committee members, to discuss the report, though I have had some contact with Government bodies closely concerned with the technology of broadcasting and useful discussions with members of public corporations closely involved with broadcasting. While it has been made clear that the Report is being closely studied, these bodies know my thinking and that of other members of the Committee, but one rarely knows theirs. One hears about various branches of government instituting studies of various aspects of the report and commissioning work by outside experts, but one learns about these things by chance or by daily reading of the *Financial Times*. Much more attention is openly paid to one's professional advice by overseas governments faced with similar problems. I am not arguing that there is necessarily anything wrong with this situation, though there is an odd Kafkaesque feel about this sudden severing of the nexus between the government and its one-time advisers. An ongoing dialogue might have its uses such as the right of rejoinder to criticisms made within government itself. This position is reinforced in the case of broadcasting where the interests of those whom broadcasting is meant to serve are clearly underrepresented whereas the large broadcasting companies are in close and frequent contact with officialdom.

My second observation relates to the recent controversy about biased television reporting sparked off by Mr Tebbit. The acid test as to whether the BBC and ITN companies can claim to be unbiased reporters of current affairs is provided by their reactions to the Committee's findings. Its recommendations imply the break-up of the 'comfortable duopoly' which could be threatened in any case by the growth of cable and satellite delivery systems. It is too much to expect that the major terrestrial broadcasting companies in the UK could express pleasure at the Committee's conclusions. The reporting that I have monitored has been principally in the form of off-the-cuff remarks, largely by broadcasters, and at the time of writing no programme has appeared, so far as I am aware, where the issues raised by the Committee have been properly presented and discussed. It is not so much biased reporting as covert censorship. Now one must not get this matter out of focus for, alongside international events, the subject of the financing of broadcasting, which is hardly a glamorous one anyway, may seem small beer and lacking in immediate appeal. It is nevertheless important and affects us all. The tenets of 'public service broadcasting', which the BBC in particular claims to follow, surely call for a more responsible approach to the study of the future of an industry in which the BBC perceives that it should have pride of place.

Summing up

The inevitable question arises, was the effort put into negotiations and discussion worth it? I am too close to events to be able to offer an objective assessment. I cannot prove it but I believe that our Report benefited from our having to defend the very fact of our existence from the beginning. It enabled us, I believe, to anticipate objections that had not occurred to us and to obtain responses to the research that we had commissioned and to our ideas on procedure which sharpened up our arguments.

A related question is how one views the chances of the main recommendations being accepted, given the intense and vehement opposition to some of them. I suppose some would answer with the old adage that the better the report, the less likely that it will be accepted. I am reminded of the delightful letter written by David Hume (1758) to Adam Smith on the appearance of the latter's first major work *The Theory of Moral Sentiments*:

> Show yourself a Philosopher in Practice as well as Profession. Think on the Emptiness, and Rashness, and Futility of the common Judgements of Men: How little they are regulated by Reason in any Subject.... A wise man's Kingdom is his own Breast: or, if he ever looks farther, it will only be to the Judgement of a select few; who are free from Prejudices, and capable of examining his Work. Nothing can be a stronger Presumption of Falsehood than the Approbation of the Multitude; and Phocion, you know, always suspected himself of some Blunder, when he was attended with the Applauses of the Populace.

But then he adds the punch line:

> (I now) proceed to tell you the Melancholy news that your book has been very unfortunate: for the Public seem disposed to applaud it extremely.
>
> (Hume, 1759:12th April)

I can think there is little likelihood that the public will be so disposed in our case but a little misfortune, in the Humeian sense, could very well befall us.

Notes

1. This chapter is based on lectures given to the London School of Economics Society and to The David Hume Institute, Edinburgh. It should be obvious to the reader that I owe an immense debt to my fellow members of the Committee on Financing the BBC – Mr Samuel Brittan, Ms Judith Chalmers, Mr Jeremy Hardie, Professor Alistair Hetherington, Lord Quinton and Sir Peter Reynolds. It will also be obvious that they had a great deal to put up with in their Chairman! I have deliberately refrained from considering the internal politics of the Committee's work, not only because this is a subject all on its own, but also because I feel strongly that our good relations assumed that we could express our views to one another in confidence. (This chapter is a reprint of Peacock, 1987.)
2. They were derived from the Report of a Committee headed by Lord Balfour of Burleigh published in 1909 which considered how the business of Royal Commissions should be conducted.
3. See Note 1 above.
4. 'Sweet consolation in my heart – I have done my duty.'

6
The Fight for Freedom in Broadcasting[1]

Sir Samuel Brittan

The origins of the Peacock Committee on the Finance of the BBC undoubtedly lie in the supposed unpopularity of the periodical increases in the BBC licence fee and the existence of a vocal lobby which suggested that the gradual introduction of advertising would provide an alternative. The normal governmental irritation with the BBC licence fee requests was reinforced by the belief that the BBC was high cost, inefficient and ridden with restrictive practices. Indeed most outsiders who took part in TV broadcasts, whether in the BBC or ITV, were amazed by the large crews and other staff involved and by a network of restrictive operations rivalled only by the Fleet Street practices in their heyday. A background influence was the belief of the Thatcher Government – as most previous governments – that the BBC was biased against it. But the main Ministerial conflicts with the Corporation – over *Real Lives*, and on particular drama and current affairs programmes – came after the Peacock Committee had been appointed in March 1985. No political complaints featured in the evidence presented by the Home Office to the Committee; nor were any made in any other way. Equally, the allegations frequently made on the Left and among the broadcasting establishment, that either the Committee had been instructed to recommend advertising or that it had been hand-picked in order to do so, could not have been more wrong. No steer of any kind was given to the Committee, or its Chairman.

Nor is it true that, as some press reports at the time of publication in July 1985 stated, that the Government was so disgusted with the recommendation not to press advertising on the BBC that the Report was 'shelved'. On the contrary, a Cabinet Committee under the Prime Minister was established to consider key recommendations. A Green Paper was promised on radio. Existing ITV franchises were extended by three years to 1992, to provide time to consider new methods of awarding them. A Department of Trade and Industry (DTI) review of cable policy was established and, above all, the Home Office appointed a consultant, Charles Jonscher, to report on the feasibility of direct subscription to the BBC.

It is, of course, far too early to say what will come of these follow-up activities. Moreover, at a more fundamental level, the Peacock Report caused the Thatcher Government some embarrassment. A minor irritant to Whitehall was that the Committee interpreted its terms of reference, as the Home Secretary who established it had always intended, to cover more than the narrow question of the licence fee versus advertising, and to probe into the aims as well as finance of broadcasting.

The main reason for Government embarrassment was that in putting forward the idea of a free broadcasting market without censorship, Peacock exposed many of the contradictions in the Thatcherite espousal of market forces. In principle, Mrs Thatcher and her supporters are all in favour of deregulation, competition and consumer choice. But they are also even more distrustful than traditionalist Tories, such as Douglas Hurd, of plans to allow people to listen to and watch what they liked, subject only to the law of the land. They espoused the market system but disliked the libertarian value judgements involved in its operation: value judgements which underlie the Peacock report.

The worth of the report does not in the end depend on how many of its recommendations are accepted by a particular government. It lies in the fact that it planted the idea of a broadcasting market akin to publishing, which will flower in its time. In what follows, I shall discuss how the Committee came to its conclusions, without in any way attempting a comprehensive treatment of all the issues covered.

How the Committee worked

The ideal procedure for a fundamental inquiry trying to report within a year was stated long ago by Andrew Shonfield:

1. Intensive reading plus discussion with small expert research staff.
2. Meetings to discover common ground and divergencies among the Committee.
3. Selection of witnesses on the basis of ability to illuminate identified issues.
4. Systematic arguments on points of disagreements (Shonfield, 1967).

The first three phases would be at least half-time occupations, and the fourth full-time.

It would be idle to pretend that we had any chance of following the Shonfield procedure in its full rigour. The Home Office had set up the inquiry on a more limited basis. We were seven people, meeting once a fortnight; and Peacock set himself the aim of reporting within a year. In practice this was very much less, as the main part of the 'evidence' did not arrive until after the 1985 summer holidays; and the main work had to be completed by the end of April 1986.

We had an excellent Secretary, Dr Robert Eagle, who was not a mandarin type, but a physicist turned administrator. He had the great advantage of being able, not only to carry out the normal drafting and organisational duties, but also of being able to brief us on the technological options (as can be seen from his Appendix on the Electromagnetic Spectrum). We also had a keen and hard-working executive Assistant Secretary in Andrea Jefferies, and an excellent typist and word processor operator, Mrs Brenda Rodrigues. That was our entire staff. But we did commission eleven research papers and the Chairman could call on three specialist economists – Martin Cave, Peter Swann and Cento Veljanovski – for advice and drafts, whenever necessary.

The Committee's work turned out to be half-way between a limited inquiry into advertising on the BBC and a full Royal Commission on broadcasting; and inevitably the cracks showed here and there. For instance, the majority of the Committee advocated that the BBC should sell Radio 1 and 2, without fully specifying that this must mean handing over to the BBC property rights to frequencies which are at present held by the Crown. The Recommendation (14) that Channel Four should 'be given the Option' of selling its own advertising time seemed to clash with the Committee's acceptance of 'the Annan principle of no competition for the same source of finance, while channels are limited and IBA regulation is needed' (Report, 1986: para. 588). Not nearly enough was said on Direct Broadcast Satellite policy. And in view of our strong anti-censorship line, we should have looked at the British Board of Film Censors and its role in controlling 'video nasties'. We should have had a chapter on the effects of advertising as such; we should have more on the US broadcasting scene; and so one could go on.

But those who wish to strike a blow for freedom cannot wait for an ideal inquiry with ideal terms of reference. They must seize any available opportunity. In practice our investigation could have been indeed more thorough only by the members sitting for years rather than months; and then we would probably have been overtaken by events, doubts, second thoughts and internal tensions. As it was our Committee was for the most part a friendly affair. Indeed what surprised me in the eventual Report was not the gaps just mentioned, but the number of key features on which we did manage to focus outside the advertising licence fee area. I like to think that our Report has a relation to that of the watercolour or drawing, which so often seems more attractive than the finished painting in oil.

How did the committee operate? The Chairman, Professor Peacock, played a predominant role which was far more than *primus inter pares.* There is nothing new or surprising here. The main guide to procedure is still a Report of a Committee under Lord Balfour of Burleigh, which reported in 1909 on Royal Commissions. Its conclusions are for the most part applicable to other Committees of Inquiry too. According to Balfour, the Chairman is responsible for carrying on business, for control of staff, for the control of business and for initiating methods of investigation. The Chairman is also 'the sole medium of official communication on behalf of the commission with government departments, public bodies and individuals', and he will have been consulted on the terms of reference.

The natural predominance of the Chairman was increased for several reasons. First, Professor Peacock was an authority on public finance, the economics of politics and bureaucracy[2] and the allocation of resources. Thus he had a strong sense of the questions that needed to be asked and the kinds of behaviour to be expected in the regulated BBC–ITV duopoly. Secondly, he was appointed on 27 March 1985 well before the other members who were only appointed on 17 May. By the time we held our first meeting on 30 May, Peacock had already a research strategy and had contacted consultants. Of course, any of us could have objected. But the mood was relief that so much had been put in hand. I remember being worried that too much of the empirical research would focus on advertising versus the licence fee. It was Professor Alastair Hetherington, ex-*Guardian* Editor and ex-BBC Controller, Scotland, who specifically suggested a study of subscription which was undertaken by Martin Cave and Associates, in consultation with physicists and technologists; and this became the most important single piece of research underpinning of our recommendations. Subsequently, Hetherington initiated the Leeds study on 'range and quality' over which opinions diverged rather more.

The dynamics of the Committee

From the start it was clear that the Committee could be divided very roughly into three groups. There were Peacock and myself, who were inclined towards market provision of goods and services and who had been stimulated by Peter Jay's writings.[3]

But market economics is so little understood that it was mistakenly identified outside the Committee, and even initially inside it, with (a) enthusiasm for advertising finance, (b) support for commercial pressure groups and (c) desire to please a Thatcher Government. At the other end were Hetherington and Judith Chalmers, the television and radio journalists, who were keen to preserve the achievements of British broadcasting and suspicious of market ideology. But Hetherington, who had felt the rough side of BBC authoritarianism in his period as Scottish Controller,[4] was – as his interest in subscription showed – far from a dug-in defender of the *status quo*. Hetherington also had the great advantage of enjoying the confidence of Chalmers who, in the friendliest way, distrusted Professor Peacock's, and even more my own, intentions. The third and middle group consisted of Lord Quinton, the philosopher and President of Trinity College, Oxford, Sir Peter Reynolds, Chairman of Rank Hovis McDougall and Jeremy Hardie, economist turned business-man and SDP candidate. These three were not committed either to the existing institutions or to any recommended alternatives; they were thus the swing voices on the Committee.

There was another important distinction. Peacock, who is Research Professor at Herriott Watt, Edinburgh, was able to give between a third and a half of his time to the inquiry. So too was Hetherington, who is Professor of Media Studies at Stirling. Thanks to the generosity of the Editor of the *Financial Times*, I was able to give the Committee a little of my normal working time now and then. The other four members were much more pressed by their regular commitments, although they all took an active part especially in the last hectic weeks.

I myself regretted that there was no one on the Committee publicly associated with the Labour Party. The reason was that Labour had declared itself against advertising in advance. But we surely could have had a Labour peer or backbencher, (e.g. Lord Barnett, or the former Home Secretary, Merlyn Rees), or a non-Parliamentarian with Labour credentials who would not have been committed to an official party line in advance of examining the issue. Such an inclusion might have lessened some misunderstandings and might have made the ill-formed, illiberal and ill-considered outburst, with which the Shadow Home

Secretary, Gerald Kaufman, greeted our recommendations, a shade more difficult to make. There were some unexpected cross currents on the Committee. Peacock and I were both far too individualistic to form the solid phalanx that some members initially feared. Perhaps my greatest difference with Peacock was on how to win over Hetherington to a broadcasting market – and, by extension, on how to explain the case for the market and its application to broadcasting to a wider public. Hetherington seemed to be less antipathetic to a market-based approach if it was founded on the English Liberal tradition of freedom of choice and opposition to censorship rather than on textbook reasoning, or econometric crystal gazing. Whether or not this was wishful thinking, Hetherington and I did form an alliance at the end on the need for a clearly written and unambiguous final chapter, and in protest against the submission of numerous drafts in rapid succession which the Committee had not had a proper chance to absorb.

My greatest fear in the early months of the Committee was that the majority might want to advocate the very gradual introduction of a little advertising into some part of the BBC, combined with a stiffening of regulation to maintain 'quality'. I was indeed disturbed (but not astonished) that liberal minded scholars and businessmen did not share my instinctive revulsion from 'regulation' in anything to do with news, opinion and artistic expression. However, a direct assault on the lines 'if the public want to have rubbish that is its business' would have been counterproductive. Fortunately, a closer analysis showed that the more benign effects of regulation might eventually be achieved by the combination of a true consumer market in broadcasting and public finance for programmes of a clearly public service nature.

Principles and conclusions

Early in the concluding chapter, the Committee stated its agreement with those witnesses who – in criticism of what they thought were too narrow terms of reference – maintained 'that before we can devise guidelines for the finance of broadcasting, we have to specify its purposes', (Report, 1986: para. 546). The Report's own central finding, far more important than any specific numbered recommendation, was

> British broadcasting should move towards a sophisticated market system based on consumer sovereignty. That is a system which

recognises that viewers and listeners are the best ultimate judges of their own interest, which they can best satisfy if they have the option of purchasing the broadcasting services they require from as many alternative sources of supply as possible.

(Report, 1986: para. 592)

The fundamental aim of broadcasting policy was stated to be 'enlarging the freedom of choice of the consumer and the opportunities to programme makers to offer alternative wares to the public'. Then followed two paragraphs which alone justified all the labour expended on the Report:

> Our goal is, of course, derived from aims much wider than any applying to broadcasting alone. They are embedded, for example, in the First Amendment to the US Constitution (15 December 1791). This lays down inter alia:

> 'Congress shall make no law . . . abridging the freedom of speech or of the press.'

It is often taken by US writers to mean both that television monopolies are to be prevented and that government intrusion of a negative, censorious kind is to be avoided.

Another way of looking at the matter is *via* the parallel with the printing press, which was subject to many kinds of regulation and censorship in the first two and a half centuries of its existence (see paragraphs 16–27). The abolition of prepublication censorship by Parliament in 1694 – leaving the printed word to be regulated by the general law of the land – was described by Macaulay as a greater contribution to liberty and civilisation than either the Magna Carta or the Bill of Rights[5] (Report, 1986: paras 548–9).

Later we said:

> The end of all censorship arrangements would be a sign that broadcasting had come to age, like publishing three centuries ago. Prepublication censorship, whether of printed material, plays, films, broadcasting or other creative activities or expressions of opinion, had no place in a free society and we would want to advise Government and Parliament to embark forthwith on a phased programme for ending it.

(Report, 1986: para. 696)

The Committee did not apply the slogan 'anything goes' in broadcasting any more that it is applied to private publishing or the theatre. Recommendation 18 stated that 'the normal laws of the land relating to obscenity, defamation, blasphemy, sedition and other similar matters' should apply to broadcasting. Exemptions, in favour of broadcasting, the main example of which is the 1959 Obscene Publications Act, will therefore have to go, as regulation fades.

The present organisation of broadcasting flies in the face of the goals just stated. The main feature of the British broadcasting system is that the BBC has a monopoly of tax finance, (the licence fee is, of course, a hypothecated household tax), and the ITV companies have a monopoly of advertising finance. The introduction of advertising into the BBC would leave the duopoly untouched, but merely substituting one source of finance for another. Not only is broadcasting a duopoly. It is a highly regulated one. The BBC has the right to interpret its responsibility to 'educate, inform and entertain'. The ITV companies are regulated by the Independent Broadcasting Authority – another government-appointed body. The right of anyone to publish material, or produce a work of art, so long as he can attract consumer support or finance himself in any other way and observe the law of the land, is simply absent in British broadcasting. The first Amendment provision that Congress may make no law abridging freedom of speech is in flat contradiction to the British system.

There was a sense in which the Committee's discussions with the BBC were at cross purposes from beginning to end. Some BBC officials are so used to the idea of being financed by what is virtually a tax on the possession of a television set that they do not realise how privileged and unusual their position is, and how much in need of continuing and detailed justification. No other consumer products are financed in this way, certainly not books or newspapers or entertainment. Even the National Theatre and Covent Garden have to finance themselves in some part from box office takings.

Much worse than the method of finance of the BBC – which may be a regrettable necessity for the time being – is the general assumption that broadcasting, unlike the Press and the theatre, needs to be regulated, i.e. censored. Cries of censorship are usually confined to particular programmes, which displease the Government. But the whole process of the IBA, both its continuing vetting of schedules and programmes and its long-term power to withdraw franchises from contracts that displease, amounts to censorship.

MPs who identify freedom of speech and of artistic expression with soft porn are merely revealing something about themselves. Many other matters are involved. Recent examples of broadcasting suppression include discussion of Count Tolstoy's book on British involvement in the forced repatriation of anti-Communist Russians and Yugoslavs, and a critical programme on the role of the IBA itself. Earlier, Churchill's warnings on the dangers of Hitler were kept off the air to please the party Whips.

Where then does the goal of a competitive broadcasting market leave *public service?* The term is often used to describe anything the BBC (or ITV) chooses to do. The Committee after a careful analysis emerged with two more limited concepts.

The *first* is an Arts Council type of definition covering minority or demanding programmes involving knowledge, culture, criticism and experiment (Report, 1986: para. 563) – a formulation which owed much to Lord Quinton. The democratic justification was that viewers and listeners themselves might be willing to support activities in their capacity as voting taxpayers which they are not prepared to pay for directly in large enough numbers. The stock example was 'Many citizens who never go near our National Galleries value their existence and are prepared to contribute as taxpayers to their upkeep' (Report, 1986: para. 562). The key change recommended here was that 'public intervention should be of a positive kind and transparent, to help finance additional production, rather than of a negative censorious kind, oblique and undetectable, which even the best system of regulation risks becoming,' and also that such patronage should account for a modest proportion of total broadcasting (Report, 1986: para. 566).

The *second* and more unusual sense of public service was what we described as mimicking the market – an expression first coined by Jeremy Hardie. Advertising-financed broadcasting does not in the Committee's view accurately reflect consumer requirements – at least, while the number of channels is severely limited because: (a) the ratings will inevitably dominate and minority tastes will be under-represented (and we all belong to minorities some of the time) and (b) even the ratings do not measure intensity of preferences – whether a viewer is keenly interested in a programme or barely conscious of what is in front of him. Maybe, if audiences were highly segmented, the conclusion would not follow and there could be a television equivalent of the *Financial Times* or *Guardian*. But audience research showed that the social profile of viewers of 'Panorama' is not very different to that of 'Dallas' viewers. There are just a few of them. Advertisers have not up to now been prepared to pay more per minute for one type of programme than another.

The existence of a tax-financed BBC and the IBA regulation of commercial television were justified by Peacock as a second-best attempt to replicate artificially the programme structure of a true broadcasting market, together with some public service in the first or narrow sense. This was not, of course, how the BBC and IBA justify their activities, but it is nevertheless the main justification available. The Committee went on to say, however, that technological developments in cable, satellite and subscription technology would in future, by providing multiplicity of choice and the possibility of direct payment by viewers, reduce the need for regulation to 'mimic' the market, although not for public service in the first, narrow, or Arts Council sense. The preconditions of a genuine consumer market include (Report, 1986: para. 552):

1. Viewers must be able to register directly their preferences and register the intensity of their services.
2. Freedom of entry for any programme maker who can cover his or her costs or otherwise finance production.
3. Operators of transmission equipment, where monopoly is likely to prevail, must have common carrier obligations and accept regulated prices.

Because the technical conditions for a fully developed consumer market will take time to develop, the Committee suggested *three stages* of implementation:

1. *Indexation* of the BBC licence fee.
2. *Direct subscription* to the BBC to replace the main part of the licence fee.
3. *Multiplicity of choice* with pay-per-view, as well as pay-per-channel available.

The Stage 1 recommendations were addressed to the immediate policy concerns which had led to the Committee's creation. They included recommendations against *obliging* the BBC to take advertising finance, and for indexing the licence fee and for exempting pensioners on supplementary benefits from the licence fee. They also included some recommendations designed to be first steps towards greater competition, such as those for putting out ITV franchises to competitive tender, for requiring both the BBC and ITV to take 'not less than 40 per cent' of programmes from small independent producers and for the privatisation of Radios 1 and 2. Lastly, they included some little-noted, but absolutely crucial, recommendations designed to pave the way for the development of a broadcasting market, such as the proposal (deliberately made *Recommendation No. 1*) that all new television sets should have peritelevision sockets designed to facilitate consumer subscription at low cost. We recommended abolishing forthwith the legal obstacles in the way of Pay-Per-Channel and Pay-Per-View and of the obstacles preventing bodies such as British Telecom and Mercury from becoming common carriers of television programmes and other services. Sir Peter Reynolds was instrumental in drafting the provision to prevent monopolistic abuse by cable transmitters or other operators.

It was our Stage 2 and 3 proposals which were designed to create a new political agenda for broadcasting policy. These, it should be stressed, were not left as mere vague hopes. For all our major proposals we suggested a timetable and ways of managing the transition. Thus in the case of the recommendation that the BBC should be financed by subscription, we argued that this should be achieved 'before the end of the century' both as a step towards consumer choice and as a means of lessening the BBC's political dependence on the government of the day, as well as for a variety of other reasons (Report, 1986: para. 607). Moreover, we saw subscription 'as a way in which all broadcasting organisations, including the BBC, can sell their services to the public', and not merely as an alternative way of collecting the licence fee.

Peacock also paid much attention to the role in Stages 2 and 3 of public service broadcasting in the Arts Council sense. Some such programmes could become commercially viable with multiplicity of choice and pay-per-view ('narrow casting'). But both because it did not wish to rely on this, and because of the risks of the intermediate stage when present-day regulation may have withered, but channels are still limited, the Committee suggested a *Public Service Broadcasting Council* (PSBC) which would be able to make grants to both the BBC and private enterprise broadcasters. How would the PSBC be financed in the all too-likely event of the Chancellor of the day being unwilling to provide direct Exchequer funds? Possible sources of revenue include (1) the economic rents paid by ITV contractors under competitive tendering; (2) revenues from increasing commercial use of broadcasting frequencies and (3) maintaining an indexed licence fee at a lower rate than the present one on all television sets to support the PSBC (Report, 1986: paras 688–9).

Contrary to what some nervous paternalists supposed, Peacock did not propose any sudden removal of all vetting and control. Indeed we advocated a phased programme of deregulation in television in the course of Stages 2 and 3. 'The first act of deregulation would be that the programme and schedule vetting functions currently vested in the IBA, and any other regulating authorities, would be no more strict than the relatively loose requirements now applied by the Cable Authority' (Report, 1986: para. 692). The final step would be the abolition of prepublication censorship or 'vetting of any kind', which would be replaced by the normal 'law of the land' applying to print media. This should happen when Parliament judged that 'an effective multiplicity of broadcasting' had arrived and was not being impeded by monopoly elements or other unforeseen snags (694–6).

So much for the principles that shaped the Report's recommendations, and the way in which we saw them being implemented. In what follows, I discuss selectively some of the main questions about our market approach that have emerged in political and public debate subsequent to the publication of the Report.

If it followed a market approach, why did the Committee not recommend that the BBC should take advertising?

The Report states:

> The main defect of a system based on advertising finance is that channel owners do not sell programmes to audiences, but audiences to advertisers. So long as the present duopoly remains in being and competition is limited to a fringe of satellite and cable service, the introduction of advertising is likely to reduce consumer choice and welfare. It could do so both by driving the BBC into a ratings war and by putting financial pressure on ITV companies, which would make it more difficult for them to meet IBA requirements. The result could be an inadequate supply of programmes which many of us watch some of the time and some of us watch most of the time, but which do not achieve top audiences ratings.
>
> (Report, 1986: para. 617)

These conclusions would stand over a very wide range of estimates for the price and income elasticity of demand for advertising.

It was this desire to promote the consumer interest which lay behind the recommendation against advertising, and not any belief that insufficient advertising revenue was available. The econometric studies did not – and could not have – decided the argument either way. The demand for advertising time on the air depends both on the number of slots available and on general economic activity. If the short-term price elasticity of demand is moderate to low, this would argue for the slow and gradual introduction of advertising on the BBC as the GDP increases. If the price elasticity were higher it would suggest a quicker introduction. That is all.

Under what circumstances might advertising-financed programmes more closely reflect consumer preferences?

Peacock's remarks about advertising finance not being able to reflect the full variety and intensity of consumer preference are always qualified by phrases such as 'so long as channels are limited' or 'while spectrum scarcity prevails'. This reflects an economic analysis developed in the US which suggests that as the number of channels increases, the differences between the programme composition of a pay-per-view and an advertising-financed system diminish. (If there are many dozen channels, the typical channel cannot expect more than a small proportion of viewers. It may therefore do just as well to go for minority or specialist audiences as compete in the transmission of soap operas).

But just how many channels would be required for advertising finance to resemble pay-per-view and how close would be the resemblance? There is a gap in the Peacock discussions. But even if we had said more, we would have had to report that no general conclusion is possible, as the answer will depend on the structure of consumer preferences, and transmission and programmes costs (Owen et al., 1974). Experience in the US and Italy suggests that rather more channels may be required than appear from the textbook examples. Indeed, we remarked on the genuine danger that satellite and coaxial cable will provide before long enough advertising-financed channels to threaten the present system, but not enough to provide a full consumer market. The Report refers (Report, 1986: para. 599) to the difficulty of 'how to move from the present system now under stress to the full broadcasting market, without having to pass in between through a time of troubles which could give us the worst of both worlds, and the benefit of neither.'

Such considerations explain the insistence on *triggers* to be set off, before the various phases of broadcasting deregulation are reached. The trigger for moving to the looser 'Cable Authority' type regulation for all broadcasting would be (a) the successful establishment of the PSBC and (b) 'a political judgement that sufficient diversity had been introduced into programme sources and payment methods'. The trigger for the final stage – 'the abolition of pre-publication censorship or vetting of any kind' – cannot be as precise. 'But a judgement would be required by Parliament that an effective multiplicity of broadcasting was working as intended, and that public choice was not being artificially limited by monopoly elements or technical snags of an unforeseen kind' (Report, 1986: paras 690–6).

Why did not the Committee recommend privatisation of the BBC apart from Radio 1 and Radio 2?

Under the present broadcasting system, privatisation of the BBC would not introduce any extra element of competition. Moreover, so long as direct charging of viewers and listeners is impossible, and the BBC is tax financed, a privatised body would be responsible neither to the market nor to Parliament and would thus have arbitrary and unacceptable power – which matters more for broadcasting than it does for gas or telephones. The BBC will eventually become one of many competitors for the audience's pound and for PSBC funds. To some, privatisation may then be the logical next step. But I would hesitate to commit myself. We are not establishing a broadcasting system in a new country. History and tradition do matter; and the continued public ownership of the BBC will do little harm so long as an eagle eye is kept open for privilege and favouritism.

Will the BBC be able to compete with ITV under subscription when ITV programmes will be provided free (i.e. the consumer will pay indirectly via the price of advertised products)?

Subscription is already being used by a million French television householders receiving *Canal Plus*, which started from scratch in 1985. Far more people are likely to subscribe to the BBC as an already established mainstream pair of channels. There are a good many supporters of subscription at a little below Director-General level at the BBC who have a strong belief that the BBC has something to sell which people will be willing to buy. Further evidence is provided by the NOP Poll commissioned by Peacock:

> Taking the more realistic version, in which the question was in terms of payments per week, some 45 per cent of respondents were prepared to pay up to £1.20 per week (approximately equivalent to the present licence fee), 50 per cent were not and 5 per cent did not know. Given that subscription is a highly novel concept to most citizens, and that the recent debate has been polarised between advertising and the licence fee, we suspect that these percentages must underestimate what people would pay once subscription was in operation and the BBC was effectively marketing its services (Report, 1986: para. 679).

The Committee's guess was that 75 to 80 per cent of television households would subscribe to the BBC.

Will charging for programmes place a heavier burden on the poor?

People with higher incomes are better able to afford any new products or services. This is part of the meaning of 'higher incomes' and has nothing to do with broadcasting. The poor will not be worse off in any absolute sense, so long as they can still watch a range of programmes as wide as the present advertising-financed ITV ones free, and the cost of buying BBC-type programmes is no higher than what the licence fee would have been.

Peacock's general approach (Report, 1986: para. 586) is that if 'Pay-TV had any adverse distributional effects then the Committee would prefer to see these taken care of by alterations in the tax or benefit structure or both, leaving those who were compensated in this manner to decide for themselves', whether to use this compensation to maintain or increase purchase of broadcasting or some other purpose. But to show that we were serious about not impairing and – if possible – improving the position of the poor, we stretched out own principles to advocate in Stage 1 exemption from the licence fee for pensioners on supplementary benefit.

Will not charging for programmes drive some viewers away whose desires could have been met at no extra cost?

Yes. But charging may still be a lesser evil than other methods of finance. In strict theory, as explained in paragraphs 554–6, and more fully in Chapter 3, a charging system would lead to 'too little broadcasting'. Once a programme has been made, the marginal cost to additional viewers is little more than zero and it is therefore inefficient to price out viewers. It thus has elements of what economists call a 'public good'. This problem is, of course, not confined to broadcasting. It applies to books and newspapers, and to a lesser extent electricity and other public utilities, where the marginal cost of providing extra units is very low.

The weakness of the argument lies in the greater defects of the other forms of financing necessary to avoid charging viewers and listeners. The Report mentions three standard objections:

1. The difficulty of ascertaining the minimum subsidy required and the likelihood (not considered in static welfare economics) that subsidies would provide an incentive to pad out costs and a disincentive to innovation.
2. The distortions imposed on the wider economy from raising the necessary tax revenue; and
3. The dubious resource allocation results from subsidising one zero or low marginal cost industry while others are forced to pay their way (Report, 1986: paras 554–7).

There is a far more fundamental objection. Broadcasting is not a homogeneous product like electricity. Each broadcaster is a monopoly supplier of his own programmes. Under pay-television he will broadcast if he can charge a price which can cover his costs. This impersonal and consumer-sensitive rationing system avoids both the arbitrariness and potential political abuses of discretionary financing by a state body, and the under-representation of minority or specialist tastes likely if sole reliance is placed on advertising.

Can't you abolish censorship without introducing market principles?

Even left-wing critics such as Richard Hoggart and Philip Whitehead said that Peacock had gone far further in opposition to censorship than any previous committee. It was the linage of the Report with the long tradition of Western writing (from Milton to Mill, and beyond) in favour of freedom of expression that gave me more pleasure than anything else.

But a free market in ideas implies a market in a more mundane sense. It is precisely because we are not dealing with baked beans or packaged holidays but the communication of ideas, and the dissemination and analysis of news and artistic endeavour, that freedom of entry by producers and freedom of choice by consumers to the maximum feasible extent are so vital. There is no need to enter into a metaphysical debate about whether the consumer is the best judge of artistic quality or the best judge of which programmes will benefit him, or his capacity for citizenship, most. The point is that no one person or group, or committee, or 'establishment' can be trusted to make a superior choice.

Is it enough to provide the viewer and listener with 'what he wants'?

Of course not. We remarked that the competitive market is a 'discovery mechanism for finding out by trial and error what the consumer might be enticed to accept (as well as the least-cost method of supplying it) and for trying out new and challenging ideas'. Indeed we cite the late Sir Huw Wheldon's criticism of the false dichotomy between giving the viewer what he or she wants and what he or she ought to have. According to Sir Huw, the producer or creator provides what is 'in him to give'. The proviso in a market economy is that a sufficient number of consumers must be persuaded to take it (Report, 1986: paras 557–60).

Is there a contradiction between the committee's belief in consumer sovereignty and its support for public finance to secure programmes involving 'knowledge, culture, criticism and experiment'?

The clue as Professor Alan Budd has pointed out (Budd, 1986) is in the distinction between paternalism and patronage. It would have helped if we had used this formulation explicitly in our Report.

Paternalism is embodied by the dictum of Lord Reith who said 'Few know what they want and fewer still what they need.' The inference was that public authority should decide what should be broadcast. Reith himself said that you have to mix a little education with a lot of entertainment. But this is tactics. Paternalists believe in deciding what is good for us.

Patronage is completely different. Under a patronage system, consumers express their desires in the market place, in the arts and entertainment as in other spheres. But market-financed activities are supplemented by support for selected activated by rulers or rich individuals. Examples are Medici patronage of Michelangelo or Esterhazy patronage of Haydn. Most of London's statues and monuments are the result of patronage. While private and corporate patronage still has a role to play, much of the work of supplementation inevitably falls today on the public purse. *Even so, are the radical reforms suggested by Peacock consistent with very generous tributes paid to the success of the existing Broadcasting Authorities in achieving the cross fertilisation of different categories of programmes?*

If I had to be prodded into lesser tributes in such drafting as I did, this was not because of any formal inconsistency, but because I recoiled from the self-praise of the broadcaster, especially the BBC. People who are so wonderful and who excel at all activities rarely need to parade their own virtues, and I was wary of reader reaction on *Private Eye* line – 'That's enough tribute, Ed.'

But the two lines of thought can be made compatible. There is no need to denigrate the present state of affairs to see a full broadcasting market as an improvement. Someone who wishes market forces to play a predominant role in broadcasting – or any other area – in the future does not *have* to regret their absence in earlier periods.

A historical comparison was in fact drawn: 'A social critic in the late 18th and early 19th century could pay sincere and generous tribute to aristocratic patronage in forming taste in painting, music and literature, while welcoming the greater freedom of choice offered both to artists and to patrons by the wider bourgeois market that was beginning to develop' (Report, 1986: para. 586). Some may think this logic-chopping. But formal consistency is important in Reports such as ours.

But will not the mixed diet disappear under pay-per-view?

Misunderstandings are difficult to avoid among those who find freedom of choice a difficult idea. The Committee did not say that pay-per-view should be the *only* payments system, merely that it must be an available option by Stage 3. We were quite explicit:

> It is a common misunderstanding to suppose that in a fully developed broadcasting market most people would spend most of their time facing a bewildering set of dials, trying to make up their minds between thousands of alternative programmes. Of course, many people for much of the time will prefer to economise on the effort of choice by paying for packages of programmes or whole channels,

just as at present people buy collections of published works in the form of newspapers, magazines and journals, as well as individual books. So it would with multiplicity of choice of broadcasting.

(600)

Again in a paragraph, somewhat difficult to spot (Report, 1986: para. 688) above Recommendation 17, the Committee declared:

> We do not need to debate whether most people would take advantage of this opportunity (pay-per-view and per-channel) most of the time. The availability of the system would enable programme makers to try out minority, experimental or high or low budget ideas, unlikely to see the light of day under systems of conventional funding; and the discriminating consumer would be anxious to avoid paying for services he or she does not require.

What are likely to be the effects on cultural quality? And who will have time to watch this great variety of programmes?

With the aid of an analogy from publishing the Report answers the two questions together:

> Any individual printed work, or journal, or newspaper is read by a minority, often a very small minority. It is the aggregation of numerous minorities which makes possible a publishing industry under which hundreds of thousands of titles are published a year. By way of comparison Whitaker's Almanack, 1986 lists (page 1071) the number of book titles published in Great Britain in 1984 as 51,555. Similarly in a multiple choice broadcasting market, there could be numerous specialist programmes or channels each with its own particular public; together with more traditional channels of broad appeal.
>
> Cultural quality is also affected by these considerations. When the printing press superseded the handwritten manuscript, the number of high quality publications and their total readership both expanded a great deal. For similar reasons, the effects on standards of a fully developed broadcasting market should not be judged by the average programme, but by the range, quality and penetration of the best. To do otherwise would be like ignoring the spectacular rise in the sale of paperback classics, on the grounds that popular tabloids sell in even greater numbers.

(Report, 1986: paras 601–2)

For a liberal individualist the mechanism of personal consumer choice is itself desirable; and any favourable consequence of this kind just outlined is a bonus. But it is a wise maxim not to force colleagues back on fundamentals if you want agreement on a course of action.

What about public concern over the excesses of violence and sex?

The Report did remark 'Whether or not it comes within our terms of reference, we can hardly fail to be aware of public concern about excesses of violence and sex on television.' It declared

> We emphasise these legal constraints on Free Speech which exists even in countries most attached to the principles of the First Amendment. Our main point is that the recourse for people concerned about these areas should lie with the normal remedies of the law. To the extent that legislation lifts some of the legal constraints in return for specific regulation, these exemptions need to be removed, as we move along the deregulation route.

We also accepted that, 'for broadcasting, the existing convention under which "adult" programmes appear late in the evening is a sensible approach.'

What relevance do the Committee's conclusions have to the alleged political bias in Broadcasting or to the problem of political interference?

Of course there is plenty of bias, although the party machines do not have the sophistication to see where the ideological stand really matters and pick on innocent examples such as *Paradise Postponed* or *The Monocled Mutineer*.

The *Guardian*, *The Times* and *Telegraph* are biased too; and even the *Independent* has a stand of its own. The development of a broadcasting market is the only real solution, which will enable people to choose among broadcasters as they already do among newspapers.

Even in Stage 1, when competition is limited, an attempt to reduce bias by government interference would be a cure far worse than the disease. There is already far too much political interference in broadcasting.

Harold Wilson appointed Lord Hill Chairman of the BBC in 1967, at least partly to curb the radical Sir Hugh Greene. Wilson's own hostility to the BBC as Leader of the Opposition on the occasion of *Yesterday's Men* in 1971 is notorious. The Annan Committee noted that the ferocity of the argument then inhibited further experiments in the coverage of politics. Michael Leapman adds, 'because of the resulting bias nobody made any sustained effort to make politicians look foolish until the 1980s with *Spitting Image*, and that was on ITV.' Threats about the next licence fee increase have in the past been used to make the BBC toe the line. At the time of writing, broadcasters are under intense and maddening pressure from the leaders of the Conservative, Labour and Alliance parties alike to provide more favourable treatment.

Second only in importance to the desire for a fully fledged broadcasting market in my mind, when I sat on Peacock, was the need here and now to protect broadcasters from political interference and intrusion.

Subscription for the BBC in Stage 2 is recommended partly because it would reduce the dependence of the Corporation on government. In the meantime indexation should make it more difficult for governments to make threats about the licence fee.

Conclusion

In a book published as long ago as 1973, I wrote 'there may in future no longer be any physical need to limit broadcasting to a small number of channels. Instead there could be an indefinite number of services among which consumers could select and pay for directly. The distinction between publishing and broadcasting would then largely disappear with a consequent extension of cultural diversity and freedom' (Brittan, 1973:298).

Without being starry-eyed about the devotion of governments and politicians to freedom, when it stands in the way of more immediate objectives, we can say that Peacock has carried this cause one step forward.

Notes

1. This chapter is a reprint of Brittan (1987).
2. 'Public Choice' is the academic term.
3. E.g. essays reprinted in Jay (1984).
4. Detailed in Michael Leapman, *The Last Days of the Beeb*, Allen and Unwin, London,1986. This much underrated book provides a suitable companion volume to Peacock, containing real 'evidence'.
5. 'History *of England, Chapter XX1*. "While the Abbey was hanging with black for the funeral of the Queen, the Commons came to a vote which at the time attracted little attention, which produced no excitement, which has been left unnoticed by voluminous analysts, and of which history can be but imperfectly traced in the archives of Parliament, but which has done more for liberty than the Great Charter or the Bill of Rights."' (Quoted in Report, 1986, note to paragraph 549–eds.)

7
It was the BBC wot Won It: Winning the Peacock Report for the Corporation, or How the BBC Responded to the Peacock Committee[1]

Jean Seaton and Anthony McNicholas

The Crossman Diaries, 28 May 1968.

> Up to the P. M.'s room to discuss the BBC licence fee, which we've already been discussing for two weary years. Wedgy Benn and Ted Short and I have all been convinced that the BBC must go over to advertising, at least in part.
>
> (Crossman, 1979:415)

'The BBC has reports like other people have mice,'[2] observed Bill Cotton, the heavyweight, charismatic Controller of BBC 1 in the 1980s. But the Peacock Committee was intended to review and – many believed – demolish the single most important aspect of the BBC's institutional independence: the licence fee. Many had talked about it, but this time the threat looked deadly serious.

The danger came from the combination of political and economic threats. However, it was not the familiar formula of clashes with governments and lack of cash: it was more profound. It was a kind of ideological exhaustion. It looked as if the arguments for the BBC were no longer viable. The traditional case for the Corporation had no purchase on the new political settlement that emerged after the election of the Conservative government led by Margaret Thatcher in 1979. There had never been such a fundamental threat before and it is only matched by the challenges the

Corporation faced in 2008 in establishing an intellectual case for itself. The Peacock Report came after a series of bruising confrontations with the Conservative government about programme standards, union power, reporting, Northern Ireland, the Falklands, and they had all added their portion of sourness to what felt like an increasingly difficult relationship. Most dangerously, every issue seemed to escalate to a fissile political row: it was an intensely febrile period in general and the BBC found it difficult to calm the rows. Meanwhile there was a changed environment as privatisation became the preferred solution to unwieldy public utilities. The BBC seemed perilously exposed as an antiquated form of public service organisation in the face of the Thatcherite economic, moral and political revolution.

Moreover, Mrs Thatcher's government was radical,[3] prepared to break institutions and at the height of its powers. It thought that 'public service' had become a flabby defence for the self-serving and inefficient. It had – it was believed – not merely altered the composition of the Governors by packing it in a way that broke the 'bi-partisan' convention, but intended to alter their function as well: 'My view of the Boards of Public Bodies' argued Mrs Thatcher 'is that they are there to do things, not represent things' (Campbell, 2003:157). Internally the BBC Board of Management was in conflict at times with the Board of Governors. The Peacock Report looked like an aggressive tank on the steps of Broadcasting House. Its apparent intention was to radically alter the basis of the BBC. There was a widespread view that it would do this by looking into, and recommending that the BBC's licence fee be replaced by advertising. The report was widely seen as the first step in some kind of dismemberment of the Corporation.

There is no doubt that the distinguished members of the Peacock Committee thought that the Corporation did not present its case well when it was presented to them: nor, apparently, did they think much of the case it put. Indeed, a priori some of them did not think much of the BBC. Certainly Sir Alan Peacock, (whose appointment was endorsed by Norman Tebbit, no friend to the Corporation) (Campbell, 2003:157) the eminent economist who had been a pioneer of liberal economics long before they were fashionable, and who had done much to train a new and more open-minded generation of government economists, but who also had a particular interest in the economics of the arts,[4] was uninterested in what broadcasting actually did – to make programmes. He brought a focused economic rigour to the proceedings – as did Sam Brittan and, behind the scenes, Peter Jay, a prophet with Brittan of economic realism in the *Financial Times*, a media guru in his articles on the future of news with John Birt (Birt and Jay, 1975, 1975a) and on Peacock, the originator of the notion of 'electronic publishing'. He was not interested in the content of programmes as he did not believe that it was a proper or relevant matter. Actually, he rather thought public service meant that programmes that he liked ought to be supported, for as Douglas Hurd informed Mrs Thatcher, his narrower interpretation of the concept 'appear[ed] to include the whole of radios 2 and 3'.[5] Any attempt to talk about 'quality', or programme reach, or values was dismissed as besides the point. Fellow committee member Alastair Hetherington confided to BBC advisor Stephen Hearst after a visit to RAI in Italy that he had been cut short by the Professor when he had asked about the effect on quality of recent changes with the words 'this was irrelevant to their own consideration.'[6] Nor was he at all interested in institutions and their role.

In their deliberations on the eventual report, civil servants noted that the committee did not appear to appreciate the social significance of broadcasting – 'It is a feature of the Committee's approach that it appears to attach little weight to the argument that it is not only spectrum scarcity but also the peculiarly intrusive nature of the medium which leads to the need for a system of regulation different to that applying to other media.'[7] Nor were officials or their political masters impressed by the Committee's liberal attitude to content regulation, fearing that their recommendations on the uses to which the late-night 'unspent' hours of broadcasting time could be put would be interpreted 'as giving the green light' for 'adult films' in the early hours.[8] In this way the Committee were attuned neither to politicians' sensitivities on questions of taste and decency nor on the requirements around balance and due impartiality in news and current affairs programmes. On the latter, there had been discussion of freedom of expression, in that the Committee felt the present duopoly inhibited 'dissentient points of view', which a true market would remedy. This was seen as reasonable as 'a theoretical statement', ran a Home Office memo, 'but in practice our broadcasting authorities are more usually criticised for giving too much coverage to unusual points of view.' Clearly feeling the Committee lacked understanding in this regard, it went on, 'It may be significant that the example in the Report is the rather ancient one of the failure of the BBC to give Winston Churchill air time before the last war.' This was a 'blind spot' in their thinking and would leave broadcasting subject to exactly the same regulation as newspapers. Again, in the case of the Committee's recommendations that Channel 4 should sell its own advertising, it was felt the Committee did not appreciate the possible effect this might have on programming.[9] Yet the single-minded focus on the economic realities and principals of broadcasting were both what made the Peacock Report so novel and refreshing, effective and many might say long-sighted.

The Committee found Alasdair Milne, the Director General of the BBC, off-hand and unconvincing when he appeared before them. He had refused to practice in advance for his appearance before the Committee[10] and was apparently aggressive. When asked at an oral session how much of the BBC's output could be described as public service broadcasting, he gave what may have appeared to him the satisfyingly succinct answer 'All of it'. This was not how the Committee saw it, and was probably the worst answer Milne could have given, as his own colleagues recognised.[11] Subsequently, first on a list of 27 questions the Committee wished the BBC to consider was an equally terse invitation for him to expand on this.[12] He, meanwhile, thought he had been polite:[13] but he seemed to epitomise a BBC ostrich-like refusal to consider realistically economic and political developments, a backward-looking resting on laurels. It was as if he was not listening to what they asked. Indeed, when Director Generals do represent the Corporation on such occasions, the style and quality of a huge organisation is (despite its variety) reduced to the manner and command of the man (or at some later point woman) in charge. In many ways when members of the Committee complained about 'the BBC's inadequacy'[14] what they meant was the unsympathetic and unbending performance of Milne. Professor Peacock, when he went to see the Home Secretary just before the report was published, went out of his way to say how inadequate and badly put the BBC's evidence was and generally disparaged the Corporation. 'He had found the BBC evidence on the economics of broadcasting was greatly inferior to that offered by independent advisers. The BBC attitude generally had been combative; they were not prepared to concede anything on any point.'[15] Relations with the Committee were tense throughout and as BBC Director of Finance Geoff Buck suspected, Peacock may have been influenced by his experience of dealing with the BBC during his earlier report on orchestras. Then, the BBC 'had been slow to appreciate the importance of the inquiry' and Peacock had found them arrogant and tardy.[16] But, in part, what Peacock meant was Milne.

How come then, that the BBC won the case? The ingeniously intelligent Peacock Report was influential and, in the long run, prescient about some, but certainly not all, features of the media and broadcasting landscape that were taking shape. It got the technology right, but misunderstood the nature of broadcasting; it got auctions wrong and in some ways it got the role of independents and their effects wrong. But by far the most important thing about the report was that it, persuasively, in the most impeccably 'dry' terms dismissed advertising as a feasible alternative to the licence fee and depoliticised the argument about the licence fee by recommending that it be indexed on an annual basis to the general rate of inflation. It came up with a convincing argument for the short- or middle-term economic rationality of public service broad-casting, based on the view that it compensated for market failure in the conditions of imperfect competition that characterised the industry by delivering programmes that the market could not. The Peacock Report marked a decisive moment in the Corporation's survival and success for the next 20 years, even though in many ways it ended up by dealing with many things other than the BBC. Advertising had been known to be the Prime Minister's and indeed the Chancellor's favourite answer to bringing the disciplines of the market to the Corporation.[17] Indeed the Treasury was (and is) institutionally sceptical of the BBC, and advertis-ing seemed a good way on the face of it of relieving the tax burden. Indeed the Peacock Report was produced in a period when Britain's economy, although recovering a little from the early 1980s depression, was still insecure.

However, while Peacock concentrated on the long-term view of the 'market' for broadcasting the BBC heaved a sigh of relief. It had been a close run thing. And the feeling within the BBC was that the licence fee was safe for now, as it was. Michael Checkland, the BBC's Director of Finance, and later Director General, an enormously decent and energetically intelligent marshaller of the BBC's resources, commented 'Maynard Keynes once said "In the long run we are all dead," When I heard the news I knew we were fine . . . yes something was due to hap-pen in twenty years – well lots might happen in twenty years.'[18]

One explanation for the outcome was, of course, that some members of the Committee saw themselves as saving the Corporation for the nation. They thought that the BBC had lost the capacity to protect its own future and that a new settlement had to be reached. Others, including Professor Peacock himself, were hardly influenced at all by what appeared to them such sentimental considerations: he was inter-ested in the economics and the markets. But Sam Brittan, (who was the brother of the Home Secretary Leon Brittan) the brilliant, witty, entirely unique commentator and economist, was not only a key architect of the *Financial Times'* dominance of government thinking (where the Chancellor Nigel Lawson had started his own career), but had also through his columns begun the conversion of the nation's political and administrative elites from Keynesian orthodoxy to liberal economics, and knew exactly what he wanted from the Committee's deliberations. Speaking in 2005, he reiterated his preference for subscription, rather than advertising as a long-term solution in order to achieve the kind of market of ideas he wanted. In this he was more concerned with the political rather than the economic consequences of any particular method of funding the BBC. Subscription, he recognised, in 1986, was technically some way off. As for the politics of broadcasting, his opinions would have surprised the vast bulk of commentators of all shades of opinion. Brittan was concerned about freedom of expression, had 'a hobby horse about censorship ... in the guise of quality control' and saw the political salience of the BBC, the constant rows with Government as unhealthy. The BBC was seen as a national institution in the way that an individual newspaper, as one among many, was not. This led to the 'vitriol' and 'feeling' which characterised politicians' reactions to the BBC. Brittan thought 'that the idea of a national broadcasting corporation whose every deed and every saying was a matter for the Cabinet and for high political talk ... belonged to 1984', and in the light of this Orwellian politicisation of expression his 'immediate objective was how to de-politicise relations between Government and the BBC'. In other words, he wished to save the Corporation, and neither Milne and company, inside the BBC, nor anyone else on the outside realised it.[19] Leon Brittan, when he set the inquiry going, meant 'the committee to interpret their brief very widely: it emerged as something of a libertarian manifesto.'[20] Sam Brittan was at the height of his influence and powers: combining intellectual mastery with great political sensitivity and charm. Brittan wanted to 'save' freedom of expression. In this way it was thus clearly the Committee 'wot saved the BBC'.

However, the BBC's influence on the Committee was far greater than the individuals recall or understood at the time. Behind the scenes, informally, as well as formally organising research, talking to people, considering and preparing, the BBC was perhaps not quite the surly, passive, inadequate that the Committee thought. Indeed, in some ways the BBC was so masterly that even the Committee did not perhaps notice how far they were being managed. How did the BBC win the battle? Who won it for them?

The BBC prepares

Alasdair Milne was not the whole of the BBC and the internal team he launched to prepare for Peacock included the very best and most politically acute minds in the Corporation, some of whom were sympathetic to government frustrations. One member was Patricia Hodgson, (the BBC's awe-inspiring Deputy Secretary), 'a woman with the best strategic mind in the place and an instinctive capacity to know what language to speak to power with'.[21] Hodgson was well aware of the government's impatience with the Corporation and horrified by BBC complacency. She was to be a vital architect of the BBC's technological breakthrough in the early 1990s, as well as an enormously influential political player. She was certainly part of the BBC's future.

The Steering Group as it was called was chaired by Brian Wenham, who during this worked well with Hodgson, although they did not get on in a wider way. He was the biggest BBC player perhaps under Milne; a complex, clever man, with a sardonic turn of mind who, typically for him, gave the Committee a nickname, 'The Magnificent Seven'. Wenham, someone who 'always had his eye on the next job',[22] saw the task not only as a personal opportunity allowing him 'an insight into the whole workings of the BBC centrally' but also as 'quite an interesting intellectual problem' about which the BBC had opinions but up to that point had not tested the arguments.[23] Third was Geoff Buck, the BBC's resourceful Director of Finance. Other members had both expertise and political nous. One was Phil Laven, an engineering wizard who nevertheless had a wily political mind. Then there was Stephen Hearst, former Controller of Radio Three and head of the 'Future Policy Unit', a central European intellectual known to his colleagues as 'Deep Thought', who together with Janet Morgan was both a member of the group and also reported directly and confidentially to Milne as a special adviser. Morgan was a political fixer, who had come to the BBC from editing *The Crossman Diaries* (and winning the court case for their publication) and the heart of government in the Cabinet Office, with an address book of contacts. Other members were co-opted later on, Peter Ibbotson for television and Richard Wade for radio. The secretary was Ian Hunter. Andrew Ehrenberg, Professor of Marketing from the London Business School, was to supervise any academic research to be commissioned in support of the BBC's case. So, the BBC's operation was a class act and while Milne had given the Committee the impression he thought he knew the answer and was not prepared to listen, behind him the BBC group was trying very hard indeed to understand the new challenges.

The BBC team set about thinking around and ahead of the Committee. Hodgson knew that the BBC was in deep political trouble, and that cosmetics were inadequate. 'We had to understand and answer the Committee, and ourselves. We had to get the right arguments not just the convenient ones. This was no time for posturing.'[24] Shortly after Morgan's appointment, she and Hearst had amused themselves by a day of carefully prepared role play in their office. Hearst played Mrs Thatcher and Morgan played the BBC. They 'boned up on their parts' by talking to people and reading. By the end of the afternoon, Morgan reports, they had 'shook ourselves rigid' with the intellectual authority of the conservative position.[25] The BBC, they concluded, as Hodgson had done, was defenceless, and it was using tired old arguments which were irrelevant to the case that was being made against it. Inside the team there was a political readjustment that was forced on it by the Peacock process: but it gave the new round-heads within the Corporation a chance to re-examine the case for the BBC.

However, the BBC team also reviewed what other previous submissions to previous enquiries had got right and what they had got wrong. Here the collective memory of the Corporation came into its own as advice and comment began flowing in from staff in different parts of the organisation. A department head wrote to Hodgson that their initial submission to Annan had been 'too BBC centred', and therefore not effective. When they commissioned independent reports from economists they had better luck. 'It was important to ask themselves the tough questions first,' the note went on, 'this report is headed by an economist. This was the first argument to win.'[26] Wenham also sought advice outside the Corporation. At a meeting with senior mandarins at the Treasury and Department of Trade and Industry (DTI), he was advised that bearing in mind Peacock's reputation as a fiscal economist, the BBC evidence should show how the licence fee compared with other items of expenditure by the public. This is indeed what they did.[27]

The BBC strategy had several aims. One was to think about who might be appointed to the Committee once it was announced. This was a classic 'intelligence' operation, and though unlike Hugh Carleton Greene at the time of the Pilkington Committee (Milland, 2004a), Milne and Wenham could not draw upon personal experience in psychological warfare to aid them in their campaign, they were not without resources. Morgan talked to people; she discussed likely candidates for membership, and established their background and frame of mind. As did Hodgson, less showily perhaps, but she was a Conservative with excellent contacts in No. 10, that grew more intimate over this period. Rather more than any one else Hodgson understood the Conservative thinking at the centre – and knew that the contest was a serious one.

Very early on in this process, the BBC files show Morgan suggesting to Milne that if they were allowed to put forward names, she would recommend Sam Brittan. Brittan, had a 'dry' reputation, but there was more to him than this though. He was, she told Milne, 'not only interested in how the market works but also in what the market cannot do', and went on that he recognised that the production of some goods could not be left to the market. The fact that he was the Home Secretary's brother might be a problem; Leon would be reluctant to appoint him and from their point of view, the BBC 'did not want to appear too clever'. It would have to be done 'very privately'.[28] In the event, the BBC were allowed to put forward names but their two public suggestions, former Governor Phillip Chappell and former External Service MD Gerry Mansell, did not make it onto the Committee. Brittan, of course, did.

However, once the Committee had been appointed, the Corporation's next task was to establish the prejudices and dispositions of the Committee, to get inside their minds to see if it was possible to predict how they would tackle the remit they had been given. This was not in any way an attempt to undermine the Committee, nor would it have been in the Corporation's interest to do so, but it was an attempt to understand and consider what the Committee might think, do and want. Of course, all institutions do such strategic preparation; nevertheless, whatever the Committee thought of the BBC's presentation to them, it was prepared with intelligence, open-mindedness and was in some ways transformative within the Corporation. Profiles of the committee members were drawn up to see what potentially useful information might be gleaned. Peacock himself, it was noted was a keen amateur composer, had written a report for the Arts Council on orchestras and was a member of the council of the London Philharmonia Orchestra. Sam Brittan, according to his profile was not, as was widely believed, a 'crude right wing prophet of laissez faire', but someone who believed in a 'social market economy'. He was not easy to pigeonhole. It was true he had written with Conservative Minister Peter Lilley, but Lilley had since moved further to the right. North Sea Oil, Brittan thought, was a national asset and he had been reputedly against the Falklands campaign, he favoured abolishing corporal punishment in schools and thought the abandonment of full employment as a goal was a mistake.[29] Brittan's wonderful book *Left or Right: The Bogus Dilemma* (Brittan, 1968) had shown how original his politics were, and shrewd. Moreover, he was a frequent BBC contributor on both radio and television. Brittan was the key mind on the Committee. Judith Chalmers, another member, though a Conservative supporter, began her career at and still made occasional appearances on the BBC.

Lord Quinton, President of Trinity College Oxford since 1982, was on the face of it a potential problem the BBC moles reported. He was 'A dry conservative, a *Times* and *Telegraph* reader'. He believed the threat from the Soviet Union went beyond the military and it was necessary to guard against the infiltration of our polytechnics, universities, journalism and broadcasting to prevent them from capturing 'institutions which had not only influence but real power'. However, though a believer in a cultural elite, he liked television and 'could not be caught out on 'Tories and his Mandoliers or the Rockford Files on TV'. Jeremy Hardie was an account- ant and a creative businessman, who had invested in independent local radio and had been finance director for TV AM. Politically, he had been a member of the Conservative Party's centre-right Bow Group but was now a founding member of the new Social Democratic Party. Anthony Sampson in his *Changing Anatomy of Britain* said he was 'an intellectual master accountant'. The profile on Sir Peter Reynolds was the slimmest. Chair of Rank Hovis McDougall and a member of the Industrial Development Board for Northern Ireland. His company contributed to the Tory party. Alastair Hetherington of course was a known entity having been Controller of BBC Scotland. Hetherington had had a mixed and vexatious career in Scotland but was a master player on the national political front, and indeed someone who well understood the conditions that an industry needed to produce impartial and worthwhile news and opinions. He was a close friend of George Thomson, the Chairman of the Independent Broadcasting Authority (IBA).[30]

All the way through the various stages of the Committee's deliberations, the BBC carefully monitored opinions, cast straws in the wind and tried to read the runes. Morgan advised Milne in early June 1985, surely with the memory of the disastrously opulent dinner served up to the Annan Committee in mind,[31] that if members of the Committee ever came to the BBC, any meals served to them should not be 'over-elaborate'. Further, he noted the particular interests of not only Peacock himself but also of other members that they and 'other potential allies should be discreetly taken to, e.g., the Proms, the BBC filming at Glyndebourne etc.', and that each member should be sent 'immediately' a copy of the 1985 Proms programme.[32] Members' views, especially those of Brittan were assiduously canvassed. The following week Morgan reported confidentially to Milne a long conversation during which Brittan had said too much pontificating was coming from senior BBC executives 'in this or that journal', which ended up sounding self-serving. This was duly noted. Brittan felt it impor- tant for them to have a fall back position. In his words, 'What is a triumph of barbarism and what is not? Would advertising Mars Bars on Radio 1 be to public service broadcasting (in Thomas Mann's word) "a repeal of the Ninth Symphony?"'[33] Hearst also had his sources and passed on a letter from a personal friend of Peacock's, outlining what he saw as the Professor's likely approach – a narrow interpretation of the funding of the BBC and more ominously, an attempt 'to establish the parameters of what has to be funded and why'.[34] At all stages, the BBC sought to second-guess the Committee. For example, when the Committee went to the USA, all the people they were to see had already been furnished with confidential copies of the Corporation's (then) unpublished first submission.[35] And so it went on.

Milne may have appeared dismissive: however, this was only the unfortunate nearly disastrous tip of the BBC iceberg. Under him, though, typically finding it hard to get any purchase on him and his performance was a quite different BBC. One that approached the Peacock Committee well informed, seriously engaged and thinking not just tactically but also more profoundly about the problems the Committee was raising.

Research commissioned

But the real intelligence of the BBC's response to Peacock was demonstrated by the research it commissioned. Peacock may have found it easy to dismiss the BBC's own research. This was to be anticipated. As Milne told a conference in November 1985, ever since Mandy Rice Davis' 'He would say that, wouldn't he?' all spokesmen for institutions were expected 'to put forward the institutional interest and nothing but that interest',[36] so the BBC commissioned independent work that could not be dismissed as special pleading, concurred with research by others and swiftly, effectively and convincingly kicked the question of financing the Corporation by advertising off the pitch.

Indeed, the real strength of the BBC's case lay in the questions it commissioned research on. It was a carefully planned, comprehensive but also a cost-effective part of the BBC strategy. 'With a £1billion annual turnover at stake' Hearst told colleagues in May, 'we must not skimp. But we also need not aim to sponsor the whole of the UK's economics and market research fraternities for the coming year.'[37] So, some work was carried out by the BBC's own Broadcasting Research Department and other (perhaps more politically effective) was commissioned from outside bodies and individuals.

The work the BBC undertook itself covered various topics: audience preferences; the size of audience for different genres, including comparisons with the population as a whole; programme comparisons with Independent Television (ITV) and with a range from other countries; radio audiences; attitudes to advertising; patterns of ownership of radios and televisions; research on those sections of population which are needy – their viewing habits, attitudes to the fee, to advertising and alternative methods of payment; on cable and on the spend on home entertainment. Much of this was worthy, worth knowing – but could be seen as grist for the mill of all public reports. The BBC's case had always been that it did not want advertising: that it would commercialise services, lower programme standards and was socially maligning. But it had never, since the 1930s really, taken the proposition of advertising funding seriously. This is what Peacock forced it to do.

On the advertising issue the BBC research looked across the board at a range of issues that might be relevant: examining public attitudes to BBC funding, and sponsorship as it operated in the USA and its UK potential. But by far the most important issue the research tackled head on was the feasibility of funding the BBC by advertising. Could it be done? What would the revenues be? What would the economic impact of the BBC entering the advertising market be – and on whom? In this key area, the one most important to the Corporation at that moment, the BBC won the case for itself – in the area it most cared about – the licence fee – by producing original and immensely compelling evidence about the actual impact of advertising. Crucially, it concurred with research commissioned by the Committee itself.

Stephen Hearst turned to Andrew Ehrenberg, a professor of marketing from the London Business School. Ehrenberg had long experience of the economics of broadcasting having produced numerous reports for the IBA. He was given charge of commissioning and overseeing independent research. He had also, incidentally, just produced an internal report on the BBC's recent acrimonious public licence fee campaign, which had some stinging conclusions. Hearst commended the report to colleagues, whose criticisms were to be taken seriously. 'I believe that the confidential comments of a candid friend who believes in public service broadcasting every bit as much as we do are salutary.' The campaign according to Ehrenberg had been unprofessional, and 'sloganising' rather than providing 'analysis and documentation'. It had been an error to try to argue that what was a tax was 'The best bargain in Britain', and he added that the Corporation had not made plain the cost to the viewer of advertising, which was a further mistake.[38] The faults he noted were not to be repeated this time.

The very first proposition that the Peacock Report had been set up to investigate – whether and how the BBC's licence fee might be replaced by advertising – was disposed of with elegant swiftness. There was no argument about what people wanted, or the public interest, or woolly stuff on programmes – the economics were stark: financing the BBC by advertising, the research showed, would not work and would have huge and undesirable consequences elsewhere. Crucially, the independent research commissioned by the BBC, broadly agreed with that commissioned by Peacock. In this way it could not be dismissed.

None of the pro-advertising arguments stood up to independent examination. Neil Barnard of the London Business School demonstrated that the ITV monopoly of advertising income had not lead to higher prices for airtime, which in fact compared favourably in terms of cost with other forms of advertising, thus undermining one of the justifications for the pro-advertising case (Barnard, 1985). Paddy Barwise examined for the BBC the claimed benefits to advertisers. Advertising rates would fall, but there would be no advantage to any particular advertiser as cheaper airtime would be available to all. In addition, research indicated that the BBC audience closely matched the population at large – that is, it was unsegmented – and would not deliver a premium as some had supposed (Barwise, 1985). The BBC was not the road to the upmarket audiences that advertisers were looking for.

Brian Sturgess of SRW Forecasting found that advertising on the BBC would not increase total spend on advertising but that as the BBC would harvest at least some of any potential growth, this would damage other media, especially the smaller ITV companies, which is indeed what they themselves told the Committee in their evidence. In another paper Sturgess argued that a free market in television could have implications for the range of programmes on offer thus restricting consumer choice. The size of the projected advertising pie was of central interest. If the BBC's services were to be paid for in part at least by advertising, then either it would have to grow or existing services reliant on this form of income would suffer (Sturgess, 1985, 1985a). Ehrenberg's evidence on this, presented in March at an oral session and based on a survey he conducted of the future intentions of major advertisers, indicated no likely expansion. This caused Peacock, who was the most reluctant to totally abandon the idea of advertising on the BBC, to remark that though new ways of encouraging advertising might be found, 'it would be risky to base a business on optimism alone.' He was further moved to concede that Ehrenberg had 'provided important evidence'.[39]

Once the issues had been gone into in detail there were some startling results. Putting advertising on the BBC would not only squeeze revenue for the commercial companies, 'That would hardly have mattered, competition is painful that's why it is useful,'[40] it would have other far-reaching effects. The BBC had been aware for some time that the broad industry consensus was against advertising. Brian Wenham told a joint meeting of both the BBC Board of Governors and the Board of Management in November 1985 that the evidence on the feasibility of advertising from other bodies was even gloomier than their own.[41] This was indeed the case. The Association of Independent Radio Contractors in their submission said that partial funding of the BBC by advertising 'would be the worst possible outcome' as it would distort the market without replacing the current dual funding system with one 'true, single, market-oriented system' (AIRC, 1985). Of course, it was hardly surprising that advertising-funded bodies were anxious about the BBC programme machine hoovering up their advertising. But more remarkably (and decisively) research from consulting economists NERA by Dermot Glyn (NERA, 1985) for Peacock himself came to the startling conclusion that the amount of money expended on television advertising would actually go down if the BBC took advertising, as rates would fall proportionately greater than the increase in airtime devoted to advertising.

The Ehrenberg research, commissioned by the Corporation, but conducted by 'impartial' external researchers, talked the same language as Peacock himself; it was empirically grounded, theoretically sophisticated and utterly convinced the Committee, which, sent off to look at the possibility of replacing the licence fee by advertising, dismissed the possibility in the first section of the report and moved on to wider issues. To generally disparage the BBC's contribution, as we have noted above, that Peacock did in his June 1986 meeting with the Home Secretary and say that the Corporation's written evidence had been 'greatly inferior' to that offered by independent advisors and 'had not been of a high standard' misses the point – the BBC commissioned its research predicting precisely such a reaction.[42] The BBC won the research battle, by listening carefully to the case against it and investigating it with an astute intellectual rigour. Ehrenberg and the other researchers did the work – but the BBC set them going on it. Indeed, on the way the research managed to scotch any idea of even a small part of the BBC being funded this way. But it did it by attending to the Peacock agenda. This research virtually removed the BBC from the report – just what the BBC wanted and needed.

Politics

The BBC was not passive on other fronts. It did the backstage politicking better than it did the front of house stuff. Although it was behind the scenes – and such interventions are hard to assess – nevertheless they were certainly part of a thought through campaign that came to appreciate the radical Peacock thinking. The Corporation's team began to address the problem of what other people and bodies would submit to Peacock, and whether and what they might say. They started with the ITV companies, who were naturally enough somewhat dismayed at the thought of the BBC competing with them for advertising revenue.

Commercial television – at the height of its powers and a creative competition for the BBC at every level – was also a very successful set of businesses: public service regulation was less, it seems, a restraint on competitive programme making and more a force that pushed ITV companies productively. However, ITV companies – just like newspaper firms – were prepared to use any means to maintain their competitive edge, including policy lobbying. The smaller companies were particularly concerned about the entry of such a large player as the BBC into the advertising market, and Chairman Stuart Young was given advance sight of a submission to Peacock from HTV which spelled this out.[43] But the support and involvement went wider. George Thomson, the head of the IBA, a television political player with a good deal of trouble on his own hands, nevertheless understood what was at issue. Thomson was a great and influential Chairman of the IBA and 'taken very seriously across the whole business; if George said you are in trouble, they would believe him.'[44] He thought that whatever the long-term future, the licence fee was the mechanism that kept the BBC independent of political control. He talked to Wenham regularly, not Milne, 'a difficult man, who you could not trust, who was the problem not the solution, though an able man, a tragically able man'.[45] He called in the 'big ITV beasts' and told them that the government was serious, that it was their advertising revenue that was at risk and so they had better do something about it. Wenham had told him of the research they had been doing and Paddy Barwise gave them a foretaste of what his findings showed, informally over lunch, which was 'instructive'. Later, Thomson[46] argued that the BBC failed to assist the IBA and ITV or indeed make a common cause with other public service broadcasters when the government guns turned on them, but during Peacock and after, he kept in close touch with the Corporation – and 'we put our head over the parapet for them a good deal.' One reason, he argued, was that the BBC was beginning to make an original case during Peacock.

The BBC tried to talk its way around those with influence – as it does. Brian Griffiths, Mrs Thatcher's broadcasting advisor, was lobbied very gently by Phil Laven, a bright, Geordie engineer with a subtle mind and a firm grasp of politics who worked at the BBC technology research powerhouse at Wood Norton. He understood better than most the market implications of the way technology was moving and he was sent to talk 'hard wires and the future' to Lord Griffiths. Griffiths later confirmed that Laven came to him 'bearing attractive fruits', suggesting that even from the Olympian heights of No. 10 you had to work very hard to see 'round the political corners' of Laven's technological expertise. He was, said Griffiths, someone whose expertise commanded respect.[47] Meanwhile, Bernard Ingham, Mrs Thatcher's loyal, aggressive and efficient press officer, was lunched. Ingham, who believed that the broadcasters were above themselves, arrogant, uncompetitive, rife with union cartels, biased and treacherous to boot, was all in favour of advertising on the BBC, 'I thought it a decent and honourable way of paying for what people used.' But at least he wanted 'better television not more drivel'.[48] Patricia Hodgson, already trying to hold the Governors and the Board of Management together, understood these concerns and talked her way judiciously through Cabinet. She listened to what politicians had to say and strategised. Civil servants were approached, departmental views elicited and politicians were entertained.

Janet Morgan had written perceptively about how policy makers experienced broadcasters from her own time in the Central Policy Review Staff, the organisation set up to be a kind of Prime Minister's department – until Mrs Thatcher finally disbanded it. Morgan described the reaction of the two sides of the policy making duo, the politician and the civil servant, to the upstart, intrusive broadcasting. While on the government side, both parts shared a belief in their own authority it derived from different sources – the ballot box on the one hand and the legitimacy of government on the other. They both saw this authority challenged by the power of the broadcaster. On the one hand the bureaucrats 'believe that they understand and can interpret the public interest, but they are at the same time cynical. Indeed, they sometimes admit that those who make successful radio and television programmes show much more skill than themselves at discerning and responding to public tastes and needs – but simultaneously, the official mind cannot be wholly convinced that this is so. Officials are irritated by the glamour and frivolity of the lives that they believe that journalists and broadcasters lead,' she suggested. By contrast, multitasking politicians 'are chosen because they have definite views and opinions. Unlike officials they are reticent neither by nature nor by profession. They talk all the time. And, unlike officials they are not self protective – in fact politicians are some of the most masochistic people it is possible to meet. Politicians believe they are deeply equipped to interpret public desires.' Both groups of policy makers saw broadcasters as 'buccaneers, who imitate the tasks of politicians – staging debates, putting arguments, having opinions, interpreting the public interest, initiating ideas as well as reporting them.' But above all broadcasters were a nuisance: 'They interrupt what is in any case a frenzied life, not only with sudden crisis like *Carrickmore* or *Death of a Princess*, but with constant daily and nightly pressures. And broadcasters *want* things, money, licences, interviews, facts – and they give a platform to other people who want things – redress, change, attention.'[49] The BBC she believed had to understand how it was seen by these players.

But the BBC knew it was civil servants and Government Departments that drove policy. Making their case for Peacock was only one part of the work that had to be done; there was another job which was attempting to influence how the report was handled by the civil service and politicians once it was published. The BBC took this second part of the backstage work as seriously as it took the first part. In some ways they were more astute than the Peacock Committee itself in managing the policy after life. Historically the Home Office was 'pro' public service broadcasting and the Treasury hostile. Robert Hazel, then a junior civil servant in the Home Office Department , explained how key William Whitelaw was to the view in the department that, 'public service broadcasting was "ours" broadly we owned it and broadly we were in favour of it.'[50]

On the other hand Nigel Lawson, the Chancellor, was quite clearly in the advertising camp. 'Television in Britain had hitherto been dominated by a duopoly in which the BBC enjoyed a monopoly of tax finance and TV had a monopoly of television advertising' he wrote in his memoirs. Lawson believed, like Mrs Thatcher that broadcasting was biased against the government. However, his solution was different to hers. 'It is a fact of life' he wrote 'that bright young people on the left tend to seek and get jobs in broadcasting and journalism, just as those on the right tend to choose the city. The only way to diminish the bias is through increased competition and choice' (Lawson, 1992:721–2). This had been his opinion in office. In a minute to Douglas Hurd following publication of the Peacock Report he wrote, apparently trying to throw a last pro-advertising fusillade into the outcome, 'So far as political bias is concerned, the existing system clearly does not work, and indeed will always favour the left. While the transition cannot of course be achieved overnight, the cause of political balance, including a fair crack of the whip for conservative values, stands a far better chance of being secured by the "newspaper" solution of a multiplicity of broadcasters, each enjoying political freedom of expression, but each constrained by the need to win and keep an audience.'[51]

Presentation

Committees take evidence and they see people: the real time impression that people make has an impact. Milne certainly failed this test – and with himself and his performance damned the BBC. But the Corporation certainly understood that such things mattered. Morgan had tried to make Milne rehearse some of the replies to arguments he would encounter. He was briefed, and a 'mock committee' armed with some penetrating questions was set up to grill him. Milne was impatient with the process, lost his temper and stormed out.[52]

However, the BBC also prepared other, later presentations to the Committee with scrupulous care and they were indeed very effective. Ehrenberg and his research was the BBC's most important card. As the mood and tone of the proceedings became clearer, what was to be said was adjusted and rehearsed. After the main submission, the BBC gave further evidence both written and oral. At the last minute it was decided Ehrenberg should lead for the BBC at the final oral session in March.[53]

Another aspect of the BBC's presentation was the carefully focused arguments of the Corporation's written submissions. Their ongoing intelligence-gathering exercise had given them insights into the Committee's thinking. The BBC's evidence did not discuss wider or woollier principals, and made no appeal to tradition or the past but was drafted and argued to address the issues that the Committee wanted to consider, in the language they would accept. One observer commented of Hodgson that 'She really came into her formidable stride at this point: she did not just understand the 'anti' case, she felt where it was coming from. She has that empathetic quality you find in all great politicians: she could see things just as the forces in government saw them.'[54]

Meanwhile, Wenham, who was chiefly responsible for this, was famous within the Corporation for 'wennagrams' – short, pithy and often barbed memos to colleagues – and his skill at making a point clearly and efficiently was put to good use. In internal discussions of the first BBC submission Wenham told colleagues he had deliberately kept the draft 'free of traditional rhetoric', which he thought could appear defensive and that too strident a description of what the BBC did might be an invitation to curtail some of its activities. Wenham may have been influenced by Andrew Ehrenberg's research into the 1985 licence fee campaign which had argued that reference to Reithian values and excellence made them seem 'inward-looking and out of touch'.[55] Public reaction to the BBC's written submission was in the main favourable, which is surprising given the hostile reaction to the previous year's licence fee campaign. The *UK Press Gazette* said the BBC had made a strong case for the retention of the licence fee and had demonstrated the likely deleterious effects of advertising to newspaper as well as commercial broadcasting interests. The BBC had presented, said the *Financial Times*, 'a further mass of independent evidence' in support of its arguments and went on that 'the BBC and indeed British broadcasting generally had been the goose that laid golden eggs' and it would be foolish to tamper with success. The only problem was to make the BBC's income as invisible as ITV's. In the trade press, predictably, reaction was positive. *Television Today* headlined its verdict 'The BBC at its best, now move on' and considered that the submission may well have been the most important document the BBC had ever produced. It was 'composed, written and edited in a manner which reflects credit on the Corporation. Its simplicity of style and relative succinctness – something very difficult to achieve with so much experience and evidence to call on – are a far cry from the stodgy BBC evidence to the Annan Committee in the seventies which was eclipsed by that from ITCA.' *Broadcast* considered the BBC submission 'confident, sure-footed and bullish', and eloquent and persuasive in its defence of the licence fee (Anon, 1986; Dunkley, 1986; Anon, 1986a; Anon, 1986b).

After-politics

Reports are political instruments: they are set up to solve political problems. But publishing a report is only one small part of its career – or impact. It is a beginning, not, as it looks, an end. The Peacock Committee was set up to provide a solution to the political and economic inadequacies – as the government saw them, of the Corporation. Actually, the Prime Minister thought that they were going to recommend a new way of financing the BBC to replace the licence fee. Instead of recommending advertising the Peacock review curtly dismissed the possibility on principled economic grounds, and moved on to an enormously cogent and clear analysis of the future of broadcasting (attached to some rather imperiously narrow recommendations of the proper consequences of these developments). Yet the effectiveness of the Committee's recommendations depended on it meeting a government agenda, or in persuading the politicians to accept its definition of the future.

However, from the BBC's point of view there was a paradox: in order to 'win' the BBC had to appear not to. For if the report was 'in favour' of the BBC, its findings would be dismissed as irrelevant. Stuart Young, the Conservative Chairman of the Governors, had been seen as having been 'turned' by the Corporation and was as a consequence dismissed in Cabinet as 'a dry gone damp'. The Report's hostility to the Corporation was actually politically vital. Indeed, when the Peacock Committee came in with what many – in the Treasury and especially among backbench Tories – thought was the 'wrong' answer, it was hard to turn it into policy. Giles Shaw, the minister with responsibility for broadcasting, minuted the Home Secretary that he regarded the Committee's 'conclusions as difficult to present from a party point of view', and Hurd, mindful of this likely adverse reaction among colleagues, decided that the Home Office would say little publicly beyond a statement that the Government needed time to reflect on 'this major report in the light of public reaction' and nothing at all on advertising. In the meantime, 'Professor Peacock and the members of his committee would be able to argue for their recommendations publicly.' This could be interpreted as saying that, because the Committee had not delivered what was expected, they were to be hung out to dry, thus ensuring that any opprobrium that flowed from their failure would adhere to them alone.[56]

However, at least the Peacock Committee never looked as if it had 'gone native' on the BBC – whatever it was captured by, it certainly was not the Corporation. This hostility to the BBC was rather ironically useful for the Corporation – it added value to the Peacock Report's conclusions, in as far as they were broadly in line with BBC interests. And, on the simple, immediate and clear basis of the preservation of the licence fee and opposition to its replacement by advertising, the report was exactly what the Corporation wanted.

In addition, once the report was received then officials began to chew over how it was to be handled. In one key way both Peacock and Brittan for rather different reasons misunderstood or misplayed the politics of the report. Brittan was and is a classic liberal – convinced that any impediment to freedom of expression is dangerous. But officials were not in agreement with the Committee's (surely Brittan's) view that the present duopoly inhibited 'dissentient points of view'. The Prime Minister was hardly handbagging them because the Corporation was too compliant a loudspeaker for the government case. Nor was she unique in her desire for a more sympathetic BBC (but persuasively, impartially sympathetic of course). Nor was she unusual in this: very few rows about broadcasting have ever taken the form of 'golly gosh they agree with us too much. Off with their heads!' So Brittan's theoretical and classically liberal anxiety was not one shared by the government (or indeed ever heard from any government of any political colour). Governments want a little more compliance. As one official pointed out 'in practice our broadcasting authorities are more usually criticised for giving too much coverage to unusual points of view.'[57] It was not only in attitudes to freedom of political expression that they were out of step.

While they looked far into the future, nevertheless, the members of the Committee had no crystal ball: some of the future they got rather wrong. But they also got contemporary politics wrong. The members of the Committee were entranced with their vision of 'freedom' on air. They were not to know of the explosion of pornography that was to fuel the spread of the Internet, but they were happy to think of bits of the spectrum that, less regulated, would cater to a wider taste band than traditional broadcasting. So they suggested using the night for 'adult movies'. This was a tactical error: not least because Mrs Thatcher had certainly not set up the Committee to increase 'adult' material, but on the contrary, believed that competition would decrease 'moral degradation'. The conservative radical free marketer was combined, perhaps irrationally, in Mrs Thatcher with the conservative paternalist – at least over morality. 'As for moral degradation', Lawson observes, 'she suffered from the delusion that tends to affect all politicians, even professedly free market ones, that they can regulate everything if they really wish to' (Lawson, 1992:722).

However, night time 'adult movies' were not likely to win No. 10, and the Home Office and Douglas Hurd (who, by the time the report had been presented, had replaced Brittan as Home Secretary,) knew it – and used it. You could say the Home Office pounced. Hurd was at pains to stress his rejection of Recommendation 9 on 'the provision of unregulated night-time services'. This would, he wrote, lead to speculation about 'adult films' and in his public statement about the report, he would specifically reject it, 'citing the current concern about broadcasting standards and the particularly intrusive nature of the medium'. He reiterated the concerns about balance and impartiality. So Hurd used the Trojan horse of Conservative hostility (both in No. 10 and in the grass roots) to 'adult material' to widen the argument back into the terrain of broadcasting values.[58] Ministers, when they met, were in agreement on the regulation of content, that 'the Home Secretary's statement should be firm in saying that any future system must be no weaker that it was now,' and, taking an opposite view, were of the opinion that if regulations were weakened then it would be necessary to change the law of the land.[59] Hurd had another, fundamental disagreement with Peacock over the question of the survival of public service broadcasting as a concept, to which he felt the Committee were hostile. In a minute to the PM he wrote 'It is not clear to me that there is general acceptance – and indeed I am not convinced that public service broadcasting in the wider sense is at the end of its useful life; and I think this is one of the less persuasive parts of the report.'[60] The Peacock Committee did not follow through on its report – and played back into the hands of the Home Office, essentially defenders of the public service idea and however much they thought it needed reform, of the BBC.

Conclusion

However offensive Milne's performance to the Committee, however 'inadequate' Professor Peacock found it, the BBC more generally pulled itself round: addressed the problems with its best minds, read the runes and perhaps most importantly took seriously the real intellectual challenge the Peacock Committee's proceedings offered. The BBC was certainly not passive: it was indeed in certain key respects immensely effective. It identified the key economic arguments that were likely to be persuasive, and perhaps most important of all, commissioned and supervised the vital research that demonstrated, in impeccably 'dry' economic terms, the impracticality of funding the Corporation by advertising. It did not do this in a merely self-serving way and that is why its arguments about advertising were so convincing and immediately accepted by the Committee. For the BBC's research was novel, imaginative, well founded and right. For the BBC, this was by far the most important outcome and the preservation of a newly legitimated licence fee was vital but by no means predictable. The Corporation considered the membership of the Committee and how best to advocate its case in the light of their individual backgrounds and interests, and put together an effective and intelligent team to steer the Corporation case. Of course, the members of the Committee did not see any of this and gave an entirely accurate account of their understanding: moreover they were right. But, as so often with history, other things were happening, other forces were at work. Our explanation does not invalidate theirs, but it does show it to be only a part of the story. In the Home Office and the Treasury, in Cabinet and in the commercial television industry, the BBC rallied arguments and forces with a precise and effective focus.

The BBC was the object of attention, but then disappeared from view in the Report. Our contention is that the BBC may not have been effective performers in front of the Committee, but they were effective campaigners behind the scenes in getting the outcome they wanted.

Notes

1. Thanks are due to Jacquie Kavanagh and all the staff at the BBC Written Archives Centre for access to BBC files and to Tessa Stirling and all her staff at the Cabinet Office for access to Home Office files.
2. Quoted in Summers (1985).
3. There is of course a dispute about 'how' radical, and when it became 'really radical'. However, there is no dispute that the mid-1980s, the time of the Peacock Report, were high water for Mrs Thatcher herself, on which all of the Cabinet memoires of that period and a number of impartial observers agree.
4. Sir Alan had written on orchestras and music.
5. Home Office File HO FIN 86 0244/0002/001 'Broadcasting and Wireless Telegraphy BBC Peacock Report', minute D. Hurd to M. Thatcher, 11/6/1986 (hereafter HO FIN 86 0244/0002/001).
6. BBC Written Archives, Caversham (hereafter, BBCWAC), BBCWAC R78/3532 D215-025-001 Finance the BBC Committee (Peacock) Policy, meeting BOG and BOM, 14/11/1985; memo S. Hearst to A. Milne, 5/12/1985.
7. HO FIN 86 0244/0002/001, minute Q. J. Thomas to Mr Hyde, 21/05/1986.
8. HO FIN 86 0244/0002/001, minute W. N. Hyde, 22/5/1986.
9. HO FIN 86 0244/0002/001, minute Q. J. Thomas to Ms Pelham, 10/6/1986.
10. Interview with Janet Morgan, 2007.
11. When asked about the affair later, fellow witness Brian Wenham could only offer the defence that Milne was 'a man given to few words'. BBCWAC, Brian Wenham BBC oral history interview with Frank Gillard, 21/4/1988.
12. BBCWAC BM (86) 26 Final Supplementary Evidence To The Peacock Committee, 14/2/1986.
13. 'I appeared, I prepared, I answered their questions. They were rather un-civil to me. I believed that they had been set up to attack us and I stood on the quality of our programmes – which I had complete confidence in. It was a golden age for programmes.' Alasdair Milne, interview, 2006.
14. See, for example, Brittan (1987:9), 'Some BBC officials are so used to the idea of being financed by what is virtually a tax on the possession of a television set, that they do not realise how privileged and unusual their position is, and how much in need of continuing and detailed justification'.
15. HO FIN 86 0244/0002/001, minutes of a meeting between Secretary of State and Professor Peacock, 9/6/1986, by Clare Pelham P. S. to Secretary of State, 10/6/1986.
16. BBCWAC, BOM 13/5/1985, minute 250.
17. Interviews with Sir Bernard Ingham, 2008 and Lord Griffiths, 2008. Lord Griffiths was head of the Centre for Policy Studies, 1991–2001. Nearly ten years later in her carefully engineered memoirs, Mrs Thatcher in the face of a defeat and something which explains much about the political reception of

the Peacock Report says 'But I did not drop my long term reservations about the licence fee as the source of the BBC's funding' (Thatcher, 1993:636).

18. Interview with Michael Checkland, 2005.
19. Sam Brittan speaking at 'The Peacock Legacy: Turning Point or Missed Opportunity?' (Conference Transcripts, 2005: Opening Plenary and View From the BBC)
20. Leon Brittan, interview, 2007.
21. Interview, Fraser Steele, Policy and Planning, 1984–7, Head of Complaints, 2007.
22. Interview with Alan Hart (Controller BBC1 1981–4), 2002.
23. BBCWAC Oral Archive Brian Wenham interviewed by Frank Gillard, 12/4/1988.
24. Interview Patricia Hodgson, 2006.
25. Interview Janet Morgan, 2007.
26. BBCWAC R78/3532 Finance the BBC Committee (Peacock) Policy, memo Head of Recording Services Radio (HRSR) Michael Starks to P. Hodgson, 29/3/1985.
27. BBCWAC BOM, 1/7/1985: 364.
28. BBCWAC R78/3532 Finance the BBC Committee (Peacock) Policy, memo Janet Morgan to A. Milne, 28/3/1985.
29. BBCWAC R44/1433/1 Publicity: Peacock Committee Biographies.
30. BBCWAC R78/3532 Finance the BBC Committee (Peacock) Policy. BBC Information Profiles of members, 22/5/1985, taken from R44/1433/1 Publicity: Peacock Committee Biographies.
31. Huw Wheldon, (in)famously in BBC folklore, miscalculated the level of hospitality the Committee required, and attempted to 'lunch them into inanition' to use Anthony Smith's phrase at their first meeting. The plan backfired. Colin Shaw, BBC Chief Secretary, witness seminar University of Westminster, 23/2/2004.
32. BBCWAC R78/3532 the BBC Committee (Peacock) Policy. Memo J. Morgan to A. Milne, 4/6/1985.
33. BBCWAC R78/3532 Finance the BBC Committee (Peacock) Policy. Memo J. Morgan to A. Milne, 11/6/1985.
34. BBCWAC R78/3532 Finance the BBC Committee (Peacock) Policy. Memo S. Hearst to A. Milne, 16/7/1985.
35. BBCWAC R78/3532 Memo P. Woon, Head of Operations North America, to B. Wenham, 13/9/1985.
36. BBCWAC R44/1403/1 Peacock Committee, background information and BBC comments, address by the Director General of the BBC to The Peacock Committee's Conference on Financing the BBC, 28/11/1985.
37. BBCWAC R78/125/1 Peacock Enquiry – BBC Committee, Steering Committee meeting, 13/5/1985.
38. BBCWAC R78/3532 Finance the BBC Committee (Peacock) Policy, memo Stephen Hearst to BBC Secretary D. V. Holmes, 23/4/1985.
39. BBCWAC R78/3537/1 Financing The BBC Committee (Peacock), BBC Evidence G57/86, note of Oral Evidence to the Peacock Committee given at the Home Office on Tuesday, 11th March 1986.
40. Interview with Paddy Barwise, 2005.
41. BBCWAC R78/3532 Finance the BBC Committee (Peacock) Policy, Joint Board of Governors and Board of Management meeting on the BBC submission to Peacock, 14/11/1985.

42. HO FIN 86 0244/0002/001, minutes of a meeting between Secretary of State and Professor Peacock, 9/6/1986 by Clare Pelham P. S. to S of S, 10/6/1986.
43. BBCWAC R78/3532 Finance the BBC Committee (Peacock) Policy, memo P. Meneer, Head of Broadcasting Research Dept, to P. Hodgson, 13/9/1985.
44. Interview with Sir Paul Fox, 2007, who worked in the BBC and in commercial television.
45. Interview Lord Thomson (2006).
46. Ibid.
47. Interview Lord Griffiths.
48. Ingham (1991:123); also interview with Sir Bernard Ingham, 2006.
49. Janet Morgan, in Morgan and Hoggart (1982:58–62).
50. Robert Hazel, interview, 2008.
51. HO FIN 86 0244/0002/001, minute N. Lawson to D. Hurd, 4/8/1986.
52. Interviews with Janet Morgan, 2007 and Alasdair Milne, 2005.
53. A. S. C. Ehrenberg, interview with author, 17/3/2005; evidence published as Ehrenberg (1986).
54. Interview with Fraser Steele, Head of the BBC Complaints Department, 2007.
55. BBCWAC A. Ehrenberg 'What Went Wrong? Comments on the 1984/5 Licence fee Application.'
56. HO FIN 86 0244/0002/001, minute G. Shaw to S of S, 3/6/1986; notes of a meeting held on 4/6/1986.
57. HO FIN 86 0244/0002/001, minute Q. J. Thomas to Ms Pelham, 10/6/1986.
58. HO FIN 86 0244/0002/001, minute D. Hurd to M. Thatcher, 11/6/1986.
59. HO FIN 86 0244/0002/001, minute D. Norgrove No. 10 to S. Boys HO, 25/6/1986.
60. HO FIN 86 0244/0002/001, minute D. Hurd to M. Thatcher, 11/6/1986.

8
Paradigm Found: The Peacock Report and the Genesis of a New Model of UK Broadcasting Policy

Richard Collins

> however admirable the past achievements of the BBC,
> what we are concerned with is the future.
>
> (Report, 1951: para. 185)

Why pay attention to the Peacock[1] Report (Report, 1986)? Few of its predictions have been borne out and few of its recommendations have been adopted: UK broadcasting is far from the 'sophisticated market system based on consumer sovereignty' (Report, 1986: para. 592; also Brittan, 1986:1) enjoined by Peacock, subscription has not replaced the licence fee as Peacock said it should (Report, 1986: para. 673), Radios 1 and 2 have not been privatised (Recommendation 7 of the committee) and so on.

Instead of the 'sophisticated market system based on consumer sovereignty' which would enlarge 'both the freedom of choice of the consumer and the opportunities available to programme makers to offer alternative wares to the public' (Report, 1986: para. 547), UK television is dominated by three players each pre-eminent in a distinct market sector.

- Pay television. The dominant pay television operator,[2] BSkyB, has been able to exert its market power to set the terms on which new channels can enter the broadcasting market, raise prices, bundle services and set the prices at which potential competitors, notably cable television companies, sell their products.
- Advertising financed television. The dominant operator, Independent Television (ITV), in a sector, as Peacock pointed out, driven by the interests of advertisers rather than those of consumers, accounted

for just over 50% of the market (satellite television c20%, Channels 4 c21% and 5 c9%, see Ofcom, 2005a: 60).

- Publicly funded television. The BBC has a monopoly over the licence fee[3] funds (non-payment of which leads to criminalisation and possible incarceration) as a condition of receiving any television services whether or not BBC services are consumed or valued. In radio the BBC enjoys unchallenged dominance with 54% of radio consumption.[4]

Moreover, as well as the empirical objections sketched above, there are powerful theoretical challenges to Peacock's analysis. Graham (1999) and others (see inter alia Davies, 2004)[5] have argued, in contrast to Peacock, that broadcasting markets are not perfectible, as Peacock had proposed, but rather are subject to endemic failure and on this basis have built a powerful 'standard defence' (Graham's term) of public service broadcasting arguing that it, rather than a market system, is likely to best serve the public interest. They claim that

- the public good character of broadcasting means the encryption of programmes necessary for subscription broadcasting is socially wasteful (welfare is lost) because some, who could consume at zero cost, are deprived of the opportunity to do so;
- broadcasting is an efficient way of supplying merit goods (that is goods which confer long-term social benefits, such as education in the arts and research, but which individuals underdemand relative to their's and society's long-term interest). Accordingly, free to air public service broadcasting should receive public funding to ensure adequate provision of merit goods;
- broadcasting has significant potential negative externalities (e.g. amplifying fear of crime and perhaps also actual criminal behaviour). Accordingly, both negative regulation (to reduce circulation of such programmes) and positive intervention to supply countervailing programming and services improve welfare;
- information, including radio and TV, is an 'experience good' (that is, one doesn't know what one's buying/consuming until one has done so) which is best provided by trusted and authenticated suppliers such as public service broadcasters.

But despite these cogent objections the Peacock Committee's paradigm has become hegemonic; indeed, the 'standard defence' itself testifies to the extent to which Peacock changed the conceptual framework within which UK broadcasting policy is considered. The prominence of Peacock's market vocabulary and analytical paradigm is doubtless due, at least in part, to the wide general salience which market doctrines came to enjoy in the 1980s in the UK when they went hand in hand with liberalisation and privatisation policies (see inter alia Leys, 2001; Moran, 2003). But Peacock differed from the general liberalisation discourses in that it gave primacy to consumer sovereignty rather than to efficiency and innovation (usually foregrounded in liberalisation discourses) and in its decisive break with a conception of the viewer and listener as vulnerable and in need of protection which had hitherto dominated UK broadcasting policy. Peacock conjured a novel[6] and persuasive vision of the user of broadcasting services as active, empowered and competent to decide and shifted decisively the dominant paradigm governing UK broadcasting policy.

The invention of the BBC

UK broadcasting has been shaped by the successive analyses and bundles of recommendations put forward in official reports at roughly decennial intervals: notably in the Sykes (Report, 1923), Crawford (Report, 1926), Ullswater (Report, 1936), Beveridge (Report, 1951), Pilkington (Report, 1962), Annan (Report, 1977) and Peacock (Report, 1986) reports. The principle focus in all reports was the status of the BBC and the extent to which it should be subject to competition.

The BBC was established in 1922 as a commercial company and became a public corporation in 1927 following the Crawford Committee's recommendation that broadcasting in the UK 'should be conducted by a public corporation acting as Trustee for the national interest' (Crawford, 1926:14). The BBC's interpretation of the 'national interest' was made manifest in mid-1926, shortly after the Crawford Committee delivered its report, when its reporting of one of twentieth century Britain's deepest social crises – the General Strike of 1926 – was governed by a BBC doctrine that 'nothing calculated to extend the area of the strike should be broadcast' (cited in Briggs 1961:373): as its Director General stated the BBC was not 'to permit anything which . . . might have prolonged or sought to justify the Strike' (Briggs 1961:365).

The Ullswater Committee in 1936 fended off nascent challenges to the BBC's control of broadcast content by recommending that 'control of relayed programmes' (i.e. cable radio) should reside with the BBC and that 'ownership and operation of relay exchanges' should be undertaken by the Post Office rather than by commercial interests likely to view favourably the offshore English language commercial services, such as Radio Luxembourg and Radio Normandie, which, particularly in the south of England, provided some alternative to the BBC (Report, 1936: para. 143 (r)).

Ullswater cemented two concepts which underpinned UK broadcasting policy until Peacock: first that the supply of broadcasting services should be limited (initially via a BBC monopoly and subsequently via the BBC/ITV duopoly later complemented by Channel 4 which was, at first, part of the ITV nexus[7]) and that broadcasters should be accountable to the Government (rather than to users). Symptomatically the section in the Report which comes closest to addressing accountability is that titled 'Control' where it states that 'the Corporation is strictly bound to observe the provisions of any licence granted by the Postmaster General and any instructions which he from time to time may issue' (Report, 1936: para. 48). True, the Report emphasises the BBC's independence from government at more than one point but the public, the users of the BBC, are mentioned only as the beneficiaries of the 'constitutional independence of the BBC [which] brings advantages to the general public and to listeners which could not otherwise be secured' (Report, 1936: para. 51). Protection of the BBC's monopoly involved denying, or at least not facilitating, listeners' access to broadcasters other than the BBC.

Beveridge, Coase and challenges to the BBC's monopoly

The first challenges to the BBC's monopoly and to the ideas which constructed broadcasters as upwardly accountable to political authority rather than downwardly accountable to users came in the early 1950s from the stable of the London School of Economics and Political Science (LSE) when the LSE economist Ronald Coase[8] published his path-breaking study *The British Broadcasting Corporation. A Study in Monopoly* (Coase, 1950).[9] Coase challenged two clusters of arguments which underpinned the BBC's monopoly, those based on technical and efficiency considerations and those based on programming considerations.

Coase observed that spectrum scarcity, presumed to be an inescapable constraint limiting competition in broadcasting, was in fact not so strong a constraint as had been supposed. Using the case of a relay exchange (cable radio service) he argued that the technical reasons for constraining competition in UK broadcasting, and thus the grounds for the BBC's monopoly, were weak. And, though acknowledging stronger arguments on the programming side, Coase commented that 'those supporting the monopoly of broadcasting... do not seem to have thought it constituted a threat to freedom of speech' (Coase, 1950:187). He summarised his critique thus:

> I have shown that the technical arguments are incorrect, the arguments on grounds of finance unproven and those on grounds of efficiency inconclusive. But, of course, the really important argument has been that a monopoly was required in order that there should be a unified programme policy. This argument is powerful and on its assumptions it is no doubt logical. Its main disadvantage is that to accept its assumptions it is necessary first to adopt a totalitarian philosophy or at any rate something verging on it.
>
> (Coase, 1950:191)

On the policy front, the former Director of LSE (1919–37), Lord William Beveridge chaired the next official review, the Beveridge Committee, of broadcasting policy. Coase observed that the committees of enquiry which preceded Beveridge had all accepted the BBC monopoly as a given and, in consequence, 'many questions of detail have been investigated, the central issues have been ignored' (Coase, 1950b:991). He looked forward to Beveridge facing these 'central issues' (Coase, 1950b:991) though he was clearly disappointed in the Committee's final findings for the BBC and stated 'One cannot help wondering whether an organisation which is so much in need of improvement, so incapable of clear thought and so unconscious of its own defects, really merits the great confidence which the Committee place in it' (Coase, 1951:51). Coase is not listed among those who gave evidence to Beveridge[10] and it is not clear from the Beveridge Report how far his arguments influenced the Committee's discussions (and Selwyn Lloyd's minority report in particular). But Coase clearly had some influence on the Beveridge Report – his *British Broadcasting. A Study in Monopoly* (Coase, 1950) was cited by the Committee (though not, as Coase observed, a section the author would have chosen – see Coase, 1951:51).[11] Despite the Beveridge Committee's somewhat perverse use of Coase's study, it seems unlikely that the Committee, chaired by Coase's former colleague and boss, did not consider Coase's published commentaries on the issues which it had under consideration – not least because of its break with the Crawford Committee's endorsement of the BBC's monopoly.[12]

Beveridge eloquently denounced the BBC monopoly:

> Continuance of a monopoly of broadcasting exactly on the present lines has dangers which call for safeguards. There are dangers in Londonization. There are dangers of remoteness, of self-satisfaction, of secretiveness. There is danger of slowness in exploring new unfamiliar techniques. There are dangers of favouritism and injustice in treatment of staff or performer, each of them an evil in a monopoly more serious than it would be in a concern with rivals. There is the danger finally that when a sense of mission such as animates the BBC is combined with security of office it may grow into a sense of Divine Right, as it did in the case of Charles I.
>
> (Report, 1951: para. 185)

But despite this denunciation, most of the Beveridge Committee firmly supported the BBC's monopoly and declared 'if the public service of broadcasting is to be effective, it must remain a monopoly' (Report, 1951: para. 151). However, one member, the Conservative politician Selwyn Lloyd, dissented and argued on Coasian lines that 'independent competition will be healthy for broadcasting' (Report, 1951: Minority report para. 16).[13] Lloyd's proposals were eventually adopted by the Conservative government which took power in 1951 (in which Lloyd served as Minister of State for Foreign Affairs) and came to fruition in 1955 when ITV began UK advertising-financed television.

ITV's competition to the BBC was highly controlled but ITV meant that viewers (but not yet listeners) were able, albeit imperfectly, to hold broadcasters to account. For the first time they were able to exercise the sanction of exit and in doing so massively reduced the BBC's television audience: in the first months of television competition 'something between two out of three and three out of four homes with sets converted to receive both BBC and ITV watched the main ITV programmes' (Sendall, 1982:134). What, in this context, is meant by 'holding to account' and 'exit'?

Exit and voice: Holding to account and giving an account

In 1970 Albert Hirschman published *Exit, Voice and Loyalty* where he identified three ways in which institutions can be held to account – through 'exit', 'voice' and 'loyalty': stakeholders can signal their preferences by 'exiting' from the relationship (e.g. by ceasing to buy products and services), by making their 'voice' heard (e.g. by voting) or by demonstrating their 'loyalty' (doing nothing in circumstances where exit and/or voice might be exercised). 'Loyalty' may be regarded as a null option (if one is loyal then one does not exercise voice or exit) and, broadly and customarily, exit as a system of sanctions exercised through prices and markets and voice through politics and voting.

Mary Warnock has usefully clarified the concept of accountability and (when a member of the Independent Broadcasting Authority)[14] defined accountability as a combination of the right to know (that is a right to be given an account) 'and' to impose sanctions (that is to hold to account). She stated:

> A is accountable to B where B has entrusted to A some duty (especially in regard to the spending of money) and where, if A fails to fulfil this duty, B has some sanction which he may use against A. This is one necessary part of it. But it follows that B has a right to be exactly informed of what A has done towards fulfilling his duty.
>
> (Warnock, 1974:2)

Applying Hirschman's model to UK broadcasting suggests that viewers and listeners, prior to ITV, [15] were unable to exercise either voice or exit – broadcasting was a system of compulsory loyalty to the BBC for there was no lawful way for viewers and listeners either to exit from funding the BBC or to hold the BBC to account through an exercise of voice. Beveridge first put forward a notion of empowering viewers with exit sanctions and this model of accountability was developed more powerfully and comprehensively by Peacock. Implementation of Lloyd's minority report, attached to the main Beveridge Report, enabled UK viewers, for the first time, to hold broadcasters to account through exit sanctions.

Pilkington and the vulnerable/incompetent viewer

The Pilkington Report (Report, 1962) further expanded UK television by reinforcing the BBC's preponderance[16] and reinforced an established view of viewers (and listeners) as vulnerable and thus incompetent to hold broadcasters to account. Pilkington described the audience thus:

> Sitting at home, people are relaxed, less consciously critical and therefore, more exposed. Further, audiences are often family groups and include children who are normally protected from outside influences, and therefore especially vulnerable.
>
> (Report, 1962: para. 41)

Pilkington explicitly viewed competition as corrupting: 'The quality of programmes (i.e. ITV's regulator of commercial television (RC)) is sacrificed to obtain the largest possible audience' (Report, 1962: para. 43).

The Report made quite clear its belief that, when given the opportunity to decide, people are likely to make the wrong decisions: 'Those who say they give the public what it wants begin by underestimating public taste and in the end by debauching it' (Report, 1962: para. 47).

Accordingly, Pilkington rejected explicitly (Recommendation 7) the establishment of a Broadcasting Consumers' Council (Report, 1962:287),[17] recommended against services that might compete with the BBC (and a stringently regulated ITV) by declaring that 'No service of subscription television, whether by wire or by radio, should be authorised' (Recommendation 100, Report, 1962:295) and 'There should be no experiment in subscription television' (Recommendation 101, Report, 1962:295). Viewers and listeners were not to have their powers of voice or exit strengthened.

Milland, the leading contemporary expert on the Pilkington Report, argues that the Pilkington Report (Report, 1962) was shaped in a contemporary context where 'the masses of people who were to be brought its (i.e. broadcasting RC) benefits – without having realised they wanted them – did not need to be consulted about the manner in which they were to be delivered' (Milland, 2004:92). In contrast, Coase (1966), in a commentary from Chicago,[18] highlighted the contradiction between Pilkington's proposals to buttress broadcasting authority and its rhetorical invocations of 'respect for the public's right to choose and of the need for the widest possible choice' (Coase, 1966:443). Coase observed that 'the committee avoids the question of how it should be decided which programme to transmit and for the phrase "what the public wants", they substitute another and better, "what the public authority wants". What the public authority should want, how it would get the information which would enable it to do what it should, and how in practice it would be likely to act are questions which all disappear in a cloud of pious platitudes' (Coase, 1966:443–4).

Annan

The next major UK public enquiry into broadcasting, the Annan Report (Report, 1977), echoed Pilkington recommending that 'The BBC should continue to be the main national instrument of broadcasting in the United Kingdom' (Report, 1977:476) repeating, almost verbatim, Pilkington's finding that the BBC should 'remain the main instrument of broadcasting in the United Kingdom' (Report, 1962:288). But Annan broke new ground in proposing that the audience was adult, competent to decide in its own interests and undeferential (Report, 1977:14–16). The Committee proposed several measures to improve accountability through voice, notably by strengthening the BBC's Governors vis a vis BBC management; introducing public hearings; establishing both a public enquiry board and an independent Broadcasting Complaints Commission. Consistent with its validation of broadcasters' accountability to users, the Committee justified control of programme standards not, as Pilkington had done, by referring to the need to protect vulnerable audiences (though the Committee did mention 'the most vulnerable with the fewest defences' (Home Office, 1977: para. 16.36) but by acknowledging 'listeners' and viewers' wishes' for programme regulation: 'the concern which people express about certain topics is justified; and the broadcasters have failed to consider seriously enough the objections raised to certain programmes' (Report, 1977: para. 16.36). However, few of the Committee's 174 recommendations were adopted other than its proposals for an Open Broadcasting Authority (OBA) and for an independent commission to handle complaints (realised in the form of Channel 4 and the Broadcasting Complaints Commission).

Sentiment had shifted between Pilkington and Annan. Rather than Pilkington's view that broadcasting audiences needed better protection by a cohort of Platonic Guardians, Annan recognised that deference had definitely declined and, rather than requiring protection, viewers and listeners should be confident that their complaints would be heard. Accordingly, Annan recommended (a modest) strengthening of viewers' and listeners' ability to exercise the sanction of voice. But the shift between Pilkington and Annan was small indeed in comparison to that between Annan and the next major milestone in the evolution of UK broadcasting policy – the Peacock Report of 1986.

Peacock

Peacock echoed the most radical elements of Beveridge's critique: competition should be fostered to strengthen viewers' and listeners' powers of exit and ability to hold broadcasters to account. The Committee advocated restructuring the tightly controlled UK broadcasting system through a 'sophisticated market system based on consumer sovereignty' (Report, 1986: para. 592) which, the Committee argued, (revoicing elements of Coase's and Beveridge's critiques[19]), would enlarge 'both the freedom of choice of the consumer and the opportunities available to programme makers to offer alternative wares to the public' (Report, 1986: para. 547).

Competition, the central element of the 'sophisticated market system', was seen as the essential instrument through which both efficiency and accountability could effectively be secured. Rather than the control and restriction of entry which had formerly characterised UK broadcasting policy, Peacock advocated encouraging entry. One of the most influential members of the Peacock Committee, Samuel (later Sir Samuel) Brittan summarised the Committee's reasoning, 'there may in future no longer be any physical need to limit broadcasting to a small number of channels. Instead there could be an infinite number of services which customers could select and pay for directly. The distinction between publishing and broadcasting would then largely disappear with a consequent extension of cultural diversity and freedom' (Brittan, 1987:20).

The Peacock Committee sought a well-functioning broadcasting market primarily because such a market was conducive to liberty (or, in Brittan's terms, freedom). Peacock has customarily been criticised by proponents of public service broadcasting for putatively reducing viewers and listeners to the status of mere consumers rather than acknowledging their (loftier) status as citizens. But the primacy Peacock gave to the principles of liberty and viewer and listener sovereignty suggest the Committee saw users of broadcasting services no less as autonomous and empowered citizens than as consumers of paid services. Although the terms consumer and citizen have often been constructed in UK broadcasting debates as antitheses, here there is no necessary irreconcilability in the concepts consumer and citizen.[20]

Peacock's notions of the importance of liberty and of viewer and listener sovereignty in broadcasting neatly fit Brinkmann's classic definition in the *Encyclopaedia of the Social Sciences* of citizenship inhering in 'the notion of liberty . . . and membership of a political unit involving co-operation in public decisions as a right' (Brinkmann, 1959:471). Essentially, Peacock (and Coase) put forward a Hayekian analysis[21] coupling freedom and a well-functioning market as Hayek had argued in his celebrated *The Road to Serfdom*:

> Economic liberalism . . . regards competition as superior not only because it is in most circumstances the most efficient method known, but even more so because it is the only method by which our activities may be adjusted to each other without coercive or arbitrary intervention of authority. Indeed, one of the main arguments in favour of

competition is that it dispenses with the need for 'conscious social control' and that it gives individuals a chance to decide whether the prospects of a particular occupation are sufficient to compensate for the disadvantages and risks connected with it.

(Hayek, 1997:27)

Peacock therefore took a stage further the change in sentiment which had taken place between Pilkington and Annan – not only were viewers and listeners seen to be robust, undeferential and no longer requiring protection but they were, Peacock believed, the fundamental criterion of value. Accordingly, the broadcasting system should be restructured to enable them to make their own choices unconstrained by the editorial filtering effected by broadcasters – whereas Annan advocated modest changes to viewers' and listeners' ability to exercise voice, Peacock argued forcefully that they should enjoy considerably greater powers to hold broadcasters to account through exit.

Few readers will need to be advised that my account of Peacock outlined is highly unusual – indeed when judged against the orthodoxies of the UK academy it may appear both perverse and deviant for it both takes seriously Peacock's claims that a well-functioning broadcasting market could be established and that through markets and process, the freedom and powers of citizens in broadcasting might be advanced. This is a view very different to that put forward in most UK scholarly literature which relies on Graham's (1999), Davies' (2004) 'standard defence' (arguing that market failure in broadcasting is endemic and that, therefore, Peacock's advocacy of competition and markets is ill founded) and on a conception of citizenship in broadcasting which is completely decoupled from the category of consumer (see inter alia Calabrese and Burgelman, 1999; Hartley, 1999; Helm, 2005; Murdock, 1999, 2004; Stevenson, 2003).

Citizenship, liberty and welfare

Dieter Helm (2005), in an important essay (in a collection animated by the BBC), builds on the 'standard defence' and argues that at the core of citizenship is a notion of 'equal status and treatment. Membership of . . . society is, in the citizen sense, not dependent on initial wealth or income. It accrues to each person on the same basis,' accordingly a market-based broadcasting system, in which viewers and listeners are unequal (in that they do not have the same level of resources to commit to the market), cannot satisfy citizenship criteria. Helm goes on to stipulate that 'this in turn translates into the democratic ideal, which gives each member of the society an equal say. Much of the welfare state is designed on this principle of equal status: from health and education services, through to the nationwide definition of mass entitlements' (Helm, 2005:4–5). Leaving aside the unwelcome disempowerment of all which attends the current configuration through which 'the democratic ideal' is realised in UK broadcasting where 'each member of the society' does indeed enjoy ' an equal say' (that is no say at all, whether through voice or exit, over the BBC, the flagship of public service broadcasting and standard bearer of broadcasting citizenship), Helm's acknowledgement of the importance of having a say is worthy of notice (it is welcome and unusual in the scholarly literature) as is his invocation of 'mass entitlements' which is more representative of scholarly discussion of broadcasting citizenship.

Murdock's (1999 and 2004) accounts of citizenship repay particular attention. Murdock has argued that 'the core rationale for public service broadcasting lies in its commitment to providing the cultural resources required for full citizenship' (Murdock, 2004:2). Murdock's argument is representative of the mainstream of academic commentary and, unlike Helm, constructs broadcasting not as a site for the exercise of an active citizenship (having a say) but rather, and here the argument is like Helm, as a site for viewers' and listeners' welfare claims (Helm's 'mass entitlements') on public service broadcasting and on the BBC in particular.

At its most positive, this situates broadcasting as a facilitator of democratic activity located elsewhere – notably in the domain of formal politics – but doesn't identify democratic control of broadcasting itself as a significant citizenship issue. And even though Murdock's argument may reasonably be read as one which identifies public service broadcasting as a necessary element of and condition for democratic participation in modern life, a fundamentally welfarist conception of citizenship informs his vision. In this Murdock is representative, and like other contemporary broadcasting scholars his perspective is indebted to the British social theorist T. H. Marshall.[22] Indeed, Murdock's claim for a broadcasting system which provides the resources required for the exercise of citizenship rights echoes Marshall's own formulation, defining a component of social citizenship, 'the right to share to the full in the social heritage and to live the life of a civilised being according to the standards prevailing in the society' (Marshall, 1950:11).

Marshall elaborated his influential account of modern citizenship in a number of works published over 30 years and bounded by the landmark

works *Citizenship and Social Class* (1950) and *The Right to Welfare* (1981).
In *Citizenship and Social Class* he argued that 'there is a basic human
equality associated with the concept of full membership of a community' (Marshall, 1950:8) which, latterly, has 'been enriched with new
substance and a formidable array of rights' (Marshall, 1950:9).

Marshall identified three major constituent elements to this notion of
citizenship as an extensive bundle of rights: 'First comes the level of precisely defined and legally enforceable rights, which may be adjusted by
interpretation but not by discretion. Next comes the right to have one's
claim assessed by exercise of discretion in accordance with current policy'
(Marshall, 1981b:96) and third comes what Marshall (1981b:97) called a
third level of 'legitimate expectations' of 'benefits or services to be provided
for the citizen' (see also Marshall, 1950:10–11). Marshall refers to 'welfare'
as an 'integral part of the whole apparatus that includes social security,
education, public health, the medical services, factory legislation, the right
to strike, and all the other rights and legitimate expectations which are
attached to modern citizenship' (Marshall, 1981a:81).

Marshall thus constructs citizenship 'passively', as a series of entitlements – or as he puts it 'rights and legitimate expectations', rather than
as an active, participatory and creative practice. He explicitly states
that there has been a 'marked shift of emphasis from duties to rights'
(Marshall, 1950:9). Citizenship is thus, in this version of things, a competence legitimately to make claims on others within a particular polity
and is clearly identified as a bundle of entitlements that are incompat-
ible with 'the freedom of the competitive market' and which therefore
justifies 'invading the freedom of the competitive market' (Marshall,
1950:9). Elsewhere he refers to a characteristic of the twentieth century,
because of the expansion of the bundle of rights embodied in citizenship to include social rights, as the proclivity for 'citizenship and the
capitalist class system' to be at war (Marshall, 1950:68).

Marshall's triadic bundle of rights (civil, political and social) provides
a template for several influential accounts of citizenship and the media.
Murdock in another important essay on broadcasting and citizenship
(1999a:29–30) extends Marshall's bundle to include a further putative
type of right – information and cultural rights.[23] Marshall and his successors thus advance a notion of citizenship as a kind of onion. Each
bundle of citizenship entitlements/attributes surrounds the others con-
centrically and is complementary and non-rival – but all layers of the
onion must be present if the entitlements of citizenship are to be fully
realised. However, nowhere prior to Helm (2005), the nature of whose
connection to Marshall's thought remains to be discovered, has the

active, deciding, dimension of citizenship, central to Peacock's notion of the consumer (and, as I propose above, may as well be regarded, like Brinkmann's, as much as a citizenship claim as a consumer claim) been mobilised as a core constituent element of broadcasting citizenship. Rather it is the Marshallian notion, stated by Helm as 'mass entitlements', of welfarist claims rather than powers to hold to account that have figured in the UK broadcasting policy debate.

Brinkmann's 'notion of liberty' and his idea of 'co-operation in public decisions as a right' as the central attributes of citizenship are most clearly and explicitly to be found in the British political economy tradition represented by Coase and Peacock rather than in either a media studies discourse represented by Murdock, Hartley and contributors to the Calabrese and Burgelman (1999) collection (in which Marshall and Habermas tie for first place as the most cited author) or the elite policy discourse defined in successive official reports on broadcasting (i.e. from Ullswater to Annan).

Here we may return to the continuing power of Peacock. If the Marshallian conception of citizenship, at least as thus far mobilised in the UK broadcasting policy discourse, does not include the power to hold authority to account and the power to decide then, flawed though Peacock's concept of the sovereign consumer may be and imperfect though consumers' power to hold broadcasters to account actually is, it's Peacock's concept of consumer which provides better ground for the proponents of improved accountability of broadcasters to viewers and listeners to stand. True, 'consumer' is not a notion where 'co-operation in public decisions as a right and sharing of public burdens... as a duty' are to the fore but Peacock's notion of consumer sovereignty mobilises a conception (albeit limited) of accountability in a way that the post-Marshallian citizenship discourse has thus far failed to do.

Conclusion

My discussion of Peacock and the long wave evolution of ideas about accountability to the viewer and listener in UK broadcasting has been informed by Warnock's notion of accountability inhering both in the giving of an account and in holding to account. My discussion has, almost, exclusively focused on holding to account. This is because the ability to hold to account is a more exacting form of accountability – albeit one which depends on a prior giving of an account (unless well informed, those able to exercise sanctions and hold to account are unlikely to exercise their power wisely or effectively).[24]

Peacock's enduring claim on our attention lies in its advocacy, foreshadowed only by the marginalised discourses of Coase, Lloyd and some peripheral aspects of Annan, of effective accountability of broadcasters to viewers and listeners. Although couched in terms of the sovereign 'consumer' rather the 'citizen', in fact, Peacock puts forward a conception of user empowerment which echoes and embodies Brinkmann's account of citizenship as inhering in the dual notions of liberty and participation in public decision-making (Brinkmann, 1959:471). It is far closer to these attributes of citizenship than the Marshallian welfarism that has, thus far, suffused UK discussion of broadcasting and citizenship.

There can be no question that the Peacockian paradigm has blind spots – the empirical and theoretical objections which I have described above testify to that. It is, moreover, incompetent to deal with the matters of programme character and quality which have become increasingly salient; its model of accountability is partial and far from sufficient (though, I believe, necessary) and its model of competition has yet to show itself able to deal with the '800 pound gorillas' (as Greg Dyke put it referring to BSkyB and the BBC) which populate the UK broadcasting jungle. Nonetheless, both Peacock's and (some of) Beveridge's concerns illuminatingly shape and inform current debate and discussion.

Technological change, Peacock believed, would make it possible for consumers to signal their preferences, and the intensity of their preferences, through price in a pay-per-view 'broadcasting' market. Consumers would be sovereign, competition would thrive and liberty and efficiency would walk hand in hand. And though the Committee's prediction that 'well before the end of the century' – the twentieth century that is – 'subscription should replace the licence fee' (Report, 1986: para. 673) is far from being fulfilled, technological change, evolution of electronic communication markets and the reframing of the policy discourse point in that direction. The Peacock Committee's report of 20 years ago, albeit building on ground staked out by Coase more than 50 years before, continues to set the terms on which broadcasting policy in the UK is debated and formulated.

However, exit is but one means to hold institutions to account and Peacock's absence of consideration of voice as an instrument of accountability constitutes another of its blind spots (though one might judge that blindness in one eye is, while to be regretted, preferable to binocular blindness). But Peacock's silence on accountability through the exercise of voice is a representative silence: other than some aspects of, and around,[25] Annan's arguments the voices of voice are silent. Despite the importance the public attributes to improved accountability.

Jonathan Zeff, Head of Broadcasting Policy at the DCMS reported, of DCMS' research during BBC Charter review in 2004–6, that

> The governance and regulation of the BBC was obviously one of the key areas of concern in the initial round of public consultation and debate in this charter review. In the responses from the public there was a strong emphasis on the importance of the BBC's independence, and there was also clear evidence of a general desire for greater accountability to viewers and listeners, for ensuring that the interests of licence-fee payers are properly represented, and for greater transparency in the way that the BBC operates.[26]

Yet the BBC has rejected explicitly the election of members even of its advisory committees (BBC, 2005:59).[27] In its rejection of improvement of users' powers of voice it runs against the grain of developments in UK public management where in education, health, policing and other domains public authorities are increasingly opening up to their users and developing practices of co-decision.[28] The BBC now seems highly exceptional, and vulnerable, in providing for neither effective exercise of voice or of exit.

The continuing power of Peacock to claim our attention lies in its advocacy of citizenship entitlements of liberty and ability to hold to account rather than its less than wholly convincing view of technological change as opening the door to well-functioning broadcasting markets. It would be misleading to argue that the conceptual paradigm pioneered by Coase and successfully mobilised by Peacock now dominates the UK broadcasting policy debate, but it's hard not to conclude that it's Peacock's key categories and values, notably competition and consumer sovereignty, that have become the central reference points in the debate. They occupy the high ground in the battle for ideas about UK broadcasting because they provide a more solid foundation for the exercise of citizens' powers of decision and for liberty than do post-Marshallian claims for a 'citizenship' of welfare entitlements.[29]

Notes

1. I will refer to the findings of committees by the name of their chairman.
2. In late 2006 BSkyB had a c8.5% viewing share, ITV had c18% and the BBC c28%. See BARB at http://www.barb.co.uk/viewingsummary/monthreports. cfm?report=monthgmulti&requesttimeout=500&flag=viewingsummary on 22 January 2007.

3. At the time of writing the licence fee was £131.50 p.a. except for those with monochrome television receivers who were liable to pay £44 p.a.
4. See Rajar data at http://www.rajar.co.uk/INDEX2.CFM?menuid=9 on 22 January 2007.
5. Gavyn Davies was Chairman of the BBC's Governors from 2001 to early 2004.
6. In fact, Peacock threw into unprecedented prominence a well-established native political economy of broadcasting which had, hitherto, had little influence in the UK.
7. Initially, Channel 4 advertising was sold by ITV and ITV was reciprocally charged with financing Channel 4.
8. At LSE, Coase was a colleague of Fritz Hayek, Arnold Plant and Lionel Robbins and was a student, and joined the LSE staff, during Beveridge's Directorship. Coase won the Nobel Prize in Economic Sciences in 1991.
9. Coase's arguments first appeared in his 1947 and 1948 articles for *Economica* which, in revised form, comprised Chapters 1 and 4 of Coase, 1950.
10. Coase noted that 'the proceedings of the Beveridge Committee have been in secret. While evidence given to the Royal Commissions on Betting, Capital Punishment and the Press have been in public... evidence given to the Broadcasting Committee has, in general, been available to no one else' (Coase, 1950b:991). The Beveridge Committee did not publish the oral evidence it heard although much of written evidence to the Committee was published in its report.
11. The Beveridge Report cited Coase in para. 153 – but only for his finding (derived from his survey of evidence received by the Crawford Committee) that the Crawford Committee's recommendation for a BBC monopoly accorded with 'a strikingly unanimous stream of evidence' (Report, 1951: para. 153). Crawford's finding was important because, as the Beveridge Report stated, 'The Ullswater Committee... did not discuss the issue of monopoly' (Report, 1951: para. 154).
12. These appeared in *The Spectator* (Coase, 1946), *The Times* (Coase, 1950a), in the political weekly, defunct since 1977, *Time and Tide* (Coase, 1950b and 1951) and in *The Owl* (Coase, 1951a). *The Owl* was the organ of the intriguingly titled English League of Youth. The keynote of *The Owl*, as proclaimed in the Foreword to the first issue, was 'individual freedom' and the recognition that 'the powers of Government over the individual must be specified and limited' (Suenson-Taylor, 1951:2).
13. Coase's article in *The Times* (Coase, 1950a) focused on provision of TV and radio by the same organisation (he noted an authoritarian potential inherent in such arrangements) and on television finance, the article mentions the Beveridge Committee but made no direct reference to Beveridge's consideration of monopoly. In *The Owl* he argued that 'diversity of ownership and finance were desirable' (Coase, 1951a:34–5) after acknowledging that using contemporary broadcasting technologies, advertising and licence-fee funding were viable funding options and that each had signal disadvantages. Coase ended his article with an explicit reference to Hayek's *The Road to Serfdom* in deprecating Beveridge's reference to jamming (or 'bargains') as a means of keeping overseas broadcasters 'under control' (Coase, 1951a:36).
14. I owe my knowledge of Warnock's argument to the late Caroline Heller's mention of Warnock in her excellent monograph (Heller, 1978).

15. Some radio use of radios Luxembourg and Normandie excepted.
16. In the mid-1960s a second BBC television channel, BBC2, and a network of BBC local radio stations were established, and an independent (i.e. commercial) local radio (ILR) followed in 1973.
17. Pilkington (1962:291), however, did recommend that 'any advertising Advisory Committee appointed by the Authority (i.e the regulator of commercial television, RC) should include representatives of the general consumer'.
18. Coase left LSE and in 1951 took up his first US university post in New York State; subsequently, he moved to Virginia and then, in 1964, to the University of Chicago following his LSE colleague Friedrich Hayek who taught there from 1950–62.
19. Professor Alan Peacock, the Committee Chair, had studied at LSE under Coase and Hayek and another leading member of the Committee, Sam Brittan, under Milton Friedman (who had been a colleague of Hayek in the Mont Pelerin Society and of both Coase and Hayek at Chicago) at Cambridge. Peacock and Coase served together for a time as members of the advisory council of the Institute of Economic Affairs (IEA). The IEA published a number of studies of broadcasting policy which drew on Coase's ideas including Altman et al. (1962), Caine (1968) and Veljanovski (ed) (1989). See Towse (2005) for an account of Peacock's wider reflections on cultural economics. These issues are discussed also in Chapters 1–3 of this book.
20. Beatrice and Sidney Webb (1920) coined the term 'citizen/consumer' which Ofcom has subsequently taken up. Consumer activists such as Potter (1988) and Sargant (1992, 1993) have made claims for consumer rights which are hard to distinguish from citizenship rights (e.g. Potter's claims for access, choice, information, redress and representation). The *Communications Act* 2003 charges the UK communications regulator Ofcom with furthering the interests of both citizens and consumers. 'Citizen' was written into the Act after a lobbying campaign which argued that the term 'consumer' was reductive and necessarily implied a market orientation detrimental to public service broadcasting. The Act defines 'citizen' as 'all members of the public in the United Kingdom' (Communications Act, 2003:1.3.14) a definition which embraces more than those purchasing goods and services implied by the term 'consumer' (which is nowhere defined in the Act). Because 'all members of the public in the United Kingdom' may be thought somewhat unspecific Ofcom (2004) has valiantly attempted to clarify the term 'citizen' (see Ofcom, 2004).
21. Coase and Hayek are, of course, uncomfortable allies. Each argues with a forcefulness that is sometimes hard to distinguish from an inability to make proportionate judgements and distinctions. Hayek, for example, wrote The Road to Serfdom out of fear that Britain in 1944 risked adopting Nazi-like totalitarianism. Coase, rather more safely ensconced in Chicago in 1998 than was Hayek in London in 1944, proposed that 'the adoption of socialism in Britain' provided an example of 'the role of stupidity in human affairs' equivalent to those of 'World war I, World War II, the Great Depression, the emergence of communism ... the triumph of Nazism' (Coase, 1998:577).

22. Marshall taught at LSE, with periods of absence for war service and service with the UK Occupation authorities in Germany, from 1925–56. He was thus a LSE contemporary of Coase and Beveridge.
23. Hartley (1999:179), in an analogous move, further extends it to include not only a fourth form of citizenship, cultural citizenship, but also a fifth which he names DIY – Do it Yourself – citizenship.
24. Latterly the BBC's Governors have striven to give a fuller account to viewers and listeners, e.g. through virtual AGMs, a better website and Annual Report, publication and more systematic consideration of complaints. In January 2007 the Governors were replaced by the BBC Trust.
25. Heller's excellent monograph (1978) is an outstanding case in point – she puts forward a very Warnockian formulation stating 'the essence of public service in a democratic society is democratic accountability and accountability cannot be fudged. Accountability is the right to know and the power to change' (Heller, 1978:69).
26. At The Future of the BBC: Westminster Media Forum Consultation Seminar on the Green Paper. June 2005.
27. All the BBC's (and BBC appointed) advisory bodies have refused to brook election of their members (BBC, 2005:94, 97, 100, 103).
28. For example, Patient and Public Involvement Forums (PPI) have been established for all National Health Service (NHS) Trusts. For statutory bodies made up of local volunteers and representatives of voluntary organisations, see Department of Health briefing note at http://www.dh.gov.uk/asset-Root/04/07/42/88/04074288.pdf on 14 August 2006. Trusts must provide information to PPIs on demand and a PPI Forum has a statutory right to enter and inspect premises where either NHS Trusts or Primary Care Trusts provide services. In another relevant domain, Neighbourhood Policing policies charge the police with the duty to engage and involve communities in crime reduction and priority setting and to work with citizens more closely (see Home Office, 2004).
29. Acknowledgements: I have drawn on the Coase bibliography at http://www.coase.org/coasepublications.htm on 17 January 2007 for some bibliographical information cited here. My thanks to my colleagues at the Open University Library for their diligence and persistence in securing for me copies of Coase's articles in *Time and Tide*.

9
The Unbearable Light of the Market: Broadcasting in the Nations and Regions of Britain post-Peacock

Kevin Williams

The regions and nations have always had a problematic position in British broadcasting. Broadcasting began in the United Kingdom as a regional phenomenon. Local stations were established in strategic population centres such as Glasgow, Sheffield, London, Manchester and Birmingham and were linked together in a network to exchange programmes to form the national service in the 1920s which became the central plank of the broadcasting system developed by the British Broadcasting Corporation (BBC)'s first Director General, John Reith (1927–38). The regions and so-called 'nation-regions' were irritants in Reith's effort to forge a broadcasting corporation which would serve the British national community. At a low level they have continually resisted the centralising tendencies of the BBC and British broadcasting. At certain times they have threatened or actually brought about significant changes in British broadcasting; for example, Siepmann's 'Report on the Regions' in 1936, the establishment of Independent Television (ITV) in 1955 and the Annan Report in 1977.[1] Siepmann's report established regional programming as an essential component of the BBC; ITV introduced a broadcasting network dedicated to the representation of the regions and Annan paved the way for a national channel in the Welsh language, Sianel Pedwar Cymru (S4C). Regional broadcasting has always played a part, if an underdeveloped and underreported one, in the history of British broadcasting.

While the Peacock Report had very little to say about broadcasting in the nations and regions, the changes it brought about have had a significant impact on the development of broadcasting outside of London.

By arguing that government policy should promote the market delivery of TV and radio, Peacock fundamentally shifted the ecology of broadcasting. The most significant change was in the ITV system. Peacock's recommendation that the ITV regional franchises should be auctioned set into motion the centralisation of the network, loosening broadcasters' commitments to the different regional and national identities of the United Kingdom. This recommendation was marginal to the main thrust of the Report which concentrated on the BBC and the licence fee as a mechanism of financing broadcasting. Since Peacock broadcasting in the regions and nations has become more visible, culminating in the pledge of the BBC as part of the 2007 Charter renewal to devolve a substantial part of its production from London and commission a certain percentage of network output from outside the capital city. Independent television companies have sprung up around the country with a consequent impact on the production of British television and the development of regional markets. The expansion is often attributed to the transformation of the broadcasting market in the wake of the Peacock Report. Changes are attributed to the so-called 'freeing up' of the broadcasting system through increased commercialisation, accompanied by technological progress. If these changes have 'freed' regional broadcasting in the United Kingdom, they have also presented threats to the continued presence of broadcasting from and for Scotland, Wales, Northern Ireland and the English regions. New obstacles have been placed in the way of the ability and capacity of the regions and nations to report and represent themselves. This chapter examines regional and national broadcasting post Peacock, focussing on the developments that have taken place in Wales and to a lesser extent Scotland; the author is aware that the problems of the English regions and Northern Ireland have slightly different parameters. It is argued that in spite of changes in broadcasting for, by and about the regions and nations, the continued broadcasting from outside of London – as well as its nature – is increasingly threatened by marketisation.

Peacock and the regions

Alan Peacock's Scottish roots do not appear to have had much bearing on the report he delivered to Mrs Thatcher's government in 1986. Rather it was his ideological commitment to the 'free market' that shaped his analysis of the state of broadcasting in Britain and the recommendations of his Committee. The few references he made to broadcasting outside London reflected the mindset of the day. The BBC's National Governor for Wales, Alwyn Roberts, noted in 1984 that 'not a single member of the Board of Governors, apart from the National Governors, lives north or west of Oxford' (quoted in Davies, 1994:375). The Annan Committee (1974–7) was seen as having addressed the problems associated with regional representation and public access. Annan's deliberations about the future of broadcasting had taken place in a climate of political, social and cultural change. Public service encapsulated in what Peacock described as the 'comfortable duopoly' of the BBC and ITV was under attack from many segments of society, including Britain's nations and regions, for its failure to represent their views and opinions fairly and fully. British broadcasting was seen as 'no longer representative of the increasingly diverse tastes, interests and needs of an increasingly diverse society' (Scannell, 1990:23). This was brought home to the Annan Committee by the range and variety of conflicting evidence presented. Pressure groups on the left and right of the political spectrum, such as the Free Communications Group and Mrs Mary Whitehouse's Viewers and Listeners Association, lobbied the Committee for a better, broader and more diverse range of programmes (Crisell, 2002:202). The interests of the regions and nations of Britain were fully presented to the Committee.

In the face of such a 'barrage' of opinions it was not surprising that the Committee adopted 'pluralism' as the *leitmotiv* of its report (Scannell, 1990). Annan recommended the 'opening up' of British broadcasting with the introduction of a number of mechanisms, committees and commissions to ensure that the voices of minority interests who felt they had not been well served by television and radio would be heard. To this end the new fourth channel was to be granted to an Open Broadcasting Authority (OBA) which had the responsibility of developing a service that would represent those excluded or marginalised in the output of the BBC and ITV. It also recommended that broadcasting should be broken up at the local level, with the Independent Broadcasting Authority (IBA) renamed the Regional Television Authority and BBC funding devolved to National Broadcasting Councils in Wales and Scotland. Support was given to the setting up of a separate Welsh channel. These recommendations reflected Annan's desire to introduce more accountability to listeners and viewers. The top down attitude that had pervaded the history of broadcasters' relationship with their audiences was no longer considered appropriate in light of the social changes that had occurred from the 1960s onwards (Collins, 2006:15–17).

Annan's recommendations were never implemented in full as the Labour government that had set it up was voted out of office in 1979. The incoming government of Margaret Thatcher decided against the

Open Authority and handed the new channel over to the ITV network. Nevertheless, Channel 4 in most respects adopted the key ideas of the Annan Report; commercially funded through advertising, the channel was directed to cater for minority interests, whether cultural, political or ethnic. It would commission programmes rather than produce them in-house, mostly from the ITV companies but there would also be a certain percentage of programmes commissioned from independent companies around the UK. Annan's commitment to a Welsh Fourth Channel was initially shelved. However, after the escalation of the campaign of civil disobedience in Wales and in the face of concerted political manoeuvring inside the government, Mrs Thatcher relented and Sianel Pedwar Cymru (S4C) was born.[2]

In light of Annan's focus on representation, of which a better deal for the nations and regions was to a greater or lesser extent a part, it is hardly surprising that Peacock did not pay much attention to regional broadcasting. Not that the Committee would have anyway. Its free market leanings meant that viewers and listeners were seen as 'consumers' rather than 'citizens'. It was in this respect that the Peacock Report shifted the emphasis in British broadcasting, away from the notion of public service centred around citizenship to a market system based on consumer sovereignty. This was supported by Mrs Thatcher, who not only favoured a greater role for the market in the organisation of broadcasting but was also critical of the way in which broadcasters, particularly the BBC, had covered a variety of political issues, including the Falklands/Malvinas War in 1982 and the Miners' Strike in 1984 (Crisell, 2002:234). In preparing the ground for what many believed would be the privatisation of the BBC, which would be forced to take advertising, the future of broadcasting in the regions and nations of the UK could be seen as of minimal consequence for Peacock's deliberations.

If the intention of the government was to introduce advertising on the BBC, then Peacock's Report must have been a disappointment to Mrs Thatcher. Advertising for the BBC was rejected but Peacock's recommendations did presage the long term restructuring of British broadcasting, fuelled by the technological revolution that washed away the foundations on which Britain's public service system rested. Several recommendations in particular played their part in changing broadcasting in the nations and regions but perhaps the most significant, at least in the initial phase, was the decision to auction off the ITV franchises. If Peacock's enquiry had been set up to examine the funding of the BBC, it had the effect of putting ITV under greater scrutiny as a result of its sustained critique of the regulatory arrangements that governed British broadcasting. The White Paper, *Broadcasting in the 90s*

(Home Office, 1988), set about introducing Peacock's recommendations by introducing light touch regulation into the independent commercial sector and a competitive tendering process to award the franchises.

Dismantling the ITV network

The birth of ITV in 1955 is often celebrated in terms of its commercial character, particularly its funding through advertising, its competitive impact on the BBC and the arrival of ITN which had the effect of making TV news more populist and entertaining. However, one of the extraordinary aspects of the new channel was its regional character. As one veteran television executive states 'regionality is one of our defining characteristics, part of our personality, a crucial difference from other broadcasters' (Willis, 2000). The decision to operate the network as a loose association of regional companies swapping programmes, providing their own regional service and jointly owning their own international and national news provider, ITN, reflects the strength of the concerns in the 1950s about the centralisation of British broadcasting, specifically the London-centric bias of the BBC. Jamie Medhurst (2005:92) notes, in the context of Wales, that the regional basis of the new network was not only motivated by hostility to the BBC's metropolitan focus but also by the fear that commercial broadcasting would ignore audiences that were not large enough to attract the advertisers. The Welsh-speaking population believed that a commercial network would not be motivated to respond to their broadcasting wants. No matter how 'bad' the BBC was for Wales it was better than any commercial broadcaster could be and the debate about the introduction of commercial broadcasting from a Welsh perspective centred on the 'potential damage that would be inflicted on the language and culture of Wales from a market driven service' (ibid). The ITV network never operated as intended; rather than an exchange between regional producers, a small number of companies such as Granada provided the bulk of the programmes shown on the network and the objective of representing the cultures of different parts of Britain across the network soon disappeared. However, the impetus it gave to regional and national broadcasting within the UK was significant.

On 19 September 1955, Granada, based in Manchester but also covering North Wales, started broadcasting the first Welsh language television programmes. The advent of an hour-long Welsh language programme, shown twice a week had a considerable impact on the BBC which had to respond to complaints that it was doing too little in Welsh (Davies,

1994:213). The Corporation started to produce more programmes in Welsh. The arrival of Television Wales and the West (TWW) in 1958 witnessed an increase in programming for and about Wales in Welsh and English. However, establishing ITV in Wales was fraught with problems. Wales (West and North) Television (WWN 1962–4) was the only independent company to fold up, lasting only a few years (Medhurst, 2005; Tunstall, 1983: 229). TWW's efforts to serve three communities, Welsh- and English-speaking Wales and the west of England were deemed by the regulator, the Independent Television Authority (ITA), to be unsatisfactory in 1967 and it lost its franchise to Harlech Television (HTV 1968–2002).[3] There were a number of technical and financial factors, not the least the inability of such a small population as Wales to generate sufficient advertising revenue, to account for TWW's difficulties. In programming terms the artificial nature of many of the ITV regions proved a significant handicap. Companies such as Tyne-Tees TV, TWW and Border may have made economic sense but they had little which held them together as cultural entities. The failure to save a franchise such as WWN indicated that the ITV network's commitment to regional identity was limited and partial. The ITA played a crucial role in ensuring that companies maintained their regional services and commitments. While regional services, particularly in the form of news and sport, contributed to reinforcing a sense of regional and national identity this was only at a somewhat limited level. This lack of commitment was the basis of complaints from the regions and nations of Britain in their submissions to Annan.

Post-Peacock the ITV network became central to the government's efforts to reorganise British broadcasting. This was the result of a key recommendation of Peacock to make British television more efficient; namely, that the ITV franchises should be opened up to competitive tender. Rather than be allocated by the regulator, they should be given away to the highest bidder in an auction. The recommendation was incorporated into the 1990 Broadcasting Act, with the amendment that in 'exceptional circumstances' in which the 'quality of the application was exceptionally high' the franchise could be given to an applicant who was not the highest bidder. The Peacock Report had argued that the regulator should have the ability to accept a lower price if this gives more 'value for money' in terms of the programme service for viewers. In 1992 the ITV franchises were sold off in what one ITV executive described as 'a blind crap shoot' that reminded him 'of nothing more than the action in a smoky Las Vegas gambling hall' (Davies, 1990) and the not-so-long march towards the consolidation and centralisation of ITV had commenced (Johnson and Turnock, 2005a).

The threat the new arrangements posed to regional broadcasting figured prominently in the lobbying around the introduction of legislation. Quality matters were the focus of much of the debate surrounding the government's proposal for reforming ITV; the pressure group, the Campaign for Quality Television, emerged in response to the widespread belief of many in the industry that there would be a reduction in the range, quality and diversity of programmes. Such a belief was reinforced by the introduction of a 'light touch regulator', the Independent Television Commission (ITC). Many believed that the obligations imposed on the ITV companies by the regulator, first the ITA then the IBA, had ensured that a broad range of high quality programming was produced. Watering down such commitments would thus reduce quality and diversity. The initial proposals did not make any reference to guaranteed hours and resources for arts, education, religious, drama and children's programmes. Similarly there was no guarantee about locally produced programmes of regional interest. Rather there was reference to a 'suitable range' of programmes of which a 'suitable proportion' should be made within the region. Access to the network schedules and budgets – particularly regarding prime time programming – for locally produced programmes was not mentioned. There was considerable anxiety that the franchise bidders – who unlike the 1968 franchise round did not have to establish a regional base – would have no genuine commitment to the region whose licence they were bidding for. There was, for example, no specific obligation placed on the Channel 3 franchise holders in Wales to produce a broad range and mix of programmes about Wales in the English language. Considerable efforts were made to strengthen the positive programme requirements franchise holders would have to meet, which focussed on the tightening up of the quality threshold test bidders would have to reach.[4]

With increased safeguards introduced, the ITV network was auctioned off. Changes in the companies operating the 15 franchises were relatively small. But in the post-Peacock world several of the operators were paying considerably more to run their franchise than before – and there were significant disparities between what the companies paid for the right to broadcast.[5] Money was taken out of the system and with the dilution of the public service commitments placed on ITV in the 1990 Broadcasting Act, the programme making risks that ITV used to take as part of its obligations slowly dried up. Audiences started to contract and the downturn slowly began to become bad for business. Loss of market share resulted in a series of mergers and takeovers which eventually led to the demise of the original ITV companies. The loosening of the restrictions on cross-media ownership facilitated the process of the emergence of a single ITV. The fate of HTV Cymru/Wales reflects the uncertainty that beset the ITV post-Peacock. The company had defeated three rival bidders to win the Wales and the West franchise but at a high price; just over £20 million (Barlow et al., 2005:133). Working within more restricted financial circumstances programme making became tougher, particularly in light of the growing competition coming from the emerging cable, satellite and subsequently digital services. HTV has gone through a number of changes of ownership being swallowed up first by Lord Hollick's United Media in 1996, then Michael Green's Carlton Communications in 2001 before subsequently disappearing into a single ITV company.[6]

With each new owner the question of the company's commitment to the region was more urgently asked – a matter of significance in Wales and Scotland where issues of cultural identity are strongly felt. The answer was to pay lip service to regional commitments but slowly marginalise the programmes produced locally to the outer reaches of the schedule. An example of the priority the new ITV companies placed on the regions was illustrated by how United News and Media, then owners of HTV, used the £17 million reduction, in 1998, of the amount the Wales and the West franchise holder paid for the renewal of the licence. Only £3 million was to be reinvested in the franchise, on reporting the National Assembly and producing more local drama, and the remainder was used to support the ITV network schedule as part of the effort to enhance ITV's competitive position (Talfan-Davies, 1999:27).

Regulating the regional

Peacock followed in the steps of Annan in sharing what Richard Collins (2006:17) describes as a 'concern with improving viewers' and listeners' ability to hold broadcasters to account'. They differed in that Peacock emphasised the market and consumer sovereignty rather than the establishment of institutional arrangements and potentially democratic bodies to hold broadcasters to account. Peacock also believed that technological change would assist in developing a sophisticated market in broadcasting, making it possible for consumers to indicate their preferences through the price mechanism as 'pay per view' television became a reality. The Report's faith in technological change was emphasised in the prediction made that 'well before the end of the century subscription should replace the licence fee' (quoted in Collins, 2006:18). The emphasis on consumer sovereignty was equated with the loosening of the tight regulatory mechanisms that had ruled over British broadcasting since its inception in the late 1920s. The introduction of the 'light touch' ITC in the 1990 Broadcasting Act marked the beginning of the struggle over the nature and extent of independent broadcasters' regional commitments which were still, in 2008, apparent in the workings of New Labour's regulatory agency, the Office of Communication (Ofcom) which came into operation in 2003.

Since 1990 regulation has been characterised by a more intense struggle between commitments to the 'citizen' and the 'consumer'. Peacock's commitment to the consumer has become more central to the operation and workings of British broadcasting. However, the traditional commitment to the objective of promoting and supporting the notion of citizenship, central to the concept of public service broadcasting as it developed, has not disappeared. The strength of the commitment was highlighted following the failure of New Labour to mention the term 'citizen' in the bill leading up to the 2003 Broadcasting Act. It took a determined campaign to have the term inserted into the final Act. Only a sustained battle in the House of Lords and an alliance between the Liberal Democrats and Conservatives ensured that Ofcom had a duty to 'further the interests of the citizen' (Harvey, 2006:95). However, the difficulty of defining what is meant by citizenship – Graham Murdock (1999a:31) has drawn attention to the competing definitions of the concept – has proven an obstacle for those who have attempted to promote broadcasting in these terms. Ofcom has struggled in its efforts to incorporate citizenship in its operation. This is primarily due to the organisation's pre-eminent ideological commitment to the consumer. This was manifest in the decision in the early phase of Ofcom's existence to use the term 'consumer-citizen' to describe its duties. Such a term implies the term 'citizen' is subordinate (Harvey, 2006:96). The nature of the regulator's commitment to promoting the interests of citizens was not clear. This was particularly manifest in the provision of national and regional programming.

The 1990 Broadcasting Act was the first time the regulators attempted to stipulate the hours, type and scheduling of regional output on the ITV network. Pre-Peacock regional commitments were dealt with as general statements of intent about serving the region and negotiations took place between the regulator and the franchise holder over whether the programming promises made in the franchise holder's licence were being fulfilled. Since Peacock, regulators have made greater efforts to respond to distinctive regional needs. This is not a specific product of Peacock but a reaction to the commercial environment in which broadcasters have to operate as well as the political changes that have taken place. With devolution the different needs and interests of people in different parts of the UK were emphasised in the 2003 Communications Act. The Act requires ITV, Channels 4 and 5 to make a designated proportion of their programmes 'outside the M25 area'.[7] The cultural requirements of the newly devolved nations of Britain were reinforced and extended in the continuation of public funding for S4C in Wales and the provision of a Gaelic Media Service in Scotland. Attempts were made by Ofcom to place figures on the service to the regions and nations, making a specific distinction between news and non-news programmes. Regional news was seen as an essential component of the commitment to geographic and cultural diversity. In 2005 Ofcom acknowledged a distinction between the 'nations' and the 'regions'; 'We believe that the needs of the devolved Nations of the UK are distinct from those of the English regions for several reasons' (Ofcom, 2005:3.4.8). This belief led to Ofcom stipulating that, Wales, Scotland and Northern Ireland should transmit four hours per week of non-news programming each compared to one and a half in the English regions (ITV Wales, 2008).

Such stipulations can be seen as balance to the increasingly commercial thrust of the new ITV system. In the increasingly competitive broadcasting market which Peacock advocated, regional programming has become more vulnerable. Left to the market, producing programmes for relatively small and economically relatively less well-off audiences is more problematic. To stave off criticism ITV drew up a 'new charter of the nations and regions' in 2002.[8] However, this did not prevent the further marginalisation of regional and local programming. On screen there has been a standardisation of regional programming. This is most noticeable in news output, with ITV regional news programmes adopting a similar format (Thomas, 2008). Programme output for the nations and regions has experienced a substantial reduction since 2003. The number of hours ITV devoted to non-news/non-current affairs output fell by 44 per cent, from 2103 hours in 2003 to 1177 hours in 2007 and regional news and current affairs hours fell by 9 per cent and 10 per cent, respectively (Ofcom, 2008:3.87). The House of Commons Culture, Media and Sport Select Committee report, *Broadcasting in Transition*, in 2004 criticised the speed and way in which ITV had proceeded with the downgrading of regional production facilities. It stated that the 'protection and main- tenance of regional commitments by Channel 3 licensees' would be the first 'major test of Ofcom'. ITV's commitment to Wales, according to a leading figure in Welsh television, could only be guaranteed by a robust regulator (Anon, 2004).

Ofcom has proven less than robust in the defence of regional televi- sion. This is not surprising as in Peacock's market-driven broadcasting environment the concerns of the nations and regions within Ofcom were secondary to commercial considerations. They were only referred to in very broad and vague terms leading up to the establishment of the body. For example, the new agency, unlike its predecessors, was to have no Welsh, Scottish or Northern Irish representation on its main board. A variety of organisations including the National Assembly of Wales and Scottish Parliament lobbied for changes to the structure of the new regulator to include regional and national representation at a number of levels. The Blair government relented and while representation on the main board was not granted, it was agreed that the Content Board and Consumer Panel would incorporate Welsh, Scottish and Northern Irish representatives. Ofcom was also required to establish advisory com- mittees to ensure Wales and other parts of the United Kingdom have an input on a range of broadcasting, telecommunications and wireless communications matters. Assurances made to broadcasting outside of London must be seen in the context of the initial reluctance of the government to include national and regional voices in the workings of Ofcom. The result is that programming commitments to the nations and regions have been made in the context of the overwhelming desire of the agency to promote a free market in broadcasting.

Regional commitments have been waived. Ofcom has agreed that from 2009 ITV's obligations to make non-news programmes specifically for the English regions can be reduced to half an hour a week when the analogue signal is switched off (ITV Wales, 2008). Ofcom conducted a review in 2008 into non-news programming in the nations, proposing that the four hours a week, which was then being produced, be reduced to three. In the same year, ITV chief Michael Grade had warned that part of ITV's five-year strategy would be to redraw the network's regional map of Britain, reducing the number of individual news services from 17 to 9 (ibid). ITV stressed that the status quo was not viable; obligations to news and non-news programming in the nations and regions were less commercially sustainable and would continue to be so as competition increases following the digital switchover.

Ofcom appears to have accepted that a radical restructuring of regional broadcasting is inevitable.

BBC and regional broadcasting

The BBC's role in regional broadcasting has become more important in light of the changes that have made it more difficult for ITV – and commercial radio – to play their part in sustaining local and regional programming across the UK. The history of the relationship between the centre and periphery of BBC broadcasting was characterised by Director General Mark Thompson in 2008 as one of 'promises sometimes met, sometimes broken' (Thompson, 2008). As part of the negotiations over Charter renewal in 2007 the Corporation promised the 'biggest injection of regional investment we've ever made' (ibid). The aim was to create 'powerful creative clusters in key cities across the UK' and it was envisaged that 'nearly half the people working in the BBC will be based outside London' by the end of the current Charter period in 2012. A pledge has been made to commission 17 per cent of network production from the devolved nations. In 2008 the BBC appeared committed to greater devolution of programme making and commissioning to the regions and nations of Britain. The intentions of the Corporation may have been clear but so too were the considerable financial, commissioning and institutional obstacles. Not only were there the 'tendrils' that have 'snared and slowed previous efforts' to break free from London but the realities of the post-Peacock market-driven broadcasting environment make it more difficult to service the interests of regional and national audiences across the UK (ibid).

Paddy Scannell and David Cardiff (1991) describe the shift from local to national programming in Britain in the late 1920s that centralised decision and programme making in London and the south-east of England. Since then demands for greater say in decision making and better representations have come from the periphery.[9] London has traditionally seen these calls as marginal to the central objectives of public service broadcasting. Pressure has resulted in concessions to the nations and regions but alternative means have always been sought – and usually found – to claw back devolved powers and resources. The 1970s witnessed a slow and barely perceptible shift with the growth of programming within the nations and regions, increased contributions to the network and more autonomy. In 1986 a separate Regional Directorate was established, headed by Geraint Stanley Jones, who became managing director of regional broadcasting with a seat on the BBC Management Board (Davies, 1994:375). This proved a high point for regional output for the network which started to decline. By the mid-1990s a loss of nearly 469 hours of programmes was registered (Davis, 1993:73).

In 1993 Director General John Birt (1992–2000) described the nations and regions' contribution to the BBC television network as 'indefensibly low' and acknowledged that they must get a fair share of network production (ibid). Putting the principle into practice proved problematic as it had to take place in the context of the Birtist revolution in management at the BBC which emphasised rationalisation, cutbacks, internal markets, Producer Choice[10] and the imposed shift to independent production. He decided in 1993 to shift two departments, Youth and Religious Programmes, to Manchester, create Centres of Excellence in Birmingham, Bristol and Manchester which with London would be 'major concentrations of talent' and increase commissioning from the nations and regions. Regional 'proportionality' became the mantra of the day with a commitment to spend 25 per cent of the licence fee outside London and the South East (Hanson, 1993:68). Commitments struggled to match with actions. Promises to increase regional production coincided with job cuts and rationalisation, whittling away the skill base in the nations and regions. *Stage, Screen and Radio* observed in 1995 that a £28 million gain of additional network funding by BBC Scotland occurred at the same time as around 90 redundancies were announced (*Stage, Screen and Radio*, 1995). The result was that BBC Scotland had difficulties in making the programmes devised by its own staff. Independent production companies – that were only required to have a production base in the regions or nations to qualify for monies allocated to regional broadcasting – were the beneficiaries, many of which were London based. The move to Manchester in the 1990s exposed the gap between rhetoric and reality. Producers and editors from London were flown up to Manchester to do the job; a similar experience occurred in Wales and Northern Ireland with the additional funds they received (Davis, 1993:74). The Centres of Excellence saw a shift from smaller regional centres to larger ones and the exporting of a London-based philosophy to the rest of the UK.

Following the award of a new BBC Charter in 1996 the struggle for political recognition of national and regional broadcasting developed more rapidly inside the Corporation. The newly constituted Nations and Regions Directorate played an increasingly important role in this debate. For most of the period it was headed by 'high fliers on their way up' (Dyke, 2004:195), such as Mark Thompson (1999–2000), who went on to become Director General, and Mark Byford (1996–8), who became Thompson's deputy, who basically viewed regional policy through London eyes. In addition the former controller of BBC Northern Ireland, Pat Loughrey, was appointed in 2000 by Director General Greg Dyke (2000–4) to indicate to BBC staff outside London that the regions and nations would have more clout under his regime (Dyke, 2004:195). This corresponded with the devolution of power to Wales, Northern Ireland and Scotland[11] which also brought extra money into the nations to cover local politics and current affairs, the so-called 'devolution dividend'. Additional money and resources did not significantly change the relationship between London and the nations and regions. Greg Dyke in an account of his time as Director General relates the opposition within the BBC to his efforts to devolve 'real decision making power' with the relocation of key parts of the BBC's operation, including Radio Five Live and BBC Radio 3, to Manchester. Senior managers threatened to resign if their area of responsibility was shifted to Manchester (ibid, 196–7).

Most of the tension between London and the periphery at this time centred on news, and in particular, the perception in the nations that devolution was not fully reflected in the BBC's news coverage. Since 1997, BBC TV news has been the subject of repeated criticisms that it has failed to report properly the differences that devolution has brought to UK politics.[12] BBC Scotland in 1998 proposed the establishment of a *Scottish Six* to replace the national UK *Six O'Clock News* to recognise the new realities of the multilayered nature of government produced by devolution. The BBC Governors rejected the proposal, preferring to provide additional funds and an op-out from *Newsnight* for BBC Scotland (Born, 2005:394). This may have resolved the matter in the short run but the row rumbled on. In 2007 the BBC Trust, responding to what it described as concerns expressed in feedback from audience councils, public meetings and audience research, announced a review of the reporting of the UK's nations on network news. In 2007 the newly established Audience Council for Wales had expressed its frustration at 'network television news's continued inadequate reflection of the reality of devolution in the UK in its output' (Shipton, 2007). In addition and perhaps more significant, given the powers of the Scottish Parliament, was the decision of the SNP Scottish government to launch an enquiry in the same year into the future of broadcasting north of the border (Carrell, 2007). The Trust took an active interest in ensuring the BBC lives up to the commitments it made as part of the licence fee settlement to becoming less London centric. It was also cognisant that the BBC had to respond to the pressures from Scotland – and to a lesser extent Wales – for the devolution of broadcasting powers. The publication of the King Report in June 2008 upheld most of the complaints from the nations about the failure of BBC London to fully represent the nations and regions and criticised the decision made in 2004 to remove the Nations and Regions Director from the BBC's Management Board (BBC, 2008).

Concessions had been made to the nations and regions in terms of investment and network targets. This has given the BBC nations and regions a higher profile and creative capacity has increased outside the M25. Some parts of the nations and regions have benefited more than others – for example, £130 million investment in digital production centres at Pacific Quay in Scotland which opened in 2007 and the boom of network drama in Wales with the success of programmes such as *Dr Who* and its programming and commercial spin-offs. Taking advantage of the opportunity provided by dividends, quotas and targets is dependent on several factors. For example, talent is a drawing factor. BBC Wales's ability to attract investment for drama has been in part due to network demand for *Dr Who*'s main writer Russell T. Davies. Complaints about the lack of talent in the nations and regions are commonly articulated by London – exemplified by Mark Thompson and Michael Grade's comments about Scotland's television performance at a 2007 Ofcom conference on the nations and regions (Vass, 2007). Such complaints must be put in the context of the talent drain from the nations and regions. For some critics 'the magnetic attraction of London has become all the more powerful since public service broadcasting capitulated to the market' (MacWhirter, 2007). The limited production base outside London and the difficulty of winning commissions has led to many leaving to pursue their careers in Britain's capital city. Perceptions that an even playing field does not exist for programme makers outside London are reinforced by decisions such as that in 2004 to downgrade the voice of the nations and regions inside the BBC's decision making structure. The smaller than expected licence fee settlement in 2006 produced a shortfall in the BBC finances of nearly £2 billion which meant that jobs cuts were planned across the Corporation including an estimated 230 in BBC Scotland and 155 in BBC Wales over the period of the next Charter (2006–16) (BBC Wales, 2007). In such circumstances there was the feeling that London-based commissioners were less likely to take risks entering into partnership with production companies in the regions, preferring to stick to trusted partners closer to home.

Different strategies to produce more output reflecting social and cultural life in the nations and regions have been adopted in Scotland and Wales. BBC Scotland's decision to focus on BBC 1 opt out[13] resulted in *River City*, a domestic soap opera with high production values (Hibberd, 2007). BBC 1 has always performed relatively weakly in Scotland. *River City*, a twice weekly, all year round programme, launched in 2002, was an attempt to make BBC 1 more popular north of the border and attract a younger audience. In Wales BBC2W, a dedicated zone for English language programmes, was the priority. Set up in 2001 the zone was seen as a necessary step to complement what S4C has done for Welsh speakers.[14] Digital technology made possible the development of the service. Both efforts have had success. 2W and *River City* have both helped in different ways to develop the skills base and broaden the diversity of representation in Wales and Scotland. The switch off of the analogue signal in 2009 will bring 2W to an end. *River City*'s success in gradually building an audience on BBC 1 in Scotland has not necessarily helped in attracting network drama commissions. Total UK network production in Scotland fell from 6 per cent in 2004 to 3 per cent in 2006, a development partly responsible for the setting up of the Scottish Broadcasting Commission and calls for the devolution of broadcasting powers. BBC Scotland has also been criticised for becoming too inward looking (Cook, 2008).

Independent production in the regions

Peacock was clear in his view that the 'comfortable duopoly' reduced efficiency, stifled competition and prevented the consumer from having any input into what they were given. The advent of Channel 4 had done little to change this situation and the stranglehold the BBC and ITV companies had over the production of programmes limited the possibility of the growth of independent suppliers. To rectify this, Peacock recommended that BBC and ITV be compelled to increase the programmes they commissioned from independent producers. This recommendation was incorporated into the 1990 Broadcasting Act which placed a statutory requirement on the BBC and ITV to take 25 per cent of their programming output from independent production companies. The main terrestrial broadcasters had to commission programmes from outside companies with a corresponding quickening of the process of change in how British television made programmes. However, the changes have not resulted in what Peacock intended. The duopoly has been extended into an oligopoly in which pay TV has joined commercial and public-funded broadcasters to dominate the market.[15] The independent production sector has remained dependent on the broadcasters and while there are more companies outside London, independent regional production is precarious, fragile and limited.

The independent sector has evolved significantly since the birth of Channel 4 in 1982. In 2008 it was estimated that there were around 800 companies in the UK who supply television programmes to UK and international broadcasters. Currently ITV, Channels 4 and 5 are obliged under the 2003 Communications Act to ensure that a suitable proportion of the programmes they broadcast on the network is made by companies outside the M25 area (Harvey, 2006:97). The number and quality of regional independent companies are seen as insufficient to respond. The development of independent production in the nations and regions has not led to the diversity of supply envisaged by Peacock. The case of RDF in Scotland is illustrative of what happened. In 2005 the London-based RDF bought Scotland's largest independent production company IWC. Merging with one of the UK's largest independents was seen as an opportunity to increase the number of commissions for Scottish-based programmes. However, the passing of much of the Scottish independent production base into the hands of one company made it vulnerable to sudden shifts in the company's fortunes. This is what happened in 2007 when RDF was at the centre of a row over a BBC documentary on the Queen which it produced. The row resulted in a freeze on the BBC's (and ITV's) ability to commission from the company, and as a result the capacity to generate programmes from Scotland was severely impaired (MacWhirter, 2007a).[16]

Consolidation of the number of independent producers has been a feature of the situation in Wales. The flourishing in the 1980s and 90s of a large number of small companies in Wales gave way through mergers, takeovers and collapses to a handful of larger companies dominating the market by the middle of this decade.[17] These companies had the expertise, connections and trust of the broadcasters to deliver their commissions on time and within budget. S4C actively encouraged the development. In 2005 the Welsh language broadcaster decided to give preferential treatment in the commissioning process to a select number of Welsh independents, including Boomerang and Tinopolis (Ofcom 2008a). This reflected the growing emphasis placed on commercial criteria in the commissioning process. Securing supply at acceptable cost was increasingly emphasised. Programme makers with good ideas but a small production base would have to co-operate with larger companies. Supply was manipulated by S4C as it sought to standardise production.

The commercial imperative driving independent production in Wales was also manifest in the development of Wales's most successful independent company, Tinopolis. In 2006 Tinopolis acquired by hostile takeover one of the big London-based players, the TV Corporation. The company actively sought to purchase a major operator outside Wales in 'recognition of how difficult it was to grow organically from Wales into other markets' (Jones, 2008). Tinopolis's acquisition of the TV Corporation was a shock for London-based Indies. The company's editorial track record was limited to daytime and evening magazine programmes for S4C. It had no track record of making English language quality programming for UK TV networks, its strength resting on financial and business acumen which enabled it to launch a successful bid for a larger company.[18] The merger made the Tinopolis group one of Britain's leading independent TV production companies, with production centres in Cardiff, Glasgow, Leeds, London and Oxford producing a variety of TV programmes for BBC, ITV, Channel 4 as well as interactive content for the public and private sectors. In 2007 Tinopolis achieved a revenue growth of around 9 per cent in spite of a fall-off in UK commissioning during the latter part of the year and its pre-tax profits more than doubled to £2.7 million.[19] Tinopolis's commercial success was not reflected in its contribution to the representation of Wales here or abroad or to the enhancement of the production sector in Wales.

Since the early 2000s there has been a decrease in network programming made in the regions and nations. A report by the independent TV producers association PACT (2007) identified what it labelled as a 'dramatic' decline; its figures showed that between 2004 and 2006 there has been a fall in Wales from 70 hours to 58.7 and in Scotland from 179.6 hours to 102.7. The regional quotas for independent regional production were met unevenly between regions, with Wales, Northern Ireland and Scotland fairing less well. ITV did not broadcast any programme made by Welsh independents in 2006 and only 9.5 hours in 2004; Channel 5 broadcast nothing from Wales in 2005 and 2006 while BBC 1 broadcast only 1 hour in 2006 and BBC 2 12 hours.[20] Part of the problem is what determines a regional company. Three of the biggest independent companies, RDF, Endemol and Thames Talkback, were designated in 2006 as regional companies for the purpose of making bids to the BBC regional indie fund. The growth of what some producers referred to disparagingly as 'fat-cat Indies' was seen as restricting the development of regionally based companies. Larger companies are commercially driven; according to one RDF media representative 'naked competition in TV production is something to aspire to' (*Broadcast*, 2004).

They are also driven to produce regional programmes, providing further opportunity for a London perspective to filter through the UK's regions and nations.

The circumstance in which regional independent production occurs highlights the tensions between commercial considerations and representational needs which are at the heart of the post-Peacock broadcasting system. The debate about the value of *Dr Who* and its spin-offs to Wales is also indicative of the tension. Made by BBC Wales, *Dr Who* helped to develop skills, talent and business in Wales. The programmes had 'critical success', 'earned vast amounts of money in overseas sales' and breathed confidence into the broadcasting industry in Wales (Little, 2006). Nevertheless many inside Wales were critical of the contribution the programmes made to Welsh broadcasting and the representation of Wales. Complaints were made that many of those involved in *Dr Who* were 'shipped in' to work on a BBC Network production with a huge budget (Mair, 2008). Welsh Independent Producers questioned the 'cultural benefit' of *Dr Who* for Wales (TAC, 2008). Their call for more down-to-earth television was supported, in 2008, by the National Assembly's Culture Minister who believed that 'Wales must be more than a place where great programmes get made. Public service broadcasters must also hold up a mirror to the lives of the people of Wales' (Bodden, 2008).

Conclusion

The 1990 Act, inspired by the Peacock Report, ushered in a new era in British broadcasting which has had a profound impact on broadcasting in the nations and regions. At a time when political events have devolved some power from London to the rest of the UK, changing regulatory arrangements, greater competition and new technology are threatening the capacity of the regions and nations of Britain to broadcast to one another and the rest of the country. Surveys show that regional programmes are highly valued by viewers and listeners. ITV, since 1956, has carried the 'lion's share' of regional broadcasting but the 1990 Act has transformed the network's attitude to making regional programmes; they gradually have become a 'tedious overhead', a demand from the regulator rather than 'something you wanted to do well' as part of your licence commitment (Strachan, 2007). Critics such as Greg Dyke are harsher. He argues that 'ITV has lost interest in making programmes' and is 'completely obsessed with making money' as 'today is predominantly judged by how much profit it makes.' In such a circumstance regional programmes, which have little potential profitability, are made at the lowest possible cost (Dyke, 2004a).

Regional programming is increasingly seen as a public service commitment of the BBC, a national broadcaster, which has historically struggled with the nature and extent of its commitment to the regions and nations of Britain. Growing public commitment through words, resources, money and now the promise of devolving production to regional centres is taking place in an environment which is beset by cutbacks, job losses, financial savings and the potential weakening of the regulatory commitment to public service. Suggestions in 2008 that the BBC should be further top sliced to support ITV regional news and current affairs increased the difficulties in the provision of regional output. By 2007 the BBC in Wales had renegotiated additional resources to make programmes for Wales's minority language broadcaster, S4C, and a further reduction of money spent on ITV Wales would have had implications for what the Corporation could do in Wales. A similar squeeze was apparent in the other nations and regions, a situation facilitated and given a rationale by the market-led solutions offered by Peacock to the problems of technological change in the world of broadcasting.

Notes

1. For a discussion of Siepmann and BBC regional broadcasting, see Pegg (1983:31–4) and Briggs (1965:293–339).
2. For a discussion of this campaign, see Tomos (1982).
3. HTV Ltd was renamed ITV Wales & West Ltd in December, 2006; from October 2002, the full name 'ITV1 West' has only been seen before local programming on that channel. At all other times, the station is simply called ITV1. However, the name ITV1 Wales is seen before all programmes.
4. For a discussion of the efforts to change the legislation and the role of the Campaign for Quality Television, see Davidson (1992) and Corner et al. (1994).
5. For example, Yorkshire TV paid £37 million while Central TV paid £2,000 – see Crisell (2002:247).
6. In 1996 HTV was taken over by United News and Media. In 2001 United sold its television interests to Granada who, as a result of competition regulations at that time which limited the extent to which a single company could control the ITV network, had to give up one of its ITV franchises. HTV was broken up and its broadcast facilities and Channel 3 broadcast licence (and hence its advertising revenues) were sold to Carlton Communications plc, owners of Carlton Television, while the production facilities remained with Granada.
7. Outside the M25 is a term commonly used to describe the country that exists outside London.
8. See for example, Wells (2002) and Ross (2002).

9. For discussion of relations between BBC and the various nations, see Davies (1994) (Wales), McDowell (1992) (Scotland), Cathcart (1984) and *McLoone (1996)* (Northern Ireland).
10. Producer Choice was the name given to the trading system designed around an internal market which was introduced at the BBC between 1991 and 1994. The adoption of Producer Choice reflected a philosophy which was based on giving programme makers the freedom to make choices about the programmes they made, including educating them about the costs involved by introducing a system of charging for services the Corporation had previously provided freely. Choice and competition, it was hoped would drive costs down, enabling more money to be ploughed back into programme making. It was highly controversial and finally scrapped in 2006 (see Harris and Wegg-Prosser, 1998).
11. In 1997 a devolved government was created following simple majority referenda in Wales and Scotland. In 1999, the Scottish Parliament, National Assembly for Wales and the Northern Ireland Assembly were established. There are different levels of devolved responsibilities and there is no common pattern. Scotland, Wales and Northern Ireland all have different forms of devolution. Broadcasting is a matter that has not been devolved. For further details see House of Commons Library Research Paper (2003).
12. In political circles First Minister Rhodri Morgan expressed his frustrations on *Newsnight* in 2001 while then Culture Minister Alun Pugh drew attention to the matter as part of his response to the Charter renewal in 2004 (see Mason, 2001; Pugh, 2004).
13. National and regional opt outs from network programmes have been a feature of TV broadcasting when local programming replaces network shows in particular slots on BBC 1 and BBC 2.
14. S4C's remit is to provide a service which is in the Welsh language in peak viewing hours. It broadcasts a full service of programmes in Welsh including news, with a Welsh-speaking perspective on international, UK and Welsh stories, as well as a range of other programme genres such as soap operas, documentaries, current affairs, comedy, sports and children's programmes.
15. For a more detailed discussion of the realisation of Peacock's objectives, see Collins (2006).
16. A BBC promo in 2007 included clips of a documentary about the Queen which erroneously showed the Queen walking out in what was referred to as 'a strop' in a photocall with photographer Annie Leibovitz. The footage had been supplied by RDF, the programme maker, and the BBC had to apologise to Buckingham Palace. The BBC Trust set up an inquiry which led to a temporary freeze on RDF commissions and led eventually to the resignation of BBC 1's controller.
17. Two of Wales's foremost independent television companies, established in the 1980s, Nant, with offices in North Wales and Opus TF, based in Cardiff, announced in 2008 that they were joining forces to create Rondo Media. Rondo Media – see Wales Screen Commission (2008).
18. The lack of an editorial reputation resulted in key talent leaving TV Corporation following the takeover. The appointment of a senior figure in the broadcasting industry, former Director of Programmes at Channel 4, Managing Director of LWT and most recently the BBC's Director of Factual

and Learning, John Willis as MD and creative director in 2006 provided the editorial clout that helped to stem any haemorrhaging of talent.

19. Figures in the paragraph are drawn from Growth Company Investor (2008).

20. This does not include programmes such as *Dr Who* and *Torchwood* which are made in-house.

10
PSB 2.0*–UK Broadcasting Policy after Peacock

Janet Jones

Set in the context of the Peacock Report's (Report, 1986) influence on UK broadcasting policy, this chapter considers the future of public service content in a media ecology where public service *communication*[1] becomes the dominant delivery mechanism and public service *broadcasting* more marginal.

It looks at the main influences of Peacock on two decades of communications policy and examines how the status of citizens and consumers of broadcasting might be reconfigured to accommodate the influences of the Internet within a deliberative democracy. It argues that any vision of Public Service Broadcasting's (PSB) future that doesn't establish a new economic framework with the user-citizen at its centre will fail. Successful public service content providers will have to foster and support public media spaces and make the important philosophical leap from 'audiences' to 'users' and 'consumers' to 'producers'. It also suggests that the future of the BBC as the dominant PSB player will depend on its ability to be flexible enough and to change fast enough to allow the 'user to lead'.

Digital disruption

Peacock's profound reinterpretation of the mission of broadcasting was both subtle in its refashioning ability to place a cultural product, which thus far had been primarily associated within the domain of merit goods,[2] firmly within the domain of the market. The 1986 Report, with its pervasive influence on two decades of communications policy, reimagined a broadcasting system unfettered by spectrum scarcity and daring enough to expose itself to the market while abandoning funding based on taxing television ownership.

Its prescience was limited to what it could imagine future technologies and future publics would support. It couldn't, however, have foreseen the new models of communications consumption that would emerge from a digital world dominated by the internet. At the heart of Peacock's recommendations was the principle that

> Eventually we hope to reach a position where the mystique is taken out of broadcasting and it becomes no more special than publishing once the world became used to living with the printing press.
>
> (Report, 1986: para. 711)

In 1986 the bookstore model, with its diverse product range satisfying both high and low brow taste and popular and elitist themes, and where consumer choice drove the production of the books displayed, seemed an inevitable outcome of the liberalisation of broadcasting. The view of the consumer as sovereign, holding broadcasters to account through their purchasing decisions, made sense within the framework of Peacock's goal of a full broadcasting market.

Two decades on, and the 'internet model' has introduced a new set of complexities for all content providers and especially for those who provide public service content. In a model defined by ubiquity, interactivity and instantaneity, the challenge for PSB is to reimagine itself as PSC (public service communications) and creatively exploit the navigation tools that define the user experience. The BBC acknowledged in 2006 that the 'on-demand world' held many significant challenges and would force the Corporation to go beyond current broadcasting models (Thompson, 2006). The most compelling reason for this strategy was to be in the vanguard of fashioning a new PSC model that would survive into the twenty-first century. In the UK, in 2008, the BBC claimed to reach 80 per cent of Britons each week. Yet, the Corporation was acutely conscious of losing younger viewers who were habituated into self-directed, interactive communication activities (Horrocks, 2006).

How much of the traditional public service broadcast model survives as the digital age matures will depend on how imaginative and daring the regulators are. In 2008 Office of Communications (Ofcom) began consultation on its second public service review where it acknowledged that, 'the underlying economics of commercial public service broadcasting are increasingly difficult,' and that, ' a new sustainable model for public service broadcasting is needed, with a range of options for funding and provision considered.' Underpinning this review was the belief that there was significant support for 'plurality of supply' (Ofcom, 2008).

This move towards a 'plurality of supply' weighed heavily on the BBC in 2008, faced with the prospect of having to share its licence fee funding. The Culture Secretary, James Purnell, put forward proposals on how to 'top slice' the BBC's funding to help subsidise other public service providers. In the same year leaked documents from Ofcom confirmed the BBC's worst fears that future public purposes would be provided by a mixture of the BBC, Channel 4 and perhaps other new entrants competing for funding, 'all paid for out of the licence fee or direct government grant, and possibly overseen by a new Public Service Authority' (Gibson, 2008).

A few years earlier in 2005, Ofcom (Ofcom, 2007b) had seeded the idea of a 'Public Service Publisher' (PSP) that would provide competition for the BBC, a proposal that was intended to ensure a necessary level of quality in PSB through the transition to digital. This was reminiscent of Peacock's (Report, 1986) recommendation of the creation of a 'Public Service Broadcasting Council'[3] for positive support of public service ventures not supported by an open market.

There was a wave of hostility to the proposals best articulated by media commentator Polly Toynbee. Writing in the *Guardian*, she laid down her fears. 'Imagine the idea of public service broadcasting increasingly dispersed among myriad commercial outlets, pepper-potted in among ads and hard to identify, while BBC channels were drained of funds yet again,' she lamented. 'He (Richards)[4] has, merci-fully, ruled out an Arts Council of the Air commissioning programmes from all and sundry across all outlets. The bureaucratic and artistic nightmare of choosing individual worthy programmes and separating them from commercial programmes bore very little close inspection' (Toynbee, 2008).

Plans for a PSP were eventually shelved in 2008. When the PSP idea was abandoned as unworkable, Ofcom's chief executive, Ed Richards, claimed that it had 'served its purpose' in shifting the debate on the future of PSB by emphasising the importance of digital media (Richards, 2008).

The debate was inevitably focused on who should be funded to provide the gatekeeping for future PSB and PSC models. Yet, the power to choose what constitutes public programming, who should make it and how it should be distributed had not fully embraced the digital communications ecology. The internet militates against an economic model that is singularly defined as a group of pub-licly funded publishing houses designed to distribute goods in a one way direction through a few chosen gatekeepers. It seems likely that future models will require far more complex delivery structures relying on sophisticated search engine branding through the internet.

Happily for the BBC, one of Peacock's indirect legacies was to stimulate the Corporation into investing heavily in interactive infrastructure, a move which went against the grain of industry developments in the early 1990s. These activities were rooted in the institutional and programme policy renewals in the late 1980s and early 1990s spearheaded by John Birt, Director General 1992–2000. On his departure in 2000, Birt had developed Europe's most popular internet site.[5] In 2005, Tony Lennon, President of the broadcasting union BECTU credited Peacock with having facilitated this aggressive push to embrace new technologies in their nascent stage.

> What the Peacock Report did was to give the BBC sufficient funding over a critical period to position itself almost irremovably in the firmament of web publishing and digital broadcasting.
>
> (Conference Transcripts, 2005: Conduct of the Committee)[6]

The speed with which internet use grew in the 1990s and 2000s put the Corporation in a strong position to launch new services in the ensuing two decades. The BBC was no longer reliant on broadcasting to maintain and grow its market share and was ready to capitalise on new programme delivery methods.[7] There was a general nervousness overtaking the industry as the 2000s drew to a close. Broadcasting executives were unsure of what future lay ahead. In the words of Peter Bazalgette, one of the UK's leading independent producers, 'So great is the digital disruption we are currently witnessing, both in scope and speed, that several things we regard as givens are in reality not certain at all' (Bazalgette, 2008:4). Twenty years after Peacock, the BBC appeared reasonably well placed to capitalise on Bazalgette's 'digital disruptivity' and to reinvent its primary mission, to inform, educate and entertain, within the framework of public service interactivity.

Peacock's legacy

The impact of the Peacock Report has been widely discussed and analysed and its legacy debated and scrutinised at length (see O'Malley, 1994; O'Malley, 2001 and Chapter 12 in this volume). O'Malley argues that the perspective developed on PSB in Peacock became the orthodoxy of politicians and policy makers during the 1990s and more significantly that PSB declined after 1979 as 'the organizing concept of UK broadcasting' (O'Malley, 2001:36–41). Rather than a revolution in broadcasting policy, O'Malley defines these changes as 'a drift' which ensured that two decades later, UK policy makers were no longer committed to public service ideals (O'Malley, 2001:33).

This 'drift' can be best analysed through the semantics of policy. Peacock has been recognised as an important harbinger of linguistic change altering the way policy makers and regulatory documents refer to the production and dissemination of broadcast goods (Hall 1993; O'Malley, 2001; Coleman, 2005 Livingstone and Lunt, 2007). The econometrically centred discussion of broadcasting in the Peacock Report was a radical departure from its predecessors, Pilkington (Report, 1962) and Annan (Report, 1977). It raised very important questions about the relationship of broadcasting providers with listeners and viewers in a changing market environment. It envisaged that, as the physical need to limit broadcasting to a small number of channels became obsolete, consumers would have the power to choose from an indefinite number of programmes which they could pay for directly on a pay-per-view basis or through subscription, rendering the licence fee unnecessary. Programmes of 'a more demanding kind with a high content of knowledge, culture, education and experiment' were to be funded by a special public service broadcast tax. In this way, public service programmes were newly defined as anything that 'viewers and listeners are willing to support in their capacity as taxpayers and voters, but not directly as consumers' (Report, 1986: para. 580). These recommendations opened the door to what Peter Jay asserted was an 'ideologically free' philosophy celebrating consumer sovereignty (Jay, 2003).

The 1990 Broadcasting Act was the first major piece of broadcasting legislation to be passed after the publication of the Peacock Report. In his review of the Report's impact, O'Malley concludes that this legislation was hugely influenced by Peacock.

> The Act enshrined in law a radically new conception of policy, one which, whilst introducing the continuations of some form of public service broadcasting, articulated its presence as marginal to a system in which commercial competition was to be the mechanism for driving expansion.
>
> (O'Malley, 2001:37)

Barnett interprets the trend towards marketisation as seeing the world through 'the wrong end of the telescope' with a tendency to ignore the fundamental importance of broadcasting in our national life (Barnett, 2004:38).

> What it (Peacock) didn't do was to engage with the notion, the phi-losophy, the idea, the concept of public service broadcasting or the contribution that broadcasting can potentially make to people's lives as a life enhancing project . . . it was the antithesis of Annan.
>
> (Conference Transcripts, 2005: Conduct of the Committee)[8]

The economistic analysis of the broadcasting market place was warmly embraced by New Labour in the late 1990s as part of a wider shift in public policy that went much further than media policy.

> Liberalisation, the free market, deregulation and withdrawal of state intervention have become the new battle cries, while rival parties quar-rel only about the speed and extent of withdrawal of the nanny state.
>
> (Barnett, 2004:36)

Peacock might have provided the script, but, the move to consumer-ism over the last 20 years has enshrined this philosophy in all areas of civil life. When viewed through the frame of contemporary neo-liberal debates on broadcasting, the language of social benefit permeating the Annan Report (Report, 1977) is easily subsumed in the discourses of freedom of choice, empowerment and liberation. Those who attempt to engage in definitions of what broadcasting can constructively contribute, risk regressing into the dangerous territory of paternalism. It is no longer acceptable to put across a picture of the viewer as vulnerable and requir-ing protection or as Collins describes, 'requiring tutelage by platonic guardians running the system' (Conference Transcripts, 2005: Conduct of the Committee).

The Peacock Committee's Chairman, Alan Peacock, took the view that 'the fostering of qualities which forge a nation's character and influence and which are generally respected, such as enterprise, inven-tiveness, tolerance, and justice, is hardly the function of a broadcasting system, rather it is the function of an educational system in the widest sense' (Peacock, 2004:52). Thus, the Committee considered that broad-casting deserved to occupy no special place outside the domain of the market and despite its role in 'raising the understanding of a nation's own cultural diversity and the threats it may face from cheap access to the trivialities of Tinsletown, this does not make the case for confining state financial support to a single, monolithic supplier of public service broadcasting' (Peacock, 2004:53). After Peacock, policy debate was dominated by what Georgina Born describes as a 'conceptual lock-down' (Born, 2005a:105). This debate was staged between those who broadly supported the position developed in the Peacock Report and those who argued for a more expansive definition of PSB as a public utility.

These post-Peacock debates represented in the works of Collins and Purnell (1995), Dahlgren (1995), Davies et al. (1999) and Graham and Davies (1997) among others, polarised around the justification for public intervention based on provable market failure on the one hand, and the civic role of broadcasting with its unique ability to advance social and cultural goals, on the other.

Ofcom–'child of Peacock'

The civic role of broadcasting was at the heart of policy discussions immediately prior to Ofcom's formation in 2003. Part of this debate revolved around an attempt to rationalise the competing interests of the citizen and the consumer. In the lead up to the publication of the 2003 Communications Act, the words consumer and citizen were negotiated and renegotiated by regulators as ill-suited soul-mates (Born, 2005a; Dawes, 2007; Livingstone and Lunt, 2007).

A critical discourse analysis of the 2000 Communications White Paper by Simon Dawes confirms that the semantic shift in the government's conception of the public from citizens to consumers was evident in the years leading up to the creation of Ofcom. He found that the citizen was being constructed in government publications in increasingly individualistic terms. The public or collective good was subservient, at least semantically, to an individual's rights and needs. He also noted that the balance of agency changed so that the 'citizen' was constructed as passive and the 'consumer' as active. Choice, he observed, was associated with quality and plurality and the consumer acting in his or her own interest. He concluded that the notion of the public sphere had been effectively bypassed and that 'public service has already been reconstructed in private terms, so there exists no possibility of an alternative to the commercial market, and therefore, that PSB, as it is traditionally understood, has already, and effectively ended' (Dawes, 2007:48).

This unsettling conclusion suggests that the discursive and operational changes set in motion post Peacock had the effect of reinterpreting the mission of PSB placing it on the periphery rather than the centre of a new media ecology and reconstructing social values and public interests in economic terms.

Livingstone and Lunt came to similar conclusions in their study of key broadcasting policy documents post 2000. Initially the language used in the Communications White Paper (DTI, 2000) was dominated by the words 'consumer', 'public', 'community' and citizen' but these were replaced in the Draft Communications Bill (2002) by the word customer, 'signalling the intention to form Ofcom as primarily an economic regulator' (Livingstone and Lunt, 2007:55).

Opponents of this discursive switch argued that if broadcasting is linguistically commodified, then discursively at least, the audience is de facto moulded into a consumer group or groups and the citizen-viewer becomes marginalised. Lord Puttnam's Joint Select Committee produced a report in 2002 (Report, 2002) arguing that the draft Bill marginalised both consumer and citizen interests by reducing them to 'customers'. A last minute change to the wording was agreed after a bitter battle. The reductionist approach was dropped and in its place two new semantic zones were created (Livingstone and Lunt, 2007).

An eleventh hour change to Ofcom's constitutional mandate forced the new regulator to take explicit account of citizen interests. Ofcom was therefore charged with the following duties as laid out by the Communications Act of 2003.

It shall be the principal duty of Ofcom, in carrying out their functions:

(a) to further the interests of citizens in relation to communications matters; and

(b) to further the interests of consumers in relevant markets, where appropriate by promoting competition.

(Communications Act, 2003: 3(1))

These objectives were to be achieved through the establishment of two separate panels, one to police citizen interests (the Content Board) and one to further consumer interests (the Consumer Panel). They had the effect of mapping individual consumer interests to economic goals and collective citizen interests to cultural goods and content issues.

This semantic battle was not just a trivial, pedantic row. There was recognition among key Ofcom executives that the stakes were high. Kip Meek, Senior Partner (Competition and Content) observed:

> It was hard fought over because as with many of these things, it became a metaphor for . . . the soul of Ofcom was being fought over and . . . if you include the word citizen, QED Ofcom will not just be an economic regulator, it will look more broadly than that.
>
> (Livingstone et al., 2007:92)

Although the Act separated the terms citizen and consumer, Ofcom chose to conflate the two in its inaugural mission statement. It stated that 'Ofcom exists to further the interests of citizen-consumers through a regulatory regime which, where appropriate, encourages competition' (Ofcom, 2007a). Ofcom's first CEO, Stephen Carter argued that 'we are all of us both citizen and consumer . . . to attempt to separate them or rank them would be both artificial and wrong' (Livingstone et al., 2007:87). Yet, the duel briefs make uneasy bedfellows and Livingstone et al. suggest that despite this last minute change to its mandate, Ofcom still risked marginalising public interests. They note that 'the consumer interest is and will continue to be interpreted narrowly in terms of price, choice and value for money, thus legitimating an economic model of regulation' (Livingstone and Lunt, 2007:64). The outcome they fear is that the public is granted the rights of consumers but not of citizens as the power elites 'reproduce and naturalise a consumerist discourse of communications regulation' (Livingstone et al., 2007:86).

This consumerist discourse was evident in a speech given by the Secretary of State for the Department of Culture, Media and Sports, James Purnell, which encapsulated what he described as a 'third-way' vision. He talked of a 'democracy enriched by diverse broadcasting' but within a set of clear goals and using language that privileges a market-driven future for broadcasting.

> Those goals would be, first, an open market, perhaps with a greater reliance on principles than on detailed rules. Second, the very best broadcasting should be open to everyone, and third, consumers should be in charge.
>
> (Purnell, 2007:11)

A new form of sovereignty

This debate on how to enrich our democracy with 'consumers in charge' suggests that those concerned with regulating our public service media were looking to a future where user-instigated activity would drive demand. Negotiated as part of this new media ecology, was an important philosophical leap from 'audience' to 'users' and also from 'consumers' to 'producers'. In a broadcast-dominated media landscape, the citizen was served by guardians of mass transmissions, in a PSC environment, and citizens become user-citizens within a far more complex, internet-enabled, public sphere. In this latter model, the argument of whether the market should deliver or the State becomes less relevant.

Curran (2002) argues for a third way that accounts for weaknesses in both strategies: market and state controlled. On one hand he suggests that liberal theories of media and democracy are conceptually flawed and that their objectives cannot be realised through the free market where the influence of the consumer is 'reactive rather than proactive' (Curran, 2002:227). He also acknowledges the limitations of public broadcasters who have been subjected to direct and indirect censorship through laws, regulations and threats to their income streams. Specifically he works with Habermas's more recent conceptualisation of the public sphere (Habermas, 1996) and uses this to draw a 'third way' model for the fourth estate and PSB. He maintains that an ideal democratic media system 'can be best realised through the establishment of a core public service broadcasting system, encircled by a private, social market, professional and civic sectors' (Curran, 2002:247). This regime is predicated on an open system of dialogue that doesn't view the public sphere as an aggregation of individuals gathered together as a single public but instead envisions a network that is multiple instead of unitary.

Yet, in a communications ecology based on interactivity and user-instigated refashioning of texts, Curran's vision of an aggregated media system takes on a new set of meanings. The web encourages, as part of the gift economy,[9] the production and consumption of content through open source software. In this context, Bracken and Balfour (2004) talk about public service interactivity or PSI as one of the greatest cultural revolutions of our time facilitated through the use of peer to peer and file sharing where the orientation is simultaneously global and local and where the cost is typically free. Critically, they see PSI as having a, 'user-created' mandate which challenges traditional supplier-based rationales for the production and dissemination of communications goods. They argue 'Why not recognize that the user leads and begin to measure demand and the effects of supply' (Bracken and Balfour, 2004: 105).

For example, hundreds of thousands of people around the world have contributed their time freely to make *Wikipedia* and *Wikinews* two of the best-known and most-cited web sources. Were they acting as consumers or citizens? What was their constituent country? This kind of market place in knowledge and ideas operates within a non-hierarchical paradigm, where everyone can contribute and the roles of producer or editor, manufacturer and distributor lose their original meaning.

Thus, the debate over whether or not we see the recipients of public service content as 'citizens' or 'consumers' is complicated by a media ecology migrating to user-instigated interactivity supported by one-to-one, one-to-many and many-to-many communications channels that are impervious to national borders. These assertions naturally expose themselves to the charge that Winston (1998) makes about the risks of fetishising the new. Broadcasting remained the dominant delivery mechanism for public service communication into the first decade of the twenty-first century. The suggestion here isn't that new communications forms will take the place of PSB, but a new hierarchy of use is inevitable where PSB becomes more marginal. As Holmes (2005) argues, 'when looked at from an economic perspective, we shall be able to see how both the internet and television, network media and broadcast media 'need' each other' (Holmes, 2005:12).

So, despite the recognition that many people won't have the time or inclination to generate their own content,[10] there will still be a large number of users whose relationship with public service content will be based around fluidity and interactivity. In this way, the paradigm of a central broadcaster charged with defining the common good and servicing that common good becomes problematic and the one-to-many broadcast ecology, where a few chosen people make decisions about broadcasting in the name of a 'healthy society', becomes irrelevant. This is part of a wider conceptual argument characterised by the 'second media age' which has been discussed by scholars since the mid-1990s. The idea of a second media age implies the demise of broadcasting and the concomitant rise of the internet culture. (This is examined in depth in Holmes, 2005.) It is concerned primarily with the liberating social possibilities brought about by new technologies and the much-disputed possibility that they might eclipse broadcast. At the very least, this digital disruption will precipitate a re-examination of what new and old technologies mean for social communication processes.

The BBC's news quandary

In its *Creative Futures Strategy Report* (2006) the BBC acknowledged the need to forge innovative relationships between producers, texts and audiences that take advantage of new technology to realise its stated 'public value' goals – that of building a new civic commons and an active and informed citizenship (Thompson, 2006). The report identified opportunities and challenges created by the disruptive wave of digital technologies and talked of 'seismic shifts in public expectations, lifestyle and behaviours'. It stressed that unidirectional, linear discourses were not interesting for the younger license payer (those that the BBC must attract to survive). The under 35s would prefer instead to interact, to change and add content or ideas.

Given the right conditions, new kinds of interaction, facilitated by disruptive digital technologies, might spur open, public debate and information exchange. Free market proponents would argue, in line with Peacock, that open debate requires open publishing. When Caxton invented the printing press, in theory, all citizens had a voice where before they had none, despite centralised control in most European states. You didn't need one central public service provider to control and filter the free exchange of views. As Oliver Holmes declared 'the best test of truth is the power of the thought to get itself accepted in the competition of the market' (cited in Curran 2002:225).

By the turn of the twenty-first century it cost approximately £20 million to establish a new national broadsheet (Curran, 2002:226) disqualifying all but a wealthy minority from having a voice. Yet, with the digital age came interactive platforms ideal for harnessing public participation and encouraging debate. Suddenly, there were fewer barriers to entry and once again it was cheap to publish and 'groups of ordinary people could set up their trestle-table, so to speak, in the main market place of ideas' (Curran, 2002:226).

The meteoric rise of blogging in the first decade of the twenty-first century was testament to this. Traditional gatekeepers of news and information could be bypassed and a more open market for production created. Picone prefers to use the word produser (producer-user) to describe the activities that surround online citizen journalism activity. As the production of news becomes part of the consumption of news, the user's role can be reconceptualised. 'He does not merely consume news, but also shares it, rates it, searches it and produces it' (Picone, 2007:104). This inevitably upsets the power base and editorial decision procedures of any traditionally run news organisation. Broadcasters must decide to what extent audience participation should be exploited, how it should be exploited and what commitment there might be to integrating audiences into the production process – into the very formation of news.

It's useful to examine what happens when the public's voice is harnessed within a traditional news culture that necessarily militates against equality of voices being heard. One example of this is the BBC's courtship of what it calls 'participatory journalism', whereby users contribute images, thoughts, stories and opinions through its website.[11] Initial experiments with the adoption of user-instigated material have created problems for the BBC as was illustrated vividly in a speech by its head of Multi Media News, Peter Horrocks, entitled 'The Value of Citizen Journalism' (Horrocks, 2008).

Underpinning Horrock's speech was a profound ambivalence towards participatory journalism. His remonstrations suggested that the Corporation remained uncomfortable fully embracing audiences as producers of news.

> I want to argue that the somewhat messianic and starry-eyed way in which public participation journalism is argued for needs some very careful consideration .... We cannot just take the views that we receive via emails and texts and let them dictate our agenda. Nor should they give us a slant around which we should orient our take on a story.

Horrocks gave many excellent reasons for this discomfort including issues of quality, impartiality, cyber-bullying, lobbying and professionalism. He relayed a powerful dilemma his news team faced just after the Pakistani parliamentary candidate, Benazir Bhutto was assassinated in January, 2008. The newsroom quickly launched a 'Have Your Say' forum which is a facility for users to post and recommend comments. They were deluged by reactionary, racist posts condemning the Islamic religion. As a consequence a nervous BBC considered turning off the comment recommendation facility on the BBC News website. Horrocks (2008) said,

> It was only a fleeting suggestion, but that we could consider, however briefly, freezing this important part of BBC News' service tells you something about the power and the potential danger of the new intensity of the interaction between the contributing public,

journalists and audiences. And it raises the question of how much attention and resource news organisations should devote to this rapidly burgeoning aspect of our journalism. The vehemence and the unanimity of these opinions against the Muslim religion were striking. So why did we briefly consider freezing this forum? A small part of our thinking was that in the context of the death of a significant international figure, who was herself Muslim, we thought that the weight of remarks could be offensive to some users of the BBC News website. Might some readers believe that such views as 'most recommended' represented an editorial line by BBC News? I suspect not, but there was at least that danger. But our real question concerned the editorial value of the comments and how far they should influence our coverage more widely. And the answers to that were: very little and hardly at all.

This shows the tensions between a genuine desire to make use of contributions from the public and host a civic debate and the need to control that debate. The racist messages were not palatable for a state broadcaster to relay and yet it could not cut off the flow of feedback without being accused of censorship. The BBC had charged itself with growing and nurturing the community it serves, but, Horrocks implies it is uncomfortable opening its gates too widely and allowing disparate voices to be heard. Instead, the normative functions of the BBC newsroom struggle to reassert themselves against this unwelcome tide of 'bilious vitriol' from its public. Yet, once the dissolution of boundaries is underway and once expectations are created that the public has a voice, these voices may be difficult to quieten. User-generated content at BBC News has grown significantly over a relatively short time, raising expectations within the BBC's news audiences that a serious paradigm shift is underway that might genuinely dissolve boundaries between those that make the news and those that consume it.

James Curran (2002:240) acknowledges that any pluralistic design of media systems may make the attainment of collective agreement more difficult. He suggests that without hierarchy promoting social integration on its own terms, you risk destabilising the system and as communication resources are allocated to subordinate or minority groups, this might promote 'fissiparous tendencies at a time when general societal ties appear to be weakening'. This is the plurality dilemma the BBC struggles with. It's a huge challenge to harness the anarchy or potential anarchy of limitless interactivity back and forth.

Hence, the BBC is wrestling with two very different models of news production that compete irreconcilably – top down control versus bottom up influence (Jones, forthcoming 2009). Yet, how far down this path of bottom up, democratic production is the BBC willing or able to go? It is dependent on public trust which up until recently has been built top down through authority and credibility and disseminated through a strong corporate ethos of impartiality. But, trust and audiences are both diminishing and it remains to be seen whether trust might be enhanced through a networked world(Horrocks, 2006).

Theatres of contemporary pluralism

The Peacock Report stimulated a seismic shift in thinking, a break from paradigms of the past with its forthright attack on broadcasting paternalism. In a one-to-many broadcast environment, paternalism reflected the presence of broadcasters choosing what audiences have a right to see and listen to. This has allowed the BBC to become habituated into a role where it has historically dominated the production and dissemination of broadcasting goods in British society. Historically, it has often been criticised for its arrogance, as again evidenced in Alan Peacock's Tailpiece in this volume.[12] It was no coincidence that it earned the nickname 'Auntie Beeb' – describing a matronly, well intentioned but paternalistic body. To earn its place in the new media ecology, the BBC needs to find a way of letting go.

We have yet to develop a sophisticated enough model for the funding and organisation of broadcasting and mass communication in the UK and as a society, we are deeply reluctant to do anything that might impinge on our fragile social cohesion or weaken our national cultural identity.

In the past, the paradigm of a healthy civic commons, where debate among all members of society could be fostered, rested on the old-fashioned concept of a national conversation stimulated by a mass, top down address, where all experienced the same communication at more or less the same time. This debate has been traditionally supported through the output of public service broadcasters in the UK. A weakened public service provider might jeopardise this process, and it would be weakened further if citizens were too narrowly defined as consumers within the new communications environment, for, as James Curran writes, 'People who are informed and active participants in civil society are a much more formidable and less biddable force than those who are only 'active' at the level of consumption' (Curran, 2002:238).

The problem is that very little meaningful distinction can be made between acts as 'citizens' or 'consumers' in a media ecology defined by fluidity and unlimited choice. These interactions are seemingly impossible to control through old-fashioned gate-keeping models. Coleman (2005) and Scannell (2005) both ponder the realities of a fragmented and disjointed civic audience and the impact on the future of PSC. Scannell is pessimistic, linking the demise of broadcasting with the demise of the BBC and aligning digital, narrowcast media with Peacockian free market concepts of individualistic consumer address and personalisation of experience (Scannell, 2004). Coleman also talks of the need to be addressed as a 'citizen' rather than 'mere consumers or free-floating egos' and acknowledges the deep pessimism surrounding the demise of a universal discourse of citizenship where 'the fragmentation of the media audience (....) is regarded as a metaphor for the tribal disintegration of the public' (Coleman, 2004:89).

Coleman, though, recognises that the internet might succeed in hosting a new civic commons where horizontal communications and interactions have the potential to revitalise the public sphere and reverse 'a veritable crisis of public participation' (Coleman, 2002:91). He acknowledges that technology is inherently neutral and warns us that our civic hopes shouldn't be vested in any 'new' media given the fates of earlier new media such as radio, television and cable television (Coleman, 2002:93).

Technology has done a lot to individualise communication processes and this can be deeply unsettling, but it can also be quite liberating. As a solution, Bazalgette (2008) argues for the creation of a new centrally funded navigation system that would promote a genuine plurality of supply. He calls this new search engine 'Boggle' and suggests it should be at the centre of all public service output and be accessible to all (Bazalgette, 2008:7).

The mass reach that broadcasting traditionally provides is often described as the glue that cements society. The fear is that once that reach is fragmented into thousands of counter-publics,[13] a comprehensive public sphere might be undermined. In an unprecedented era of choice, the concept of a single broadcaster, empowered to be 'the glue' that binds the nation together, seems a very outdated notion. Yet, the creation of a nexus of public spheres that feed off each other with the BBC as fulcrum may also serve the same broad public purpose. The notion of choice is at the centre of this debate. Does endless choice encouraging citizens to gravitate to channels reflecting their own world views necessarily bring about the collapse of the public sphere, or can a body such as the BBC, through its size and status, engage the nation with fragmented discourses, appealing to a multitude of counter publics who are in turn both producers and users?

Born recognised this tension in her 2006 attempt to rethink the nature and scope of PSB and to 'justify its existence anew' (Born, 2005a:102). She attempted to reconcile the binary divide that exists between those who think that broadcasting must be associated with the creation of an inclusive public sphere and those who accept a system that is designed to support a multitude of public spheres or 'sphericules'.

> Scholars writing on PSB and digitisation tend to divide between those who emphasise the democratic benefits of media that afford a universal public address and those who advocate media systems that enable a pluralistic address among multiple competing publics, or 'counter-publics'.
>
> (Born, 2005a:107)

Born argues that 'media organisations – both in their social make-up and in their output – can be understood as the primary 'theatres' for contemporary pluralism' (Born, 2005a:114). She concludes that PSB needs to be able to host pluralism and a panoply of diverse voices where counter public can speak to counter public. This she believes needs to be supported by a mass broadcasting system (the one-to-many model) that should be at the heart of the space for exhibiting and experiencing diversity (Born, 2005a:114). She underpins this point by quoting Stuart Hall, 'the quality of life for black or ethnic minorities depends on the whole society knowing more about the black experience' (Hall, 1993:36).

Conclusion

In 2008, the BBC continued to provide broadcasting free at the point of delivery to all UK households in return for approximately £2.5 billion per annum of licence fee money. Yet, the very idea of Public Service Television is fast becoming redundant requiring the BBC to redefine its role substantially without losing its identity.

The Peacock Committee (1986) looked to a future where new technology would liberate broadcasting from the necessity of state intervention. It argued for a fundamental reappraisal of the long-term funding of the BBC, and by association British broadcasting. It concluded that 'British broadcasting should move towards a sophisticated market system based on consumer sovereignty. That is a system which recognises that viewers and listeners are the best ultimate judges of their own interests' (Report, 1986: para. 592). At the time, Peacock's conceptual model of a full broadcast market 'no more special than publishing' (Report, 1986: para.711) was constrained by technological realities; but, by the turn of the twenty-first century, the forces of globalisation and technological change had significantly altered the media ecology.

The Report was prescient in its vision of a broadcasting arena where there were few barriers to entry, and where there was the potential to sell broadcast products like books; however, it couldn't have foreseen a world of *MySpace*, *Wikipedia* and *YouTube*, employing the productive talents of the user in an incredible symbiotic relationship that belies conventional producer-consumer models. Choice was at the heart of Peacock's recommendations, yet, in the digital age, the ultimate 'consumer sovereignty' lies in an ability to choose, rewrite, refashion and redistribute communication goods and the portals to entry are theoretically unlimited. This fragmentation of supply and demand has the potential to lead to significant disruption.

As Henry Jenkins argues 'Throw away the powers of broadcasting and one has only cultural fragmentation. The power of participation comes from not destroying commercial culture but from writing over it, moulding it, amending it, expanding it, adding greater diversity and perspective, and then recirculating it, feeding it back into the mainstream media' (Jenkins, 2006:257).

Raymond Williams (1974) reminds us that we shouldn't allow ourselves to be lulled into a belief that new technologies have a special power to shape and transform society. Old and new media exist side by side and old media never disappear. Yet, the introduction of a new communications medium can engender debate about how society should best organise itself and in doing so, suggest new possibilities and create new communication paradigms. Cowling and Tambini argue in their book, *From PSB to PSC*, that broadcasting policy must adjust to a radically altered landscape and that 'the harbingers of change, such as Alan Peacock were not wrong, they were just ahead of their time' (Cowling and Tambini, 2004:171). If, as Steven Barnett forcefully argues in this volume,[14] broadcasting has a unique ability to advance social and cultural goods, then it is important to consider how future models might map onto a media ecology where public service *broadcasting* becomes public service *communication*.

The funding and organisation of PSB in this country cannot continue unchanged, it has to evolve to meet the needs of society in a digital age.

It seems clear that the debate about PSC must advance quickly to revisit the civic role of communication, and embrace, and perhaps even reconcile the twin identities of citizen and consumer within the framework of participatory media.

Happily for the BBC, investment in new technologies was always central to its future blueprint. Thus, for historical reasons, if none other, the BBC may well take its place in the new media ecology through the sheer force of momentum. Yet technological innovations and new consumption patterns have caused a crisis of identity for broadcasters in general. The BBC must therefore carve a very careful path through the rocky terrain of convergence and user-generated content.

The 2003 Communications Act was intended to last for about ten years, although with the pace of change it might have become redundant well before 2013. The BBC's size and its success in holding onto a significant share of the market, puts it in a strong position to continue with its mission to provide meritorious cultural goods to a large number of citizens.

Those who argue that with convergence PSB has lost its purpose are misguided. This view does not reflect renewals that might make it possible for PSB to survive digital transformation. Thus, PSB's future must rest in establishing a new legitimacy as a democratic and inclusive public sphere by attracting young viewers (those with new user-generated content skills) and encouraging participation through a prominent institutional strategy.

Peacock gave the world permission to release broadcasting into the domain of the commons, technology has also liberated it almost wholly, yet policy is reluctant to take that final step. The Peacock Report also created a far humbler, more innovative and democratic BBC, one that knew it must find a new rationale to survive as a public institution into the next century.

Current policy debates point in two directions. Their rhetoric, they owe to Peacock, and their ambivalence to the full marketisation of broadcasting they owe to the wonderful and unrivalled national and international success of one of Britain's most loved organisations.

Notes

*   PSB 2.0 is a term used to refer to public service broadcasting in the age of the Internet. Web 2.0 is an umbrella term for new interactive web services and possibilities characterised by the freedom to share media content and to participate in its production.

1. Public Service Communication can be described as the evolution of Public Service Broadcasting from a one-to-many, one way broadcasting ecology using television and radio to a dynamic system where one-one, many-to-many, and many-to-one interactive interactions become possible through the Internet.

2. The concept of merit goods was first introduced in Musgrave and Musgrave (1973). Merit goods, by definition, aim to interfere with consumer preference since they are determined by government to be good for people, regardless of whether people desire them for themselves or not, and this contrasts with the idea that individual consumers' autonomy and preferences have normative value.

3. The Report's authors envisaged the creation of a Public Service Broadcasting Council which would support programmes that, 'viewers and listeners are willing to support in their capacity as taxpayers and voters but not directly as consumers' (Report, 1986: para. 693). A type of 'Arts Council of the Airwaves'.

4. Ed Richards was appointed Chief Executive Officer of Ofcom in 2006. He had made a speech ruling out the development of a public service publisher in a recent speech for the Royal Television Society (Richards, 2008).

5. See this volume, edited conference transcripts, p. 341.

6. The quotation can be found in Chapter 12 of this book, p. 338.

7. The most significant testament to this in 2008 was the huge success of the BBC's 'IPlayer' which allowed viewers and listeners to download programmes through the Internet after transmission.

8. The quotation can be found in Chapter 12 of this book, p. 330.

9. The gift economy in this sense is characterised by the free sharing of ideas and knowledge without any direct payment or reward, with the idea that some greater good is served and that reciprocal altruism might result.

10. User Research from 2006 (US) concluded that 'in most online communities, 90 per cent of users are lurkers who never contribute, 9 per cent of users contribute a little, 1 per cent of users account for almost all the action' (Nielsen, 2006).

11. The rise of participatory journalism can be traced back to the prominence of citizen journalism images that accompanied both the 9/11 terrorist attacks in New York and the July 7th, 2005 terrorist bombings of the London Underground. Stuart Allan refers to these contributions as being from 'digital citizens' (Allan, 2006:144).

12. See Chapter 11.

13. Fraser (1992) defines counter publics as 'parallel discursive arenas where members of subordinated social groups invent and circulate counter discourses to formulate oppositional interpretations of their identities, interests, and needs' (1992:123).

14. See Chapter 12.

11
Impressions, Influences and Indebtedness

Sir Alan Peacock

The invitation to add a tailpiece to the proceedings enables me to offer some observations on impressions gained, lessons learnt and debts incurred. This serves the purpose of trying to remove some of the misunderstandings surrounding the work of the so-called Home Office Committee on the Financing of the BBC (Report, 1986) (hereafter the HOCFB). This requires me to mention previous attempts by the author to do so (see Peacock, 1986, 1987, 2005, 2006).

The Peacock Legacy Conference had a rather different focus than that suggested by the Terms of Reference of the HOCFB which were to cover the whole field of future broadcasting provision. The general expectation had been that we would recommend that the BBC should take advertising. The fact that we did not do so led some commentators to assume that the HOCFB had been markedly influenced in its conclusion by an allegedly persuasive case made by the BBC itself. This explains why what follows concentrates on the particular issue of the HOCFB's relations with the BBC.

Impressions

Let me preface impressions with a tribute to several producers of BBC programmes who coached me in my salad days in the art of talking on radio. I recall particularly the patience, skill and sheer professionalism of P. H. Newby of the old Third Programme and of George Bruce of BBC Scotland. Both were authors of fine repute. Newby will be remembered for his novel *A Picnic at Sakkara* and George Bruce 'for his much-acclaimed poetry earning him the title of 'the last of the makars' (an ancient Scots term for poets). He had been my English master at Dundee High School before he entered broadcasting. Although I have appeared now and again on television, particularly frequently after the appearance of HOCFB, and observed at close quarters the skills of producers, I am poor material for them. I was perhaps a shade better and certainly more comfortable with radio discussions when I served my apprenticeship with Steve Banerjee, well remembered as a producer both efficient and humane.

My debt to such unforgettable members of earlier BBC staff means that I have been faced with a major disappointment. To explain this I have to go back to the BBC's approach to the HOCFB. I had imagined from the outset that the BBC would try to engage our interest by reasoned argument backed by relevant evidence. This approach would be the natural result of having considered the background, experience and integrity of the members of the Committee and would pay us the courtesy and compliment of assuming that we were competent at carrying out our task. It was a considerable surprise to find that this was not to be.

I had known from previous close encounters with the top brass of the BBC, notably when chairing The Committee on the Financing of British Orchestras for The Arts Council of Great Britain (1969–70), and some later consulting work for the Performing Right Society in dispute with the BBC over performance rights (see Peacock and Weir, 1975, 1993), that the BBC had a well-honed strategy for dealing with any publicly declared set of criticisms. Its underlying principle was clearly assumed, as in the orchestral enquiry, not that the BBC had to work its passage with whomsoever was assigned the task of investigating its activities but the reverse.

A quick response to a suitably polite demand for submission of evidence might evince from the BBC a promise to co-operate, without commitment as to the timing and form of a reply. If required, careful attention might be paid to the status of the Chairperson and whether or not he or she should be personally invited to the BBC for some suitable entertainment – not too lavish, of course, to avoid any suggestion of seeking to exercise undue influence. The investigators might have to wait anxiously for the reply to the criticisms made of the BBC who were known to use the tactical device of submitting evidence at the last minute. Any suggestion that they might be called to modify it – though the Corporation might be willing to give oral evidence – would be resisted. The investigators were expected to accept without question that evidence submitted was an authoritative reaffirmation of the BBC's inalienable right to be the primary authority on matters concerning its own functions.

This is not a strategy employed only by the BBC. I recall that the erstwhile professor of surgery at Edinburgh, appearing before the royal commission on the remuneration of doctors and dentists in the 1960s, countered a request for empirical evidence for one of his assertions by what he regarded as the appropriate riposte, 'what other evidence do you require than the fact that *I* have said so?'

If the resultant criticisms appeared in part or in full in some publication issued by a public authority of some consequence, there was a well-framed additional strategy. Criticisms could be ignored, though perhaps briefly reported without comment in BBC News programmes, but not at peak hours. If that gave rise to irritating Parliamentary Questions (PQs) or requests to appear before some parliamentary committee or other, a document would already be in draft to show that criticisms believed to have some substance in the eyes of the BBC had already been recognised by the BBC and would be put right by much more suitable remedies than those proposed, if there were any, by the investigators. Apart from any official means for promulgating a reply, the BBC might find a slot in a suitable news bulletin indicating its sensitivity to public concerns.

Now I admit to a certain amount of journalistic licence in what has just been said. However, if I thought that this might cloud my judgment, I would have been only too glad to find evidence in the BBC's treatment of the HOCFB that I was palpably wrong. I have given a fairly full account of negotiations with the BBC in *The 'Politics' of Investigating Broadcasting Finance* reprinted[1] here, one of several of my post-HOCFB publications (see also Peacock, 1986, 2005). There is little in it to substantiate a different perception of the BBC's strategy compared with earlier days when it was under less pressure to justify its position as a public corporation which saw itself as the flagship of the broadcasting world.

This caricature does not suggest that the BBC does anything unusual in developing an offensive strategy in coping with inquiries into its affairs. However, what was revealed at our meetings was the lengths to which it appeared to go in order to gather intelligence about the credibility of the members of the HOCFB. One can expect sections of the Press to base their hostility to one's activities on 'ad hominem' arguments such as one's incompetence or bias – as happened in my own case with *The Observer* and *The Scotsman*. However, in both cases those whom they consulted for evidence questioning my competence did not act the part assigned them. Two of these had very different views from my own about economic policy, but gave me good references. At least the broadsheets both made their position clear and, to their credit, published the views from those they had expected to give a rather different opinion.

Sam Brittan's initial reaction to the revelation that Janet Morgan (now Lady Balfour of Burleigh) had headed such an intelligence-gathering operation for the BBC was the same as mine – how flattering to be assigned such importance! But, the fact that this took place at all suggests that the BBC also regarded 'ad hominem' arguments as useful and effective weapons. I would prefer to be mistaken in this. It is extraordinary to me that someone with the formidable reputation of Janet Morgan had been asked to undertake an unnecessary task. The standard of evidence produced by the BBC appeared to be as much a disappointment to those present at The Peacock Legacy Conference, who would support the BBC through thick and thin, as well as to ourselves. Alistair Milne is perceived as having let the side down. I consider it unfortunate that he was not able to be present at The Peacock Legacy Conference to give his own observations on his treatment.

Influences

In preparing for this conference, I came across a welcome letter from Jeremy Hardie written to me just after the HOCFB had reported. In it he remarked that 'I think that a lot of what we say shows how useful applied economics can be – and particularly that market economics and commercialism are not the same thing.'

The distinction drawn by Jeremy is fundamental to the thrust of argument and the conclusions of the HOCFB. At several times during our conference he offered graphic illustrations of its importance. Let me remind you of its substance.

If listeners and viewers, acting passively or interactively, are to be the decisive influence on the type and quality of broadcast programmes, then some means has to be found for expressing, evaluating and giving effect to their choices. These must also encourage presentation of alternative choices easily available. The long-established method for achieving this result is a 'free market'. The free market is therefore nothing more or less than a mechanism which does not define a political or philosophical stance of any kind. If for any reason listeners and viewers are to be denied sovereignty status supposedly for their own good, as in the Reithian concept of the philosophy of broadcasting, then the 'free market' is not the appropriate way for achieving the desired aim.

Even those who accept the 'sovereignty of the consumer' as the ultimate criterion for judging how broadcasting should be conducted have advocated government intervention, originally because of technical factors such as spectrum scarcity and limitations on methods of transmission including difficulties in charging customers in direct proportion to their use of the service. The HOCFB considered that these difficulties would not be long in being overcome. This explains its concentration of argument on two matters (a) the free market could not guarantee the degree of competition necessary to present suitable alternatives to customers and (b) the undersupply of programmes, particularly of a cultural nature, which customers wished to be encouraged but which could only be supplied by some form of co-operative action reflecting agreement on how such encouragement should be given. We used the Arts Council analogy, as an example of such action, but in the full knowledge that there are many practical difficulties in implementation. In other words, the HOCFB envisaged that the major purpose of state intervention was to enable the market to work as efficiently as possible. Intervention would never achieve perfection but could ensure 'workable' competition.

Whereas this argument was given a fair run for its money during the conference, one senses that Sam Brittan, Jeremy Hardie and I did not exactly enlist enthusiastic support for it. At this stage, I cannot expect to change this situation, and in any case my persuasive powers do not match theirs. The reasons for non-acceptance are somewhat complex and I cannot categorise them in any sensible way without more time to think about how this might best be done. As a rough guess there is a major division between those who begin with the outright rejection of the consumer sovereignty principle and those who, while accepting it, perhaps reluctantly, consider that there are too many barriers to its implementation, including opposition from those whose material interests seem likely to be adversely affected by the changes in the system of broadcasting that a move to consumer sovereignty entails.

Jeremy Hardie contended that economists suffer from a lack of knowledge of and interest in the organisational features of public corporations and private industry. There is truth in this but it is interesting to note that an institutional approach to the study of broadcasting was the very foundation of Coase's famous pioneering study of the BBC (Coase, 1950). I do agree, however, that economists have not spent enough time learning how to convince those whose business behaviour is the subject of their investigations that they fully understand the decision making process in broadcasting, particularly a non-profit making corporation such as the BBC. Clear indication of this is found in the appreciation expressed by the HOCFB members present at the detailed accounts of 'inside' experiences offered by several contributors headed by David Nicholas on the rough passage experienced by ITN.[2] We could have spent much more time on this matter.

So the criticism of institutional neglect is well founded and I take it to heart. One still may harbour the suspicion that opposition to economic analysis can originate not only from legitimate criticism of the gaps in economic investigation but also from the likelihood that they can come in the end to unpalatable conclusions. This gloss arises from my own analysis of how the BBC has adapted to a world where they indicate that they must now pay more attention to what economists have to say. It is apparent to me that those whose help they have sought subsequent to our Report have been under pressure to act as hired guns. I consider that a strategic error on the BBC's part (see Peacock, 2006).

So far as the influence of the BBC itself is concerned, an attempt is made in the enjoyable and racy account of the comings and goings of the BBC's top brass in their perception of the appropriate strategy for dealing with the HOCFB.[3] The authors clearly believe that they have provided abundant evidence that this strategy worked. The fact that HOCFB did not recommend that the BBC should be financed by advertising has been mistakenly ascribed to the influence of the BBC's submissions on the HOCFB's thinking.

It was because the HOCFB took seriously the intensely practical matter of setting out how the whole broadcasting system would need to adjust to changing economic and social conditions that it arrived at the position that the BBC, subject to some very important changes that it recommended, should continue to be financed primarily by a licence fee, at least for a limited period. This approach owes little if anything to the BBC's submissions which paid scant attention to consideration of the future, other than to lay out what it considered to be its reasonable demand for a sizeable increase in its funding to allow it to establish a monopoly in new methods for delivery of programmes. Our conclusion about continuation of the licence fee to support the BBC was reached not because of but in spite of the poor case that the BBC presented on its own behalf.

Indebtedness

Let me begin by expressing warm thanks to Tom O'Malley and Janet Jones both for bearing the burden of organising The Peacock Legacy

Conference and preparing its proceedings for publication. I cannot identify those, who under the cloak of anonymity aided their efforts, but I must thank them as well.

Peter Jay is a key figure in this whole affair. His close association with the organisers, a product of his sojourn as a visiting professor at the University of Aberystwyth, has had a marked effect on the choice of themes and the mode of enquiry, and, above all, through his characteristically penetrating observations on the problems at issue. Those who have identified him as a major influence on the HOCFB are correct. That was bound to be the case because he opened up the whole debate on the future of broadcasting before the Committee was appointed by his examination of the potentialities of electronic publishing and its implications for both the nature and dimensions of broadcasting services. He has outrun the sceptics. Nowhere is this better demonstrated than in his own contributions to the conference.

Finally, I must emphasise that the 'Peacock Report' may be useful shorthand but its conclusions are a collective effort. It was therefore a particular pleasure for me, and of clear benefit to the Proceedings that fellow members Sam Brittan and Jeremy Hardie found time to participate . Bob Eagle, our secretary, strangely enough, is a missing player in the BBC's perception of the role of the HOCFB members. He had special skills derived from his training as a physicist. Without his organising ability and professional knowledge the HOFCB would never have been able to meet its self-imposed deadline of reporting a year after its members first met. He was only prevented from joining the conference because, in what turned out to be his last senior appointment, he had to cope with the immigration problem. His qualities as a scientist and administrator were recognised by the award of the CBE on his retirement.

Edinburgh, August 2008.

Notes

1. See Chapter 5.
2. See Chapter 12.
3. See Chapter 7.

12

Conference Witness Testimonies: Extracted from 'The Peacock Legacy: turning point or missed opportunity?'

Contributors to the Conference

Introduction

Some of the most influential figures behind the Peacock Report met to discuss the forces which have shaped the world of UK broadcasting since the 1980s at a conference on 'The Peacock Legacy: turning point or missed opportunity' between 18 and 20 March 2005.

The conference was organised by the Department of Theatre, Film and Television Studies at the University of Wales, Aberystwyth, and took place at the University of Wales residential study centre, Gregynog, near Newtown mid-Wales.

Its main purpose was to review the Peacock Committee's history, its politics and its policy context. Over three days its main sources of inspiration, its conduct and its subsequent impact on communications policy were discussed in detail. Those directly responsible for the authoring of the original report along with researchers who have monitored broadcasting policy in the ensuing years spoke as witnesses and academics. These sessions were recorded and the full transcripts are available in The National Library of Wales.

The conference was structured around the following sessions: 'Opening Plenary'; 'Establishing Peacock'; 'View from the BBC'; 'Conduct of the Committee'; 'Influence' and 'Closing Plenary'. A selection from these transcripts has been edited and reproduced here and the full transcripts of the proceedings have been deposited in the National Library of Wales.

Origins

Sir Alan Peacock:
It never occurred to me that I was going to be asked to be the chairman. I got a telephone call – I've got a note here – from Leon Brittan[1] to say, 'I wonder if we could talk about this. I'd like you to be chairman of this committee.' There ... is no letter. I never received a letter of appointment.

.... In the case of a committee – although questions might be asked if it were not published – there's no obligation to publish the findings. There's no obligation to accept any of the findings at all. Therefore this has big advantages, because it means that there is less incentive for politicians to want to try to rig the conclusions, because ... the government will draw its own and the opposition will draw its own conclusions from what you've said, and there is no commitment. So I think it was very easy for the Home Secretary to take a relaxed view about what we said and did. Later, that's not quite what Douglas Hurd,[2] who had to receive the Report, said. ... I have somewhere a note of what he said. Oh, yes *(reads)* 'Home Secretary speaks to the Royal Television Society Convention dinner, 6 November 19' – it says 85; it means 86, obviously. Here Douglas said 'When I gave a cautious welcome to the Peacock Report in the House of Commons, my cautious words of appreciation were handled by the media with characteristic scepticism. When I said that we intended to study the Committee's conclusion with great care, this was treated as a few polite words uttered by the graveside as the coffin was lowered out of sight. Perhaps it's now clear that that was the wrong impression. The Peacock Commission was given relatively restricted terms of reference' – note what he said – 'but, understandably, being a lively set of people ... they overflowed their terms of reference and produced a report which touched on most of the possibilities for the future. The members of the Committee would, I think, agree that they set an agenda rather than worked out full conclusions.' Well ... that's not quite what he has said later on. If you read his memoirs, you will get a slightly different view.

Sir Samuel Brittan:
Well I remember very brief, informal discussions both with Alan and with my brother Leon. I can't remember with whom I discussed it first, but I do remember it was agreed very firmly that the invitation to me, at least, should come from Alan so that it looked, so that it didn't look

like – I don't know what the word is, you can't say nepotism – didn't look like fraternalism. But I also remember Leon saying to me, 'You do watch, you do watch quite a lot of television?'

But even in those days, I was very, very discriminating in watching television. ... I think while the Committee was sitting, I watched a few shows that I otherwise would not, but otherwise I just regarded it as an alternative to going to the cinema to the theatre or listening to a concert. In fact my favourite viewing was never current affairs, because I had enough of current affairs during the day. We obviously antici-pated there would be a fuss that the Home Secretary's brother had been appointed. That does show that people don't understand the difference between brothers and clones.

I had actually – nobody knew this actually – something I wrote 13, no 12 years before the Committee was established, and I had said the ideal system for broadcasting was not advertising but direct subscription.[3] And I knew even less technically then than I did afterwards; it was just one sentence in a book I wrote. ... So, people knew roughly where I was coming from.

Jeremy Hardie:

What I remember about it is that I got a telephone call saying, 'Would I like to be on the Peacock Committee?' I think it was known there was going to be a thing called the Peacock Committee, because Alan had been appointed. For me, the business about the licence fee and rows between the BBC and the government and so on was not in the front of my mind at all. ... I had however been involved in, well first of all, bidding – unsuccessfully, defeated by Peter (Jay) *(laugh from PJ)* for the breakfast franchise.[4]

Sir Alan Peacock:

... Economic analysis provides a well-established body of thought. If you are analysing policy questions, you identify policy aims, you look at the economic environment in which these aims are being achieved, and particularly you need numbers for this; ... you want to express these aims in some kind of numbers. You also need to know something about the trade-off between the aims and ... how this has been presented in the theory of economic policy.

... This kind of technology, if you like, can be transferred to all kinds of different situations. So it didn't seem to me a problem necessarily that, in moving to an area where you hadn't considered institution-ally a particular set of institutions of this kind – broadcasting – that necessarily there was any particular problem, at least in general terms.

... I have some contact with those who specialise in public finance. One of my close colleagues at London School of Economics (LSE) in my early days was Ronald Coase,[5] and those of you who know anything about the economics of broadcasting will know that he was a pioneer. One of the first things that I had to read as an assistant editor of a journal called *Economica* in which, interestingly enough the joint editors were Friedrich Hayek and Roy Allen,[6] imagine working with them, there was an article on wire broadcasting, or rediffusion as it became called later, by Ronnie Coase, which intrigued me.[7] About all the restrictions which were placed on the poor little electrician near Southampton who set up a rediffusion system with his neighbours and ran foul of the Post Office for not having a telegraphy licence, the up-and-coming BBC and the politicians thought he might broadcast programmes 'from foreign countries' – wouldn't that be terrible! It stimulated my interest and I read his great work on the BBC as a study in monopoly,[8] which was a classic, and as you know he later became a Nobel Prize winner.

Jeremy Hardie:
If you are an economist you believe that economic analysis is generic, meaning that you can apply it to every problem, and I certainly came to it from that point of view. Very, very surprisingly the first serious books I ever read was a book called *An Introduction to Positive Economics* by a man called Lipsey.[9]
..... So if you want my intellectual background and baggage, the first thing of any serious analytic polity I ever read about economics was about the duopoly problem. Now I don't say that because there was any line of causation through to me sitting here today, but I ... did have all that intellectual background. I used to teach economics, and I was a microeconomist, industrial economist, that sort of person, so this was the water that I was used to swimming in, or waters I was used to teaching others to swim in, so all that's true.
... I was also a businessman. I am also a qualified accountant ... I did money in a different sense. And I think that did make me a different sort of person. I wasn't, as it were, just 'economist number three'.

Sir Samuel Brittan:
Well I perhaps 'did money', but in a very different sort of way. Trying, probably unsuccessfully, to elucidate to my readers why Friedman[10] thought money important and Keynes[11] also thought it important, but many Keynesians did not.
.... When broadcasters said 'broadcasting is different' and you can't just treat it like the market for cheese or bananas, I tended to agree. This was

not systematic reflection, the thoughts I had – but I came to opposite conclusions. I thought that it was much more important to let the viewers and listeners choose. ...

Therefore the ability of would-be entrants to compete and for viewers and listeners to choose what to hear was extremely important. Perhaps the nuance I brought to it is that some people, including even some economists, made a difference between 'quality control' and 'censorship'. Well, I think they merge into each other quite readily. ...

Sir Alan Peacock:

If you're thinking about broadcasting as in some general sense a market – meaning in a broad sense transactions between those who are producing the broadcasting and those who are receiving it – I think that you'd have to know a little bit more than would be fashionable at the time in economics, where macroeconomics was associated specifically with policy, in going into, for example, the theory of duopoly. I certainly had to scratch my head a bit over that in trying to apply it to the chapter on 'The "Comfortable Duopoly"'[12] which no doubt you know all about. But I can't think of anything fundamental which presented some barrier, by looking at broadcasting. Any more than there would be in other cases where the public goods problem arises. ...

... This is, I think, very important – the public goods problem. The thing that struck me before I came to broadcasting is the similarity to the lighthouse situation, that maybe technology will alter the whole nature of the possibility of having a more direct relationship through, for example, subscription or pay-for-view, between the listener or viewer and the producers.

Jeremy Hardie:

.... Economics contributes nothing to how you might arrange the intervention that is going to put this thing right. For example, do you just keep the BBC going because it does public service broadcasting very well, do you Arts Council-ise it – which is one of the recommendations here – or whatever? How is it that, if there are these, as economists analyse them, public good or merit good questions, how do you structure the intervention so it's going to work? And that seems to me what we all go round and round and round on. It's easy if the market could just deliver because the merit good or public good thing is not there, or is trivial, and economics does the job for you perfectly. If that problem, however, is substantial, how you sort it out and how you do it is very, very difficult, which is why twenty years later the debate looks almost the same as when Peacock reported it.

Sir Alan Peacock:

... I wrote a report for the Arts Council on the future financing of orchestras,[13] in which the BBC was involved, and I had been a member of the Scottish Arts Council, was later Chairman of the Scottish Arts Council, and there the same problem arises about quality.

This is the problem. If you're going to use performance indicators as a way of financing opera, for example, they'll all come back to you and, quite reasonably, say, 'But you don't take into account the quality of the performance; how are you going to measure quality?' Who are the best people to determine quality? 'We, the producers, are the best people.' You see? Well exactly the same things happen, as we know, in broadcasting as well. One wants to have some mechanism by which this is at least subject to review and to questioning. .... The Committee provided some very interesting ways in which you could do this and which of course have continued and been adopted widely in broadcasting not only in this country but elsewhere.

Sir Samuel Brittan:
I have a question, actually – as an insufficiently believing economist who heard a lot of econometric predictions about the advertising market and how it would have a devastating effect on independent television ... if advertising were allowed on the BBC. This wasn't anything to do with quality and public goods – it was to do with so-called 'quality', but nothing much to do with the public goods, because it was the idea that the advertising market would not grow ... sufficiently, and it was very much self-interest on the part of the Independent Television Authority (ITA).[14] Now this was bought by some of the econometricians, and I question it. This is a serious question, not a debating question. Has anyone followed up these econometric predictions to see how far they were justified in the end, by events?

Peter Jay:
.... What is your understanding now of the immediate political factors which led to the establishment of the Committee? My reaction at the time was exactly the same as all of yours; that, okay, a relatively trivial squabble between politicians and the institutions may have led to the establishment of the Committee, but the moment a Committee was established, the thing to do was not to focus on this rather trivial squabble between politicians, but to ask the real questions.

Sir Alan Peacock:
That's right. I was asked personally to advise Sir Keith Joseph[15] on the possibility of introducing a scheme of educational vouchers, and that got quite a long way. ... The reason that he[16] gave for asking me was 'Oh, you have experience of government Alan' – because I spent three years full time as Chief Economic Advisor to the Department of Trade and Industry (DTI)[17] (where, coincidentally, I did discover something about

telecommunications). And this was produced again as a reason. … The reason that was given 'to try to mollify the kind of attacks by gentlemen like Gerald Kaufman'[18] (although it didn't stop him from attacking the appointment) was that I had been Chief Economic Advisor during the period of both the Tory and the Labour governments from '73 to '76. Again I have to get rid of a rumour here – I was not a political appointment. At least, it's inferred. I was just asked to come on secondment for three years …. So as far as the members are concerned, that follows a fairly well-established procedure in government, namely that one had no say in the decisions concerning membership. One was asked one's opinion on individual cases and was expected to, and was allowed to offer suggestions, …

Jeremy Hardie:

….. I absolutely take the point that in a certain straightforward sense it wasn't a 'fixed' committee. As I think you, Sam, said last night, if it had been meant to fix it, they ought to have fixed it better. It wasn't fixed, but still it was a committee of a particular kind. For example, it was heavy on economists or quasi-economists, which is one of the ways of approaching public policy issues, but not the only way. The second thing, as I say, it didn't do this classic 'spread' thing of having the trade unionist, and in terms of politics I always believed that I was there as 'the dangerous lefty', as I was a member of the SDP.[19]

Peter Jay:

Were you conscious of any discussion at all, Alan, with Leon, as to whether you were sufficiently representative, politically speaking?

Sir Alan Peacock:

Well I don't know. The only time I've ever been a member of any political party was an enthusiastic member of the Liberal Party. I lost a lot of shoe leather going round, years ago, but I left them on social policy, at which I was appalled. Sam will remember being a member of something called 'the unservile state'.[20]

Sir Samuel Brittan:

I do.

Sir Alan Peacock:

Which had connections with the Liberal Party, but after the mid-60s I had no connections at all.

Sir Samuel Brittan: (laughing)

…. I was probably the nearest connection they had with the Labour Party because my only political activity was, many years ago, to have been Secretary of the Cambridge University Labour Club. And I can say I didn't leave the Labour Club, the Labour Club left me (*general laughter*).

Sir Alan Peacock:
That's absolutely right.
Sir Samuel Brittan:
I did say it was a pity that there was nobody who was associated as an adult with the Labour Party. By that, I didn't mean somebody like Gerald Kaufman with predictable prejudices ... but if you'd looked around, there were people who knew something about ...
Sir Alan Peacock:
That's right.
Sir Samuel Brittan:
.... Economics and broadcasting, either/or ... were not party line people, but who were actual members of the Labour Party. Admittedly, some of them were en route to the Social Democrats, but not all, and it would have made it just a little bit more difficult for Gerald Kaufman if there had been one or two such people. I did think of one or two people at the time, but I can't remember who I had in mind.
Sir Alan Peacock:
We did pay particular attention to any particular memoranda of some substance and seriousness from politicians ... Merlyn Rees,[21] you may remember, wrote a very long and interesting piece for us. And I seem to remember Joe Ashton[22] – yes, who went to town on the whole question of the licence fee and its effect on the poor, that kind of thing. They were not simply bits of political carpet bagging or anything of that sort. I think you're right, though. I think we would have welcomed more reaction.... I was asked to appear before the Broadcasting Committee of Parliament. Can I say a little bit about that, very quickly? Simply, that I spent my time listening to them fighting with one another. I didn't have to do anything. But the Labour Party refused, nobody would come and talk. That would have to some extent solved this particular problem if one had had some reflective views.
Sir Samuel Brittan:
I have to admit that I had not read the Annan Report;[23] I had not read the Pilkington Report;[24] but I had seen them – at that time we had proper broadsheet newspapers, and as a dutiful newspaper reader had read their conclusions as they came out. I had also been lectured to by Noel Annan[25] at Cambridge, so I could actually hear him delivering some of his paragraphs. And I read essays by Richard Hoggart,[26] but not particularly on broadcasting, and may have referred to them. But I was aware of the sociological tradition. I am not as hostile to it as some economists because there are alternative sociological traditions. Sociology doesn't have to be Left interventionist. There were people like Durkheim and Max Weber who would have wiped the floor with a lot of you, to tell you the truth.... I

don't know what attitude they would have taken to broadcasting, but I was very conscious of the freedom of speech and freedom of artistic production element. To be more specific, you can be absolutely sure that the relevant parts of Annan and Pilkington, all these documents, were produced.

Jeremy Hardie:

I agree with Sam that we/I, like other reasonably well-informed people, knew what had been in Annan, and we knew the kind of debates you could have about broadcasting and so on. I agree with him that, surely, if there is an alternative, generic set of skills coming from sociology or whatever, you'd have expected Robert Eagle[27] or the BBC or whatever to draw these to our attention as part of the argumentation. However, in terms that Peter has put it, I don't think that's good enough ......
The thing about economics that we all believe is that it is a well-developed, systematic method of analysis that works pretty well a lot of the time, having as it were, a manual. And the manual is fairly specific and it includes all these categories, these old chestnuts I keep on repeating about public goods and merit goods so on.

.... But if the question is 'Was I, as a member of the Peacock Committee, aware of alternative ways of looking at the problem which had the same systematic or whatever status as economics', then I wasn't – and I don't think I got it from my reading of the serious newspapers, or from my half-understanding of Annan, or from what the BBC says.

Sir Alan Peacock:

First of all, for the record, may I point out that I think the Committee as a whole was very conscious of the fact that the Pilkington Report and the Annan Report had had a different perspective on these matters. In fact ... Lord Annan came and talked to the Committee, and emphasised (and this is my own account of what happened) why issues we faced required careful attention to the economics of broadcasting. And he said at the time that perhaps they had not paid enough attention to these issues. Annan said ... by the way, that we should pay due regard to the ethos of public service broadcasting; he was very insistent on that. But I would claim the Report does that, and does it to the full.

What one must remember also is that it all depends on what you think, in an economics education, are your views about human action. Because I was brought up in a completely different tradition in Scotland, of political economy, where, of course, everybody worships (as they should) Adam Smith, and ... *The Theory of Moral Sentiments* was just as important a book as *The Wealth of Nations;* in which you could say what we might call the welfare/utility function of individuals included concern for the welfare of others.[28] And ... if you look at sections in which we talk about the case for a public goods approach, we actually ... mention that one of the interesting aspects of broadcasting is the extent to which people would support broadcasting initiatives which are testing their understanding, in the course of which people may change their views about what is good for them, and secondly what they think is good for their children and possibly what is good for posterity. So I think to some extent sociology has penetrated, in at least one particular respect, what we have said in the Report. And we specifically said, as Adam Smith said, this is not a laissez-faire approach to the question at all. I think what we can say is that, in relation to Annan and Pilkington, there was a missing element in this which was, namely, the economics (or political economy) of broadcasting to which not sufficient attention had perhaps been paid. And also that this in fact is what Annan, in a very nice sort of way, was saying when he came to see us.

Sir David Nicholas:
... I don't think ITN made a submission, as a company. If I remember correctly, we were part of the Independent Television (ITV) system. So, even now, looking back on it, I don't think that Peacock did have much effect on news as such – which was of course our prime consideration – so I don't think we expected anything particularly. Looking back on it, I think I'm disappointed really that Peacock didn't give sufficient consideration to the role of news in broadcasting. ...

Conduct

Sir Alan Peacock:
I think the first thing to note is that the pressure to report in a year initially came from me and not from Leon, although he did say – and that's what he said in Parliament – he hoped the Committee would be able to report by the summer of '86. ... The terms of reference and the ultimate form of the Report, and my application of course affected the conduct of business.

The first thing we did was – I think this is quite interesting – we knew that the Committee couldn't meet until May because members had to be appointed ... so the secretary and I drafted the first chapter on 'Background' before the Committee met. ... I don't know if we sent it out in advance of the meeting or not, I can't remember that.

'Did you divide responsibility for different areas?' Well, not in any rigid sense. I think members of the Committee devised their own perceptions of how they could help. And I would say it took us some time to get to know one another and make an assessment of how much time they had to spare to make a contribution. In other words, you must dismiss from your minds any idea that the Chairman sat down and assigned duties to the various members. You just need to have met them to realise what difficulty that would have created for the Chairman to have laid down ... rigid ideas. Of course we all had clearly ... read and heard evidence from the broadcasting regulators and companies at home and abroad, and an account was given in tabular form of where we went and what we did in the Report. Of course not all members could attend all sessions for hearing evidence, but I think we had a fairly good turnout generally. I think there was no problem here.

Visits – the great thing about visits, I thought ... was we got to know each other very quickly that way. I think the expertise and experience of members was much more evident and pertinent when an attempt was made, largely by myself and Bob Eagle initially at least, to produce a coherent draft of the Report. ... Then of course we had to make decisions about recommendations. There we enter another sort of Ball Park.

Let me just say that, on Bob Eagle ... he was a necessary condition for the whole thing to take place at all. He was, I think – and I hope you would agree with me – he was superb. First of all he was a physicist and with expertise in this particular area of communication technology. He wrote an excellent appendix, which you may have seen, on the radio spectrum, and also a short one on electronic publishing. He was an expert summariser of evidence, and his first draft of expository chapters I think was exemplary. He not only reacted immediately to what the Committee asked him to do, but I think he anticipated our needs. ....

Jeremy Hardie:

This is not attributing great virtue or other things to Alan and to Sam, but it's true – they were the most important people on the Committee. Meaning that they were the ones that in certain senses set the tone, and I think the rest of us were less important partly because we put, in certain senses, less into it than those two did. And of course, Robert was key because he was the Secretary and was doing the drafting and so on.

.... The second thing is that, if you get all this stuff – and this is not particularly to do with the Peacock Committee but with the Monopolies Commission as well – quite a lot of it is terribly repetitive.

... Once you've got down to there, if you've read what might be the good ones, you've sort of got it. And then you go down here, and there is some sort of passing the time, going through the motions. You've asked for submissions from such-and-such, a listeners' organisation, and you read through it and you say, 'Oh yes, that's what they're saying. I know that.' So the reading is both impossible and actually perfectly practical.

Sir Alan Peacock:
Could I just add that Bob did a very good service here, because what he would do is draw a member's attention to what was available and they could pick and choose, and he provided of course a masterly summary ... of all the evidence.

Sir Samuel Brittan:
The point about the logistics is, as I think Jeremy has mentioned, the Chairman was announced, I think, in March, and the members of the Committee were not announced until May and I think they met in May. When we were there, when we first met, we found that Alan had already organised a secretariat, asked for a lot of the evidence, and none of us regarded that this was in any way a conspiracy. I was also doing a job of sorts at the time, not an executive job but a scribbling job, and I think that the attitude of all of us, even of Alastair Heatherington and Judith Chalmers, was relief that all the organisation had already been put in train, and we did not have to spend time discussing who the Assistant Secretary should be. I think Alastair, because of his knowledge, had one or two other ideas on whom we could take evidence from, but basically this was done by Alan and the Secretary, so we were all grateful for it!

One sceptical thought I want to have is about the quality of the oral evidence that we took. Jeremy spoke of how you can skim through written evidence quickly. It's difficult to do that with oral evidence. I don't know what the alternative is because Committees, even slightly unusual ones, are expected to talk to all the interest groups. But I've found that ... even though I hadn't read all the detailed literature, I knew roughly what the arguments were of all these bodies, and they did not come out with a single thing I hadn't heard before. ... Even supposed market research or empirical investigations really reiterated what they had said before. I really do wish I'd had the courage to do my own reading while they were giving evidence. I don't know what the alternative is ...

Sir Samuel Brittan:
.... The one session of all evidence which was interesting and which did influence us was towards the end, when the independent producers came over .... We hadn't been sufficiently aware – we knew roughly they existed but weren't sufficiently well informed – and they did say things which we hadn't thought of before, and they influenced our recommendations. But the mainline evidence was really a waste of time, a lot of it.

Sir Alan Peacock:
I really don't need to say anything about that. My only concern about the BBC ... was their attempts to influence our reception by ... broadcasting companies in other countries. I think most of the state

broadcasting systems which we visited had, I think, immediately asked the BBC, not us, for a briefing. ... They placed articles in the media journals I think certainly in Germany and in France, and I think in Italy, I suppose defending the licence fee. ....

The Head of Independent Broadcasting Authority (IBA)[29] and I had been at the same school ... although not at the same time; he's slightly older than I am. That meant that the ice was broken very, very quickly ... George Thomson,[30] yes. He even said that one of the things that had influenced his education was my father was one of the first broadcasters. ... Every time that we met he would mention this, which was rather nice. So I had no problem – and then of course we did meet Independent Television Contractors Association (ITCA) members as well.

I had no contact with any of the ministers. I'd never received any communications from any minister, from the Prime Minister downwards and not even an indication from any of their staff – 'The minister would like you to know this – that and this,' I think ... and I've offered at least one possible reason for this, namely, that nobody need pay any attention to the board unless they wanted to.

Sir Samuel Brittan:

One obvious thing. Because of my professional activities as well as personal relationships, I did have contacts with ministers, but I don't remember any discussion about the Peacock Committee or about broadcasting. Such conversations as I had were mostly afterwards .... Perhaps I was both the greatest cynic and the greatest idealist on the Committee, and these things often go together. I read this stuff on the advertising market's future. I held my peace on this. I was not very much in favour of advertising. ... I did think, in retrospect, after the Committee had reported, there was one piece of investigation we could have made, and that is 'How much of a dis-utility advertising is' – how much advertising detracts from the enjoyment of viewers. ...

Jeremy Hardie:

If the question is 'What reasons persuaded you to reject advertising on the BBC,' well one answer obviously is 'read the Report' – there are the reasons. The Report is rather carefully written ..... I think if I was just to sort of say informally what I think was going on, I think the econometric forecasting was important, not actually because it showed a decline in advertising, but because it presented you very firmly in the face with the fact that if the BBC was going to take advertising, and if that was going to be of a quantum sufficient to replace the licence fee, then something very substantial was going to happen to the players in this market. ... there would be a terrible financial problem which would fall on somebody. ... this would change the whole thing. So you then had to go on to the big questions, which are 'What's all this for, anyway?' ... And I was quite surprised, it really became a non-question very, very early on. And I don't mean by that we had decided to make a recommendation of the following kind, or that the arguments were convincing, all that sort of stuff. As a matter of fact, we moved off it very, very fast – and I think that was important, and we got on to what you might call 'the real stuff'.

Sir Alan Peacock:

Could I just say something? I think that ... certainly in the press and I think elsewhere it was assumed, that I was the villain of the piece in this, and was going to defend advertising on the BBC, ... but I wrote a memorandum deliberately, which I have here, 'Questions raised by financing options' – ... in which I ... tried to set out ... that whatever conclusions we reached about sources of revenue, diversity and intensity of consumer choice could only find expression in paying directly for programmes. But that was not something which the technology enabled one to do at that particular moment, and there were other problems about this. One possibility was that the BBC should finance 50 per cent of the licence fee to allow for the public service. ... I thought these arguments had to be presented, but as far as I was concerned, I certainly didn't stand out for anything other than the conclusions which we came to.

Sir Samuel Brittan:

I have to make one confession; that, before the first meeting, I think before I even received your memorandum, I decided that ... I was not going to make an issue of advertising, and I would go along with the probable majority against advertising on the Committee, because I was interested in establishing a broadcasting market and I had this hobby horse about censorship ... in the guise of quality control, and I just thought that if we recommended advertising it would have discredited the Committee's findings even more than they have been already by people like the people in this room.

I also wanted to try to do my little bit to disabuse the idea that market economics was the same as business interests. I just thought that I would leave advertising aside and concentrate on other issues and as other members of the Committee came, perhaps for different reasons, to this conclusion, I just thought I'd be dormant. I don't say necessarily that I would go to the stake to prevent five minutes of advertising once a week on the BBC.

Jeremy Hardie:
I think it was interesting that, as far as I remember, what you might call 'the advertising agency argument' – which was advertising is very expensive and the reason it's very expensive is because it's artificially constrained. I think we didn't pay any attention to that at all, as far as I can remember. Which is odd, because, if you think in terms of market economics ... the supply of advertising space is a commodity. Why isn't it properly provided through a more competitive system? ... I think that it may be because, deep down, some of us were quite snooty about advertising. We wouldn't actually think about advertising as being a commodity which ought to be supplied in that way.

Peter Jay:
Were you tempering the line for the newspapers?

Sir Alan Peacock:
No, I don't think so at all – no tempering at all. Of course, I'd forgotten I had a lunch with the newspaper people, yes, and they went hammer and tongs, of course, about the effect. ... Perhaps we should have paid more attention to the question. ... There was some evidence about this, but I don't think that we were concerned about this at all. ... Sam should answer this because he would have been much more personally affected than I might have been, if there had been something in the Report which ... was to the detriment of the newspapers. ...

Economists talk about consumer sovereignty in the same way as Adam Smith, as a kind of useful operational device to talk about policy. That's to say, admitting it's a value judgement ... a consensual judgement that can't be proved scientifically to be better than any other policy, but it has the strength of general acceptance. But I think the point that we were trying to make about this is that we weren't thinking in terms of very narrow sort of abstract static models of markets. We were thinking in terms of a situation where, through innovation and change and competition, the whole structure of the economy might change. ... So ... the idea of consumer sovereignty is not some narrow idea of given tastes ... that people don't change and their tastes don't change. It also is, in other words ... a value judgement quite distinct from the interests of the consumer. And of course I think one of the problems is that many broadcasting pundits believe that it should not be decided by consumers themselves – 'we know what's good.'....

As I've said, it's a value judgement which economists not only regard as an operational concept and it doesn't necessarily mean ... that the consumers can simply say 'We know exactly what we want without further information about what choices we want to make.' And I think we bring that out very strongly in the Report. What I'm saying in short is that the crude idea that commercialisation of broadcasting is what we are supporting, and that the consumer just takes what's given now from a set of broadcasting stations, which provide advertising, is an insult, I think, to those who think about how they spend their money and what they believe in as far as investment in, say, educating themselves and their children is concerned, which will affect the way in which their tastes change.

Sir Samuel Brittan:

What is really wrong with Reith[31] is not perhaps his attitude to the public, but the belief there are people like himself who know better.

Sir Alan Peacock:

That's right – that's the problem.

Sir Samuel Brittan:

By all means, have support for the arts – this is the place to discuss 'The Arts Council of the Air' – but in the end you can drag me to the Caravaggio exhibition; you can't necessarily make me like it ... I am going to it and maybe I'll learn something about his appeal. It seems to me he belongs in the same category as Lucien Freud and Bacon. ...

This is a bit of a digression. But could I say something about economics, because some of you may find out that there are different sorts of economics. ... In the last few years – in the 90s and after – the BBC has mobilised a whole lot of economists, led by Andrew Graham of Oxford, who have taken some arguments about public goods but they've blown them right up. ... They made a great fuss about ... merit goods ..... But you'll find a lot of these people just say that we're wrong and the broadcasting market is different from other markets .... Some people are libertarian by instinct and therefore are quite happy with consumer sovereignty, and there are other people (sorry to keep on mentioning Oxford) who are educated as economists but hate this presumption in favour of consumer sovereignty, and they will find one argument after another to go against it. ...

Peter Jay:

Before I come to Jeremy, Samuel would you just say a couple of sentences about what I think is the important and helpful distinction between the utilitarian sort of Marshallian arguments for consumer sovereignty, and the libertarian or Hayeckian arguments for consumer sovereignty, because there is a pretty fundamental difference, and they tend to get lumped together rather unsuitably.

Sir Samuel Brittan:

Yes, Alfred Marshall[32] as a person had far broader and more interesting ideas on the mainsprings of progress and human conduct than he put into his models, because he said economics ought to be like biology. ... but in fact the only way he could develop it was by analogy with mechanics. But the basic difference is (I think it's partly pedagogical) that elementary economic textbooks start with the idea of given consumer wants, then you can move from utility to demand, then you put in a supply curve and you can examine first year students.

But the Hayeckian's (not only the Hayeckian, but quite a lot of other people) have seen ... the economy in rather different ways, as a sort of trial and experiment system in which different ideas are put to people. Innovations are tried, some are accepted and some are not. It ... certainly is a caricature to think that we are born with certain tastes which some megalith like the so-called market supplies. But to be fair, I don't think anybody in what I might call the pedagogical mainstream, thinks that either; they just regard it as a good way of introducing the subject, and perhaps a good way of bringing in econometric research. And all they have got against ... Hayeck and these so-called Austrians, is that they use too many words and not enough mathematics or charts; although Schumpter[33] in fact tried to be mathematical and really failed. To his own disappointment he was remembered more for his words than for his mathematical analysis.

Peter Jay:

Well I think the basic difference between people who see markets as a way of achieving happiness and a form of efficiency on the one hand, and those who see it as a way of achieving a degree of freedom and choice and experimentation on the other is an important one. Jeremy.

Jeremy Hardie:

Again, there are several levels at which you can answer that. Alan is quite right, that the concept of consumer sovereignty comes from bog-standard economics – that's one answer. The other thing, that you have said Peter, is that the notion of consumer sovereignty and what publishing was like – meaning, above all, book publishing – and the analogies, or not, between that and television was, I think, are a very, very important way of getting the consumer sovereignty debate into what you might call operational shape for discussion. Your very simple question, 'Why shouldn't it, in the future, given changes in technology, be like book publishing?' ... We all agree that book publishing is something which is for the public good, achieves high ideals and so on. Why shouldn't it be like that? I think a lot of the debate just straightforwardly came from what you were saying. And it wasn't original, in the sense that you were using conventional tools but it was a very striking way of putting it, and I think it was around in the air enough to inform the way that the Peacock Committee, and so on, were thinking about things.

The other thing I would say is – again I don't want to say Mrs Thatcher influenced the Committee. It was a decade during which notions of freedom, where people were falling out of love with the idea that the state could run things well, and were rather falling in love with the idea that markets were a good thing. ...

... It is quite right that what is unattractive about the Reithian practice is that Lord Reith knows better than I do what I want. When the Peacock Committee recommends an Arts Council of the Air – and I was on the Arts Council – that it's run by people like me, who say on the whole what they ought to have is the ballet. It's Reith really.

... Let me put it absolutely straightforwardly. The really wonderful thing about economics when market economics ... is applicable, is that the question of value is ducked. That is to say it is an idea about choice, and what you say to people is, here we have, we've got a system. Choose what you want, and if bananas sell for more than coffee, it's because people value bananas more than coffee. And that's just a private thing that they've all decided. And as soon as you get outside that into all these other areas, the notion of 'value' becomes something you've got to decide about. And you've got to decide about it not by saying 'I want bananas rather than coffee,', but by saying, 'I think ballet is more important than street dancing.' And then you're paternalistic, and we have no way of getting out of that; we have no sensible way of talking about that.

Peter Jay:

Paternalism punctuated by the rotation of the arts figures.

Jeremy Hardie:

You change the fathers and you change the fashions and you change the hunches and you change the tastes and all that sort of thing. But it's still people sitting in a room, in those days in Piccadilly, saying 'I think – more money for theatre'.

Sir Alan Peacock:

I think that the problem was the old question of what you do about a scarce resource in which if you don't have some control, you have over-use. The radio spectrum ... it's like the over-fishing problem; the same kind of problem that you have over the fact that you can't, or it's very difficult to assign property to areas of the sea. You get round this one by all kinds of devices, like territorial limits accepted by negotiation, but the way they try to do this ... to stop over-fishing, is by hitting the poor fisherman. What happens is, therefore, ... that you have a radio spectrum and it is scarce. It's partly of course an artificial scarcity created by the Government having grabbed a large part of it initially, ostensibly for defence purposes. The interesting initial assumption, which of course Coase questions, is why should it be assumed that governments owned the spectrum in the first place?

Well, you have a public goods problem here, so you have to have some means by which you allocate this. I remember George Thomson saying, 'The way we do this is by a sort of rather informal beauty competition, and we know the people we can trust and all the rest of it, and we do the best we can. We award the franchises in this way.' But he said, 'I'm sure there are all kinds of objections to this, and your Committee no doubt will be looking at the possibility of some kind of other way of doing this.' All one thought of was, well, auctioning is a well-known device for allocating scarce resources, which confers, at least for a limited time, exclusive use to the winner. ... This might be a useful way, of course, as Mr Brown[34] has found, of obtaining some income which you might perhaps use for the purposes of an Arts Council of the Air, for example. Some kind of hypothecation which the Treasury of course hates, as we all know. And also it seemed that a fair way of doing this was to simply say it is just for a limited period of time, and companies could bid or companies could be formed to bid for this subject to a quality threshold – which was of course to deal with the problem of public service broadcasting obligations. And I invented a scheme, which in fact was developed after the Committee. But there were written objections from Jeremy, and Judith Chalmers and Alastair Heatherington to this particular thing, for reasons which I thoroughly respect, but we didn't think we wanted to make a great issue of it and so we put in recommendation and then a note of dissent – quite rightly – that there were three members of the Committee who didn't think this was a good idea. But at least we raised the issue. .... One thing where we ought to make ... clear there are differences, and what those differences are. Jeremy, I know, has got it very clear in his mind what they were, and that this didn't seem to be a suitable way of what was dealing with an obvious problem. ... And a problem which, of course, varied in intensity depending on what part of the spectrum was necessary, ... the efficiency of its use, and whether there'd be any differences in the amount the government was willing to offer for the purposes of broadcasting transmission.

Jeremy Hardie:

The trouble about the auction is, it is designed to take away the super-profits from ... the bidder. The bidder is therefore in the position to be much, much less likely to have what I might call 'spare money', and the business of enforcing the contract to do public service broadcasting is much, much harder, and that contract in itself is a vague contract. Let's say it's poorly specified, and very difficult to enforce, and those difficulties are substantially increased if you take away the super-profits.

Peter Jay:

Without claiming any higher authority in the matter, my recollection is that I did play a role in this particular point in, as I would call it, injecting this suggestion, through Samuel, in a document in which we to some extent worked on together, and the motive was quite clear – namely that, if there is value in a public opportunity, it belongs to the society, and if it is then allocated by public authority to private interests without cost, that quite dreadfully robs the public. ... You didn't have to auction the access to the spectrum ... you just auctioned the existing contract, which would have the consequence, under normal market forces rules, of capturing for the public the value that was the public's and leaving with the franchise winner the opportunity for which he had bid at the price he was prepared to pay. And that, it seemed to me, remedied completely what I regarded as a very major wrong – namely, that the public was being robbed of the value of the franchises which properly belonged to them. And in my opinion now, contrary to the general consensus, this exercise, far from having been a failure or a disaster or a muddle or anything else, was a great success. The Treasury got a large amount of money, which thereby relieves the taxpayer of raising that money in other forms. That certainly was the thinking that was going through my mind at the time, and it overlaps evidently with what you and Alan said. But it has different nuances, and it had this very strong, if you like, moralistic premise about the public's right not to be robbed of what belonged to them. Sam.

Sir Samuel Brittan:

... The way to appropriate for the public its monopoly rent, is to have some kind of auction. Now the auction theory is very, very difficult, and there are people in the LSE[35] who do nothing else. So it's possible – I'm just expressing a view on this – that the auction was not ideal, I don't know. But I think this principle was demonstrated to a much wider public with the auction of mobile telephones. ..... There is another thing I wanted to say. Speaking purely for myself and only for myself. I was very conscious of the political background to it and I was very political (with a small 'p' not a large 'p') and of course I knew about these various rows going on, but it was at this point that I told some BBC people informally they didn't know who their friends were.

I thought of the indexed licence fee at a very early stage, probably before I even confessed to Alan ... about it. When you had all these rows between the Government and the BBC, I reflected. ..... I really thought then that the idea of a national broadcasting corporation whose every deed and every saying was a matter for the Cabinet and for high political talk – I thought this ... belonged to '1984' and it belonged to a different world altogether.

I believed in a broadcasting market for which subscribers could pay directly; I thought it was a long way off. My immediate objective was how to depoliticise relations between the Government and the BBC. .... How could you depoliticise it? The best way was to have indexation. ... An indexed licence fee was the best way to depoliticise the BBC, because as long as that system was in force it didn't have to be renewed every five years. It would be not impossible, but more difficult, for the Prime Minister every time he or she got irritated to threaten the BBC with the licence fee. It wasn't a perfect system but it was a step towards depoliticisation and that was what I cared about much more than whether people watched one soap rather than another.

The view from the BBC

Alwyn Roberts:
.... I can't however refrain from quoting one little snippet. Many years ago another Peacock, the novelist Thomas Love, prefaced his novel Headlong Hall with a quotation from Swift:

All philosophers who find
Some favourite system to their mind,
In every point to make it fit
Will force all nature to submit.

I have the same kind of feeling about consumer sovereignty.

The BBC, it has been pointed out, was in a period of pretty desperate unpopularity particularly from Government where for a number of years issues had been raised which brought the BBC into conflict on issues of perceived partiality. Starting from Carrickmuir, which was my first meeting as a governor, it went on and involved things like the Falklands War, the Miners' Strike, the handling of the Bobby Sands[36] case – all these were fairly constant events during that period. At the same time there was a press campaign, particularly in The Times, and it seemed to some of us as if the Peacock Committee was yet another episode in this hostility. Nobody – and I wish to make this absolutely clear – nobody believed that the Peacock Committee was a 'fix'. The reputation of its members was such that it simply wouldn't wash. On the other hand, it did seem that there was a chance at least that a Committee of this composition would come from its own convictions and its own principles to an answer which would not be unpleasing to Government, and which the BBC might in fact rue.

The earlier thoughts about a full switch to advertising were, very quickly I think, dismissed. It was quite clear within the BBC and common sense that the whole burden of the broadcasting systems of this country could not be borne by the advertising industry. There was a fear that some part might be so funded. That, for example, the ... licence fee existing at that point might be frozen and that any progress beyond that point would have to come from partial advertisements on some of the channels. The fear in that case of course was that as inflation – which in those years was much higher than it now is – took its toll, then the percentage deriving from advertisements was inevitably going to increase, as has been the case in other systems: in New Zealand and (so I was told) in Canada as well.

I think some people within the BBC, faced with those possibilities, considered at least, subscription. I must confess that I was a total heretic on this, and still am. I think subscription is more of a threat to any public system of broadcasting than any advertisement campaign. It becomes 'narrowcasting'; you pay your entrance fee, you join the club. Now I know there are arguments in favour of this; there are other points on which I feel distinctly unhappy about it.

From the standpoint of the Governors, we were given occasional reports, usually at the Board meeting and usually from Wenham, as to how things were going and what the gossip was down in the forum. In Wales, we were asked to produce a report and of course in Wales there were some aspects which made the threat of advertising, as we perceived it, particularly dangerous. Sianel Pedwar Cymru (S4C) had just been created and was totally dependent on Government monies, at that time top-sliced from the levy on the IBA companies and passed on. We had doubts; we had wondered how this kind of system would ever fit into an advertisement or indeed a sponsorship-driven, subscription-driven type of broadcasting economy. It seemed to us that if you were talking of things like public service, or a Welsh language broadcasting system, then it had to be publicly funded as a matter of public service. So we did, I think, prepare a memorandum but the whole approach in the BBC at the time was to present a centralised, unified document. ... When the Report was received there was, I think, a huge sigh of relief. The immediate threat was seen to have passed; there was a mood, I think of not self-congratulation but appreciation for the way in which the Committee had conducted its affairs, and even though the answer which it seemed to be aiming at in the long term – namely a subscription service – seemed to some of us extremely dangerous, nevertheless the immediate response was this sigh of relief.

I was concerned about some of the definitions of public service broadcasting and the basis on which they were drawn. I seem to recollect that part of the Report refers to 'those services, which a person is not prepared to pay for as a customer, but which as a citizen he approves of' – and there is a list. I wondered, for example, what the harassed single mother of yelling twins in a tower block would think of that particular list. I think public service to her might mean a much better cartoon service.

The public perception became fairly selective, and I still believe that attempts to define public service broadcasting by category of programme is a dangerous one, and that it is very difficult to sustain. Even to give it objectivity – who, after all, draws up that list of types of programmes? Is that in itself not a Reithian activity? So you don't escape the public service broadcasting issue by categorising programmes. I think there is a different way and I haven't really developed it nor would I think of expounding it now other than to say that it seems to me that public service broadcasting implies a particularly direct relationship between broadcaster and audience where other considerations do not intervene or become the primary thing.

Tom O'Malley:

Thank you very much. I just want to ask Alwyn one question that puzzles me. How frequently ... was this discussed at the level of the Board of Governors, and in what kind of tone? Because we know this is a period when ... the relationship between Alasdair Milne and the Board was fractious, to put it mildly.

Alwyn Roberts:

What I have to say is partial in two senses. It depends on a memory which is by no means faultless, and it is partial also in the sense that I have a standpoint, I was committed to the BBC's cause.

It was I think frequently reported to Governors' meetings as a matter of – a progress report, really. Certainly the evidence and the commissioned material was made known to governors, but they didn't, I think, in any sense direct the inquiry; that was done by Milne and his group. There was no great argument within the Board as to the viewpoint that should be put forward, nor was there as I recollect on this issue ... any cause of friction between the lay members of the Board and the Director General.

Influence and closing thoughts

Professor Steven Barnett:
I can sketch out what I think are five key legacies of the Peacock Committee's report.

First, there is the question of whether the BBC should be funded by advertising. I think that what Peacock did is essentially to make it absolutely clear that advertising was a non-runner. And since 1986 advertising for the BBC has never been taken seriously ... I think the rejection, the intellectual rejection of advertising on the BBC, has actually been a very important legacy of Peacock which is sustained to the present day.

The second legacy is that it showed how the free market/consumer sovereignty ideologies and arguments can be applied to the broadcasting industry, and others have made this same point. I think that is quite important. Maybe if the Peacock Report hadn't done it, others would because that was the political environment of the time. But I doubt that it would have been done with quite the same intellectual rigor. What it didn't do was engage with the notion, the philosophy, the idea, the concept of public service broadcasting or the life-enhancing contribution that broadcasting can potentially make to people's lives. I don't think the Report engaged in the way that Annan and Pilkington and their predecessors had before with the cultural and democratic contributions that broadcasting can make to the life of the country. I have read the current spate of reports, in particular from Ofcom and its Public Service Broadcasting Review, and what I see isn't a one-sided, consumer-dominated piece of work, but actually a much more sophisticated synthesis of Annan and Peacock. What I think Ofcom has managed to do is to take a very important step in synthesising the intellectual robustness of the Peacock arguments on consumer sovereignty with a much more sophisticated approach to arguments about public service broadcasting, which they call 'consumer citizen arguments', and to say 'here are a number of things which we need to address. We do not believe in the market gap theory of public service broadcasting, but nor do we believe that we need a single, dominant public broadcaster who can define for itself what public service broadcasting is all about.' ...

The third legacy is that the whole idea of a PSBC, the Public Service Broadcasting Council, was put on the agenda for the first time. This was the beginnings of 'the market gap theory' .... I think that it was the first intellectually respectable argument around the whole notion of a publicly funded body that would 'fill in the gaps' left by a wholly commercialised system, such as arts programmes, serious current affairs and so on. The same idea has materialised since then in different forms and with different acronyms, but the essential concept of an 'Arts Council of the Airwaves' actually began with Peacock.

The fourth, and I think the most important legacy, that what the Peacock Committee really did in terms of television output is to turn commercial broadcasting upside down, in a way that was both damaging and enhancing to the broadcasting ecology. It did this in three main ways, two damaging and one I think enhancing. The auction of ITV licences, which took money out of programming and gave it to the Treasury – although I entirely understand the economic intellectual justification for it – I think in programming terms was a travesty, and I think to some extent we still see today some of the problems that emerged out of stripping commercial broadcasting of some of the money that was going into programming. Yes, some of ITV's revenue was going into the hands of greedy and lazy trade unionists who were indulging in restrictive practices and making sometimes outrageous demands from their employers partly because they could see the money flooding in. But they could have been dealt with through trade union laws, not through auctioning of ITV licences.

The second damaging impact on actual programmes was the separation of Channel Four from ITV. I think the fact that we had a funding system within Channel Four that allowed it the luxury of not having to compete for revenue, but did compete for audiences within a very tight public service remit, was of benefit both to audiences as consumers in that it offered more genuine choice, and to audiences as citizens in that it made a distinct cultural and democratic contribution (like Channel Four News). The separation may have been good for advertisers – I still think that's unproven – but I think the impact on programming was unfortunate and I think again the fact that Channel Four today is not being driven by the same kind of innovation as it was at the very beginning is in some respects due to that separation.

The enhancing impact on programming was the independent quota, set at 25 per cent in the Broadcasting Act, which I think certainly encouraged a new wave of creative independents, building on the creation of Channel Four in 1982, who were given access to the broadcasters for the first time. It also of course contained the roots of Producer Choice which revolutionised the internal structure of the BBC in the early nineties. If it hadn't been for that independent quota, and if it hadn't been for the Peacock Committee, we would not have Producer Choice at the BBC. As soon as you introduce the 25 per cent quota, the BBC had to have a means of comparing its internal accounting procedures with what things cost outside. This was tied incidentally, to the impact of new technology and new wave of desktop computers. But Producer Choice and internal accounting procedures – which I don't think were particularly a bad thing for the BBC – were all owing to the Peacock Report.

The fifth legacy is that I think we ended up with a humbler and more democratic BBC which suddenly realised that actually telling Committees of inquiry that they 'knew what was best and why don't you go away and do something else' is not the best way to approach them. But that's slightly facetious.

In summary, I think what the Committee did was to put the economistic arguments with such intellectual rigor that actually they've never been bettered. But in doing so, and by not balancing them as Annan and Pilkington had done with cultural arguments, they produced a blueprint for change in the commercial sector which ended up doing fundamental damage to Britain's broadcasting ecology. The legacy of that damage is still with us today.

Sir David Nicholas:

What I am going to talk about is the experience of being on the downstream side of all this. It was the ITV Council – that is to say, the fifteen managing directors of the companies who were responsible for dealings with Peacock and other major industry bodies of that kind. What I am going to tell you is how we in ITN were really caught in a kind of cross fire in the aftermath of all this – and I really mean crossfire, coming in from all kinds of directions. I'd like to tell you an anecdote about our World Service, if I may just digress for a second. We read in the papers – in the *Sunday Times* – that the BBC was approaching the Foreign Office for a thumping amount of money to produce a television version of the Bush House World Service. Now we were already providing this service to the ITV satellite feed to northern Europe for a tiny sum of money, and the implication was that if the BBC got their thumping money from the government, that would put us out of business. So we wrote to the Foreign Office and said, look we don't think that taxpayers' money should be used at all for this service but if it is, then it should be open for us to tender. We could hear the intake of breath from the Foreign Office as far away as we were in Wells Street. They'd never heard of our World Service, probably never heard of ITN. So we invited Mrs Thatcher to dinner in ITN, and she came along one night. Now I ought to tell you that the World Service, which was presented by John Suchet, was done from a Portakabin which had been lifted on a crane in Wells Street on top of the flat roof of our main studio. So, Mrs Thatcher came to dinner and we took her into see the broadcast. There was a howling gale blowing and she had to walk across a sort of perilous gantry to get to the Portakabin and she had to hold her skirts down like this because the wind was blowing, and we shuffled her in. There was hardly any room; I couldn't go in, it was just Mrs Thatcher in the Portakabin. So she came away very impressed to see how we were producing our world news. A few weeks later there was a reception in Downing Street for some visiting dignitary and I went along there and as I came along the line, Mrs Thatcher said, 'You've heard the news, have you?' I said, 'No, Prime Minister, what's that?' She said, 'We've told the BBC they're not going to get the money.' Later that year the Director General of the BBC, in a speech at the Cambridge RTS,[37] said that they had been thwarted in their plans for, at that stage, their World Service because they had been 'stabbed in the back' – and he glared at me as he said that.

As the Government was preparing legislation in the post-Peacock period, the ITV companies were invited to make separate submissions to the Home Office. Looking back on it, with the prospect of the licence auction looming, I suppose in a sense ITV suffered a corporate nervous breakdown. I remember the first shock I had was this. One of my colleagues got a 'leak,' got a tip – actually it came from Bernard Ingham's office, the press secretary to Mrs Thatcher. Bernard and I had been on *The Yorkshire Post* together. We learned that the first draft White Paper[38] had nothing at all in it about the need for news. There was no mention of 'must carry'. If you don't want news, you needn't have news. Now, of course, that was a fairly Hiroshima-style bomb on my desk. There were four government offices involved in that phase of preparing for the legislation. There was the DTI, there was the Treasury, there was the Home Office, and of course, eventually, the Prime Minister's office. So we went to work and we made it plain to Mrs Thatcher with a paper and a meeting that we thought that the whole underlying philosophy was a matter of choice, but if you don't have to have news – and there would have been those among ITV companies who would have preferred a sort of rip and read or whatever, then you were reverting to the pre-1955 situation in which there was only one national news network, that is, the BBC. Well I suppose the definition of a split second would be the time it took Mrs Thatcher to cotton onto that. We were told later, by the way, that the paper advancing this case was put in her box to read when she flew to Balmoral for the annual meeting with the Queen. Then lobbying began in a big way. I think, from memory, two of the ITV companies in their submissions to the Home Office had indicated that

they would like to be free to take their news from sources other than
ITN – so I didn't exactly feel that I had the All Blacks' pack behind
me on this occasion. We were now faced with a very serious position
indeed. Brian Griffiths[39] was helpful in this way as well. Eventually
Mrs Thatcher brought this matter of the 'must carry' dimension back
into play. And the next sort of lobbying we had to do was, at that stage
or later on. Mr Mellor[40] was the minister midwifing the Bill through
Parliament, and we lobbied very hard to get two words into the Act:
the word 'quality' news, so there should be a requirement not just
for news, but quality news. That we felt – looking back on it, it seems
perhaps a little academic – but to us it seemed the best safeguard we
could have, having the words 'adequately financed and resourced',
and also the words 'prime time'.

Tony Lennon:

I'm meant to be dealing with two questions really. What did the
unions think about the Peacock Committee? What did they do about
it and, implicitly, what did they think about anything that happened
next? The tone of the era as far as the trades unions were concerned
was set. Our analysis from the announcement of the Committee was
that this was BBC-bashing of the worst possible order. The Committee
was an a priori apparatus which was going to do something dread-
ful to the BBC, and apart from shouting, there probably wasn't a lot
immediately we could do about it. I think, again talking about the
'80s, what Thatcher was doing was unpicking the post-War compact.
She'd already unpicked us quite a lot, as trades unions, with new
legislation and the Miners' Strike and the rest of it. And in a sense it
was only natural she would move on to unpick something like the
BBC, which I felt was very much part of that social democratic, rather
presumptuous order of things. The Beeb was part of the firmament in
the way that organised labour had to be part of the firmament. ... We
didn't want any privatisation of the BBC, which we knew was on the
agenda, because privatisation was beginning to happen throughout
the economy and it was a bad thing as far as we were concerned. We
did not want an independent quota of any sort whatsoever because
for us, at that stage, the independent sector actually was a ragbag of
little cottage industries where they expected people to work for nothing. They had a terribly disorganised approach in many cases and
certainly were never going to enter, we thought, a proper agreement
with the trade unions to set standards and terms and conditions. So
we didn't want an independent quota. We certainly didn't want the
auction of ITV franchises, because again, we predicted at the time the

sort of damage that this would do in our terms to the ITV network. So for all those reasons we did have a position on Peacock, and we were mostly against.

The Unions were in turmoil because we were going through mergers. We historically had very blunt instruments in terms of intervention. We knew how to deal with the employers and the blunt instrument was if you want to intervene, you have a strike. We thought we knew how to intervene with government, and what you do there is, you have a lobby in Parliament and you go and see the minister. How to deal with these sorts of semi-Parliamentary things like this ad-hoc Committee? Actually I don't think we had a clue how to do it, to be perfectly frank. We had a political problem, which was the '80s were still relatively early days in the development of sophisticated lobbying techniques within the British body politic and frankly, if anybody in the union had suggested why don't we really get organised and do some proper professional lobbying, they'd have been strung up, actually. It was just a complete anathema. There was something dirty about all this professional lobbying. It took us five years actually, to get our heads around the concept and not engage professionals but second one of our staff to parliament during the Broadcasting Act progress. Even that was a bit uncomfortable for some people and it took a full ten years after Peacock before we'd dirty our hands by hiring professional lobbyists, in 1996 when the BBC was trying to privatise its transmitter network. That was the first time we'd ever used professional lobbyists to get the message across.

So in terms of what we did – well, we made a submission. We did whatever bit of lobbying we could in a slightly disorganised and amateur way and most importantly, we went and moaned to labour about it. They'd listen very patiently, all through. Norman Buchan, Mark Fisher, Ann Clwyd, Mo Mowlem[41] – the sympathy was absolutely wonderful. Actually I look back and I think, God what were we doing! Because we were basically moaning to a Party that had lost two elections by this point, was going to lose another two and was up against the most ferocious numerical majority on the other side and were actually not in a very good position to leverage our attitudes. But that's what we did – we went and moaned to Labour, and I think that was probably a key part of our strategy in dealing with Peacock. The last thing I will say about the period, and this partly explains why there was not so much noise from the unions during the Peacock process, there was in the Labour movement at the time a very strong sense, especially among the more senior people that – 'Look, lads' (if I can be sexist, and that's how they used to talk) 'Look, lads, the trick here lads is, you keep your head down in the trench and then when Labour come back, we'll get out of the trench and we'll wind it all back, it'll all come good,' you see.

I've re-read the Report – not every single paragraph – and it struck me several years on there are things missing, some of which jar a bit. They are in some cases things that you could never have predicted. What's missing? I don't think that the impending arrival of the 24/7 culture in all kinds of services was taken into account. We had the proposal that the dark hours of transmitters should be sold off commercially. Now if anyone had anticipated that in about seven or eight years time we'll have a society where people expect to see a picture at any hour of day or night, that proposal would never have been in there, let's be honest. I doubt that anybody at the time fully predicted the extent to which new digital technology was gong to turn the industry and our culture on its head.

Now, I'm dealing with the question, what really is the long-term legacy of Peacock? My way of approaching it is, what might have happened if Peacock hadn't happened – right? Coming from an engineering background, I think that three technologies overtook quite a lot of the conceptual material that was in the Peacock Report. And they are Hypertext Transfer Protocol (HTTP), the MPEG compression system that's given us the explosion of band width and, arguably, an end to band width scarcity; and direct, digital video broadcasting, sub terrestrial (DVBT). They were all nascent around the time of the Peacock Report, but there's absolutely no reason why the Peacock Committee or anyone else outside the academic community should have known about them or needed to know abut them, at that stage. But actually when I look back at the BBC's response to these technologies, what the Peacock Report did was to give the BBC sufficient funding over a critical period to position itself over almost irremovably in the firmament of web publishing and digital broadcasting. Because by the time the BBC was next under scrutiny in '96 Charter renewal, it had already set out its stall in both those key arenas of development. Developments that really I don't think could have been predicted in their scale and scope in 1986 whatsoever.

And it's quite interesting how it happened – and this is where John Birt[42] gets a tribute. The BBC's web activity has one of these weird and cranky histories that could only happen in a place like the BBC. There was a transmitter specialist at BBC Research Department in Kingswood Warren in Surrey. He happened to be a bit of a computer geek and, completely without any permission at all, started 'tinkering' as they were allowed to at the BBC Research Department, 'tinkering' with the

Internet. In the process, he was the guy who actually registered the BBC's Internet web address in about 1992 – 93. Now this was kind of light years ahead of what a lot of other people were doing. ... The BBC got its foot in through the door; the real driver of that was John Birt's position on platforms. He had this pointy-head type phrase, which was 'The BBC is platform neutral' – in other words, if there's a way of publishing it, we'll put it there. Now, *mea culpa*, to a lot of us union people this was not just a revolutionary idea, it was wrong, it was completely counter-intuitive. You don't run a newspaper on the basis that you hand out free copies to anybody else who wants to put it inside theirs and increase the value of their offering. It seemed totally counter-intuitive. Until we eventually got our heads round the true meaning of the multichannel society. Looking back, we realise that we didn't get it for about three years and in fact the BBC, much derided for concentrating on blue-sky stuff that no-one's got yet while on the home front audiences on BBC One are falling, actually had spotted a trend that a lot of us in the industry hadn't taken seriously enough. That is even truer of the BBC's web presence. So where did it put the BBC ten years after the Peacock Report? The money that Peacock willed to the BBC, indirectly, by ruling out advertising and sticking with the licence fee, coupled with the buoyancy of better policing of evasion and the growth in households, and the tail end of people switching to colour from mono, actually gave it a period of continued buoyant growth which enabled it to invest big-time in those two key areas. I think that by the time 1996 came round, had the BBC not had a foot in those activities, I suspect there would have been a big argument as to whether or not it should be given money to go and do it. The reality was, it had already received the money and had already spent it at a time when no one else had really spotted the long-term implications of those technologies. So it was well done to the BBC over that crucial period in the nineties on the back of money that was willed to it by the Peacock Committee. But I can't blame the Peacock Committee for not seeing any of that stuff coming up, because a lot of us didn't.

Closing thoughts from Professor Sir Alan Peacock

If you read the Report, perhaps we didn't stress enough that when it came to the question of public service broadcasting, that we saw this as something which should preferably be financed from inside the system, and that one of the most important ways of doing it might be to use the proceeds of the franchise auctions in order to finance public service broadcasting, which of course would help with the finances and of course be a better way of dealing with the issue of inducing the independent sector to continue doing the kind of things which public service broadcasting should include. Perhaps we didn't stress that enough. ...

The licence fee should be used to finance public service broadcasting and be open to bids for this, for the independent sector as well as the BBC. So you wouldn't 'ghetto-ise', to use a horrible word, the cultural contribution which broadcasting is supposed to make continuously to a British society. Now these ideas are floating around and they are taken quite seriously by Ofcom and other people. If one reads some of the Ofcom material, you will find that they have been thrown in the pot.

... But as I say, the logical extension of that could be that in fact the licence fee could be the source of this, and that in time, the BBC should be looking for other sources of revenue. Now I don't want to go into how that might be done. I've written enough about it and that can be read about, but it raises the very interesting question in the long run of whether you shouldn't disestablish the BBC rather like you disestablish the church. Anybody who has anything to do with the BBC over a long period of time, as I have, must note that it has all the characteristics of a church. It sees its position vis a vis the government in the same way as the Church of England. ... I place considerable weight upon professional reputation. I want to feel that peer group assessment is favourable. One of the things I was very much concerned about in the writing of the Report was that this would be something which would be accepted, if critically, by fellow economists in the widest sense and we would see it as representing a respectable analysis and where if the empirical work was faulty or at least imperfect, that at least we would admit this and say what we knew and what we didn't know. That is the first thing. It's not for me to say whether that object was achieved, but I think it was rather important in my mind.

... The second thing that I think that I was concerned about is that what we should write – and this is a big test for economists nowadays, because they speak a language of their own and it's often impenetrable – in a form in which what we were trying to do was understood as far as possible, not misunderstood.

I think the third thing was to be realistic in the sense that if you read Adam Smith and the classical economists they say nothing should be done overnight; ... You have to remember that people's lives and expectations might be falsified in a very definite way if suddenly you tried overnight to introduce the things which this Report produced, and that is wrong. And that therefore is why the emphasis (in the Report) on how the system might develop stage by stage, which leads of course always to this problem that you are having to make some kind of projections or forecasting about the future ...

Jeremy Hardie:

I think the Peacock Committee certainly wasn't a missed opportunity, but it was a turning point, sort of. I think it was plainly a turning point and a significant milestone in respect of two things. One is, the in-your-face introduction of the notion of consumer sovereignty as something that might be the dominant consideration long term in the way all these things operate, which I don't think had been done anything like as straightforwardly by a public, quasi-public forum report before. And the second, closely allied, was saying 'what's coming up now is technology that would allow subscription, so what do we do about it?' I think it put those two big things bang on the agenda and that has echoed on. Not alas, in a way that has plainly resolved the problem, but to that extent it was sort of a turning point.

..... Institutions, some institutions work well for quite a long time and stop working well. And to be truthful, we don't really know why that happens, but one of the terrible truths is that you have to recognise when it happens. The analysis of whether an institution is an appropriate one is not a matter or timeless analysis of whether the market is better or whether the BBC-type thing is better. It is also very much to do with whether in some straightforward sense it works. I think we have to bear that in mind because institutions do just come and go, and they come and go for reasons which aren't really susceptible to proper academic or similar analysis, but you've got to keep your head screwed on if I can put it that way, about what's really happening here.

Notes

1. Home Secretary, 1983–5 (see Bonner and Ashton, 2003:483).
2. Home Secretary, 1985–9 (see Bonner and Ashton, 2003:483).
3. Brittan (1973).
4. The franchise for the UK's first commercial TV service was awarded to TV-am on 28/12/80. Peter Jay was a leading member of the successful group (see Bonner and Ashton, 2003:300).
5. For details, see Ronald Coase Institute (2007).
6. On Freidrich Hayek 1899–1992 see Brittan (2004) and on Roy Allen 1906–83 see Anon (1983).
7. Coase (1948).
8. Coase (1950).
9. See Lipsey (1966).

10. Milton Friedman 1912–2006, see Goodhart (2006).
11. John Maynard Keynes 1883–1946, see Cairncross (2004).
12. Report, 1986: Chapter 4.
13. Arts Council of Great Britain (1970).
14. Independent Television Contractors Association (ITCA).
15. Sir Keith Joseph 1918–94, Tory politician and government Minister, see Harrison (2004).
16. Leon Brittan.
17. Department of Trade and Industry.
18. Gerald Kaufman MP was the Labour Shadow Home Secretary in 1986.
19. The Social Democratic Party was formed in 1981 by a group of former right wing Labour party ministers and aimed to represent the 'centre' ground of UK politics (Thorpe, 1997:179).
20. The 'Unservile State Group', founded in 1953, aimed to influence the liberal party 'in a more individualistic direction' (see Cockett, 1995:128).
21. Merlyn Rees, 1920–2006, was Labour Home Secretary, 1976–9 (see Pearce, 2006).
22. Joe Ashton was a Labour MP who campaigned to make the BBC take advertising (see O'Malley, 1994:28–9).
23. Report (1977).
24. Report (1962).
25. Noel Annan, 1916–2000 (see Cannadine, 2004).
26. Richard Hoggart, an academic with an interest in broadcasting who sat on the Pilkington Committee (see Milland, 2005).
27. Civil Servant who was appointed Secretary to the Peacock Committee in 1985.
28. Adam Smith circa 1723–90, moral philosopher and political economist (see Winch, 2004).
29. Independent Broadcasting Authority.
30. George Thomson, Chairman of the IBA 1981–8 (see Bonner and Ashton, 2003:481).
31. John Reith 1889–1971, Director General of the BBC 1927–38.
32. Alfred Marshall 1842–1924 (see Tulberg, 2004).
33. Joseph Schumpeter 1883–1950, economist (see Anon, 2008).
34. Gordon Brown MP, Chancellor of the Exchequer, 1997–2007.
35. London School of Economics.
36. For details of these incidents see Miller (1994) and O'Malley (1994).
37. Royal Television Society.
38. Home Office (1988).
39. Lord Brian Griffiths of Fforestfach served at No. 10 Downing Street as Head of the Prime Minister's Policy Unit from 1985 to 1990.
40. David Mellor, MP, was Minister of State at the Home Office, with responsibility for broadcasting between 1986–7 and 1989–90 (see Bonner and Ashton, 2003:483).
41. Labour Shadow Ministers who, at various times in the 1980s and early 1990s, had responsibility for aspects of broadcasting policy (see Freedman, 2003).
42. Director General of the BBC, 1992–2000.

Appendix 1

Committee on financing the BBC–Recommendations[1]

592. Our own conclusion is that British Broadcasting should move towards a sophisticated market system based on consumer sovereignty. That is a system which recognises that viewers and listeners are the best ultimate judges of their own interests, which they can best satisfy if they have the option of purchasing the broadcasting services they require from as many alternative sources of supply as possible. There will always be a need to supplement the direct consumer market by public finance for programmes of a public service kind (defined in paragraph 563) supported by people in their capacity as citizens and voters but unlikely to be commercially self-supporting in the view of broadcasting entrepreneurs.

Stage 1
605. For some years to come – probably until well into the 1990s – the bulk of broadcast television will be supplied by a very limited number of channels: the two BBC and ITV channels and a couple of supplementary channels formed by utilising the 'silent hours' (see Recommendation 9). Satellite and cable are likely to advance, but still be confined to a minority of viewers. We call this period Stage 1. During this stage our main tasks are

1. To secure the continuity and stability of BBC finances.
2. To ensure an adequate range of diversity and programme quality in a period when the 'ratings war' is likely to increase.
3. To prepare the way for the more direct exercise of consumer choice in later stages, while giving existing broadcasters and suppliers of equipment adequate time to adjust.

606. At the time of writing, a likely route to the full broadcasting market we envisage appears to be the development of an optic fibre network by the telecommunications industry, which could be used for broadcasting and other services (see paragraph 493). In our first stage proposals we suggest the removal of obstacles to such a development. But we certainly do not want to commit ourselves to one specific means

of delivery, especially when the possibilities of satellite and other forms of cable are still far from fully tested.

607. We make below a simple technical recommendation (see Recommendation 1), which will not commit the Government to BBC subscription, but which will much reduce the cost of changeover to such a system, if time is allowed for the natural obsolescence and replacement of present receivers.

1. It is a step towards consumer choice. If there is to be a consumer market in broadcasting, it will help if viewers become accustomed to paying for at least one or two channels directly rather than through a licence fee or through the cost in the shops of advertised products.
2. Once it is clear that viewers are themselves deciding to pay for BBC services, and not being forced to do so as a condition for being allowed to own or rent a television set, there will be no reason to resent the payment.
3. Last, but far from least, subscription would reduce the political dependence of the BBC on government, and political pressures upon the Corporation, even more than the indexation of the licence fee which we recommend in Stage 1 (see Recommendation 3 below).

611. Recommendation 1: All new television sets sold or rented in the UK market should be required from the earliest convenient date, and in any case not later than 1 January 1988, to have a peri-television socket and associated equipment which will interface with a decoder to deal with encrypted signals.

612. Recommendation 2: BBC television should not be obliged to finance its operations by advertising while the present organisation and regulation of broadcasting remain in being.

620. Recommendation 3: The licence fee should be indexed on an annual base to the general rate of inflation.

628. Recommendation 4: To permit the BBC to be the managing agent in the collection of the licence fee, and the Post Office should be released from its responsibility as agent to the Home Office for collection and enforcement procedures associated with the licence fee. The BBC should become responsible for inviting proposals for collection and enforcement procedures and for identifying the most efficient and economic collection and enforcement system. (The Post Office, of course, could tender for the role of agent.)

632. Recommendation 5: On the understanding that the proceeds would be used to reduce the cost of the television licence and not to

increase the total sum available for broadcasting, a separate licence fee of not less than £10 should be charged for car radios.

634. Recommendation 6: Pensioners drawing supplementary pension in households dependent on a pension should be exempt from the licence fee.

637. Recommendation 7: The BBC should have the option to privatise Radios 1, 2 and local radio in whole or in part. IBA regulation of radio should be replaced by a looser regime.

In addition five of us* go further:

Recommendation 7a: Radio 1 and Radio 2 should be privatised and financed by advertising. Subject to the Government's existing commitments to community radio, any further radio frequencies becoming available should be auctioned to the highest bidder. IBA regulation should be replaced by a looser regime.

*AP, SB, JH, Q, PR.

644. The two members (JC and AH) who were unable to support Recommendation 7a above, where it deals with privatising BBC Radio 1 and Radio 2, believe that it would seriously damage the residual BBC radio services, would indirectly harm the BBC's overseas services and would cripple a number of ILR[2] companies. They draw attention to paragraphs 388 and 389. The two concur, however, with the recommendation that the IBA's regulation of radio should be replaced by a looser regime. They accept the logic behind the AIRC's proposals noted in paragraph 369.

647. Recommendation 8: The BBC and ITV should be required over a ten-year period to increase to not less than 40 per cent the proportion of programmes supplied by independent producers.

652. Recommendation 9: The non-occupied night-time hours (1.00 am to 6.00 am) of the BBC and ITV television wavelengths should be sold for broadcasting purposes.

655. Four of us propose Recommendation 10: Franchise contracts for ITV contractors should be put to competitive tender. Should the IBA decide to award a franchise to a contractor other than the one making the highest bid, it should be required to make a full, public and detailed statement of its reasons.

656. This last recommendation is an important one and requires further discussion. As at this stage the duopoly would still remain in being, we would be very concerned if the quality of service were to be reduced. Therefore we would still expect the IBA to lay down the minimum quality, schedules and range of criteria which companies bidding for the franchise for programme packaging must meet. Once

the bidders have satisfied the IBA that they could meet the minimum criteria (which we would expect to include all the requirements of the 1981 Broadcasting Act Section 2), the franchise for each area would be awarded by a tendering system. The IBA could decide that a company offering a lower price was giving more 'value for money' in terms of a public service and, accordingly, award the franchise to them. Breach of the public service undertakings by an ITV contractor would be a serious matter subject to all the normal penalties of the law, including in the last resort invalidation of the franchise. Where there was only one bidder for a franchise, the IBA might lay down a 'reserve price' on the allocation of a channel.*

* Three of us (JC, JH, AH) do not recommend this system, certainly as long as the duopoly lasts. First, it would be very hard for the IBA to choose between a high cash bid and a bid which offered less money but a better chance of high quality public service broadcasting. The present system of allocating the franchises has been much criticised as being arbitrary and unpredictable. The proposed system would reinforce those criticisms. Second, we do not think that the public service undertakings given by bidders can be made sufficiently precise to be legally enforceable; and if it is the IBA, not the courts, who decide when there has been a breach, that again will give rise to concern about natural justice and arbitrary decisions. Third, a system of competitive tenders is designed to reduce profits. It therefore makes it more likely that companies, through bad luck or bad management, will make losses or poor profits. The examples of TV-am and many ILR stations show how hard it is in practice for the IBA to enforce standards in these circumstances.

657. Recommendation 11: Franchises should be awarded on a rolling review basis. There would be a formal annual review of the contractor's performance by the Authority.

658. Recommendation 12: Consideration should be given to extending the franchise periods, perhaps to 10 years.

659. Recommendation 13: DBS franchises should be put to competitive tender.

660. Recommendation 14: Channel 4 should be given the option of selling its own advertising time and would then no longer be funded by a subscription from ITV companies.

665. Recommendation 15: National telecommunication systems (e.g. British Telecom, Mercury and any subsequent entrants) should be permitted to act as common carriers with a view to the provision of a full range of services, including delivery of television programmes.

667. Recommendation 16: The restriction of cable franchises to EEC-owned operators should be removed.

668. Recommendation 17: All restrictions for both pay-per-channel and pay-per-programme as options should be removed, not only for cable but also for terrestrial and DBS operations.

669. Recommendation 18: As regulation is phased out the normal laws of the land relating to obscenity, defamation, blasphemy, sedition and other similar matters should be extended to cover the broadcasting media and any present exemptions should be removed.

Stage 2

673. In Stage 2, which is likely to begin well before the end of the century, we recommend that subscription should replace the licence fee. We regard it as a way in which all broadcasting organisations, including the BBC, can sell their services directly to the public. We do not see it as simply an alternative way of collecting the licence fee. We feel that three years' advance notice should be given of the date when Stage 2 would begin, to allow both the BBC and ITV companies to decide how to proceed in the new regime. In Stage 2, the BBC and ITV would continue to provide a range of entertainment, information, cultural and educational programmes, using their discretion and drawing upon their traditions to allocate expenditure. We envisage that the BBC would look to subscription and ITV to advertising revenue for mainstream income, though there would be no reason why, if they wished to do so, the BBC should not finance some of its operations by advertising or the ITV companies sell some of their programmes by subscription. The subscription services should be such that ITV, BBC, cable and satellite services can use them without the need for duplication (see paragraph 613). Should ITV decide to finance their operation entirely from advertising revenue and not from subscription, we would see no case for enforcing encryption on them.

682. Nevertheless we must face the possibility that if broadcasting finance is confined to subscription and advertising, there would be some erosion of public service broadcasting in the narrow sense.

683. Our concern as a committee, therefore, has been to identify how the essential elements of public service broadcasting could be retained. Public service broadcasting has been described as a commitment to produce a wide range of high quality programmes to maximise consumer appreciation. However, not all these programmes would be in jeopardy if competition for revenue or audiences were to occur. A number of programmes which are currently produced by both the BBC

and the ITV would continue to be produced under a more competitive system. Our concern was to find a means of separate and secure funding of those programmes of merit which would not survive in a market where audience ratings was the sole criterion.

684. Inevitably some body or bodies would have to determine what is to count as public service and to decide what programmes to support. We will use the term Public Service Broadcasting Council (PSBC) as a shorthand, but this is not intended to prescribe any exact organisational form in advance.

685. The PSBC would be responsible, in Stage 2 for the secure funding of Radios 3 and 4, local and regional radio and public service television programmes on any channel. Whenever a PSBC grant was given, the PSBC would have the right to stipulate where programmes should be broadcast, and these should be broadcast in non-encrypted form. The external services would continue to be provided by the BBC and funded as at present. A new charter for this newly defined BBC would be required.

690. The 'regulation' of broadcasting content through the IBA, the BBC Board of Governors and the looser controls of the Cable Authority can be justified:

1. as a way of stimulating the effects of a genuine consumer market, in all its range and variety, against the distortions inherent in a duopoly financed by advertising and the licence fee;
2. as a way of introducing minority, high quality or experimental work, which might not be commercially viable in a fully developed market.

691. Once the second requirement is met by a body like a Public Service Broadcasting Council or other arrangements for the positive patronage of creative broadcasting, and the first requirement is met by the development of a full broadcasting market, incorporating direct consumer payment as an option, the need for anything resembling current regulation will decline. There will be no justification for subjecting broadcast publications to any different regime of restraint from that which applies under the general law to printed and spoken publications.

694. The second and final step would be the abolition of pre-publication censorship or vetting of any kind of broadcasting.

Stage 3

700. The shift of BBC to subscription, the greater role of independents and the spread of various kinds of satellite and cable will not in

themselves create a fully fledged broadcasting market. Indeed in the early parts of Stage 2, many viewers and listeners, who do not invest in DBS or link up with local cable companies, may still find themselves effectively dependent on the present duopoly, supplemented by the hire or purchase of video cassettes.

701. We hope, however, that the time will come for what we have called Stage 3 – that is, full multiplicity of choice. Its essential characteristics – which are not to be confused with any particular delivery system – include the following:

1. Freedom of entry for any programme makers who can recover their costs from the market or otherwise finance their production.
2. Viewers to be able to register directly the intensity of their preferences through pay-per-programme or pay-per-channel and not rely entirely on indirect expression through advertising ratings.
3. A policy to prevent monopolistic concentration among programme channellers or producers.
4. Common carrier obligations upon owners of transmission equipment.

Notes

1. The numbers refer to the paragraphs in the Report. Members of the Report are referred to by their initials. A list of the members can be found in Appendix 3.
2. ILR is Independent Local Radio.

Appendix 2

Notes on Contributors

Steven Barnett is Professor of communications at the University of Westminster specialising in areas of policy, regulation, political communication, journalism, press ethics and the BBC. He has directed a number of studies on the future of broadcasting, and from July 2007 to July 2008 he was special adviser to the House of Lords select committee. After the appointment of the Peacock Committee in 1985, he joined the Broadcasting Research Unit for its international study of funding models for public broadcasting.

Sir Samuel Brittan is a columnist at the Financial Times. His most recent books are *Capitalism with a Human Face* (Edward Elgar, 1995; Fontana, 1996), *Essays, Moral, Political and Economic* (Edinburgh University Press, 1996) and *Against the Flow* (Atlantic Books, 2005). He was a member of the Peacock Committee on the Finance of the BBC (1985–6). He was knighted in 1993 for 'services to economic journalism' and also became that year a Chevalier de la Legion d'Honneur. He has been awarded the George Orwell, Senior Harold Wincott and Ludwig Erhard prizes.

Richard Collins is Professor of Media Studies at the Open University. Formerly, he was Deputy Director and Head of Education at the British Film Institute. He has written 12 books including *The Economics of Television: the UK Case* (Sage, 1988) (with Nicholas Garnham and Gareth Locksley) London, *Culture Communication and National Identity. The Case of Canadian Television.* (University of Toronto Press, 1990), *Broadcasting and Audio-Visual Policy in the European Single Market.* (John Libbey, 1994) and *The Consequences of Convergence. Media and Identity in Contemporary Europe.* (Intellect, 2002).

Jeremy Hardie was until 1975 an academic economist, and then until 1999 in business and public life in a variety of companies and institutions in Britain. He was a member of the Peacock Committee on the Finance of the BBC (1985–6). He is now a Research Associate at the CPNSS. Drawing on his experience outside academia his research concentrates on the relationship between rationalist theories of deciding, and the role of intuition, judgement, expertise and emotion.

The Hon Peter Jay has spent about half of his working life as a journalist, mainly on economic themes, for the Times from 1967–77 and for the BBC from 1990–2001. He served in the Treasury from 1961–7 and H. M. Ambassador to the USA from 1977–9. He has also presented news programmes on television including ITV's Weekend World 1972–7, Channel 4's Week in Politics 1983–6 and BBC News, Panorama and The Money Programme 1990–2001. He founded breakfast television in Britain and has been chairman of the National Council for Voluntary Organisations 1983–8 and worked for Robert Maxwell 1986–9. He was appointed a Director of the Bank on 1.6.2003.

Janet Jones is a Principal Lecturer at the University of the West of England. She began as a television producer and journalist at the BBC where she was series editor for 'BBC for Business' and worked across a range of financial and political programmes including The Money Programme, Financial World Tonight, In Business and Panorama. She has written several academic articles and books on the subject of journalism and democracy, the study of the Internet and the public sphere, the future of public service broadcasting in Europe and public participation in multiplatform media.

Tony Lennon has played a pivotal role in most major industrial disputes at the BBC for almost 20 years. He has been the elected president of BECTU (Broadcasting Entertainment Cinematograph and Theatre Union) since 1991 and has argued and lobbied on behalf of union members from every industrial section. He has also campaigned vigorously on public ownership and funding of the media and entertainment industries. For more than 10 years he was National Chair of the Campaign for Press and Broadcasting Freedom (CPBF), and continues to lobby for editorial freedom and public funding for the UK's media and arts industry.

Dr Anthony McNicholas is a senior lecturer in communications at the University of Westminster, where he is a member of CAMRI, the Communication and Media Research Institute. He is author of *Politics, Religion and the Press: Irish Journalism in Mid-Victorian England* (Oxford, 2007). He publishes on press and broadcasting history and is editor of *Interactions: Studies in Communication and Culture*. He is currently chief researcher on a joint AHRC/BBC-funded project to produce volume 6 of the official history of the BBC covering the years 1974–87.

Sir David Nicholas was Chairman of Independent Television News where he had worked since 1960 until his retirement in October 1991.

During this time he started *News at Ten* in 1967, *News at One* in 1972, *Channel 4 News* in 1982 and *World News*, in 1986. Sir David produced ITN's special news events, general election coverage, US Presidential elections, the Apollo moon exploration programmes, budget day programmes and royal events during his career at ITN. Sir David was appointed CBE in 1982 and knighted for his services to broadcasting in 1989.

Tom O'Malley is Professor of Media Studies at Aberystwyth University. He has written on media history and media policy. His publications include *Closedown? The BBC and Government Broadcasting Policy 1979-1992* (Pluto, 1994); *Regulating The Press* (Pluto, 2000), with Clive Soley; and *The Media in Wales: Voices of a Small Nation* (Cardiff University Press, 2005) with David Barlow and Philip Mitchell. He is co-founder and co-editor of the journal *Media History* (Routledge).

Sir Alan Peacock has been a sailor, Professor of Economics in four major universities, a senior civil servant as Chief Economic Adviser to the Department of Trade and Industry (DTI), the first Vice-Chancellor of the independent University of Buckingham and economic consultant to a wide range of international agencies, governments and professional bodies. Allegedly retired, he continues to add to a long list of professional publications while making occasional sorties into journalism and struggling to compose serious music. He is a Fellow of the British Academy, Italian National Academy and the Royal Society of Edinburgh. He was knighted for public service in 1987.

Alwyn Roberts has been a long-serving BBC Governor for Wales. Roberts has accrued a great deal of admiration within the BBC thanks to his track record of supporting programme makers over management. Recently he stood alone among all the Governors in refusing to call for the banning of a documentary profiling the life of Sinn Fein politician Martin McGuinness. He was in post at the time of the Peacock Report.

Jean Seaton is Professor of Media History at the University of Westminster and currently visiting Research Fellow at St Anne's College, Oxford. Her recent books are *Carnage and the Media: the Making and Breaking of News about Violence* (Penguin, 2005) and *What Can be done? Making the Media and Politics Better.* (Wiley-Blackwell, 2006) (with John Lloyd). She is writing the 1974–87 volume of the official history of the BBC. She is Director and Chair of the Orwell Prize for political writing and journalism.

Kevin Williams is Professor of Media and Communication Studies at Swansea University. He has been a visiting fellow at the Danish National School of Journalism and is on the advisory boards of several international journals including Journalism Theory, Practice and Criticism and Media History. He was a member of the Glasgow University Media Group and has been a judge for the Commonwealth Media Awards and acted in an advisory capacity on broadcasting and media matters for several bodies including the Welsh Affairs Select Committee and the UN Department of Public Information.

Appendix 3

Biographies of members of the Peacock Committee

Biographies of Sir Alan Peacock, Sir Samuel Brittan and Mr Jeremy Hardie appear in the Notes on Contributors.

    These are the biographies that were published with the Report (1986: Appendix 1: 219).

Miss Judith Chalmers: Television and radio presenter and travel journalist. She presents *'Wish you were here?'* for Thames Television and is a commentator for Independent Television on Royal and State occasions and other special events such as the Derby and Royal Film Performances. She is regularly in the Chair for BBC Radio 4's *'Tuesday Call'* programme and is travel editor of Woman's Realm. She has been a Member of the National Consumer Council since November 1984 and is Chairman of the Appeals Committee of the Women's National Cancer Control Campaign. She is a director of Durden-Smith Enterprises Ltd and Chelsea Restaurants plc.

Professor Alistair Hetherington: Research professor of Media Studies at the University of Stirling. He is a former editor of *'The Guardian'* and a former Controller of BBC Scotland. Professor Hetherington served as a member of the Royal Commission on the Police 1960–2 and was Journalist of the Year in the National Press Awards, 1970. He is the director of a small independent television production company, Scotquest, and is a member of the IPPA.

Lord Quinton, FBA: President of Trinity College, Oxford. He has held a number of academic posts and Fellowships in Britain and America. He has served as a member of the Arts Council and is a former President of the Aristotelian Society. Lord Quinton has published a number of works in the field of philosophy. He is the chairman of the British Library.

Sir Peter Reynolds, CBE: Chairman of Ranks Hovis McDougall plc. He is a former Managing Director and Chairman of Walls Ltd, a director of the Guardian Royal Exchange plc and a director of Boots plc. He has been a member of the Irish Development Board since 1982 and has been a member of the Food and Drink Economic Development Council since its inception (1976) and Chairman of the Employment Committee since 1982.

Bibliography

Adam Smith Institute (1984) *Omega Report: Communications* London: ASI.

AIRC (1985) *Initial Evidence to the Home Office Committee on Financing the BBC* London: AIRC, August.

Allan, S. (2006) *Online News* Maidenhead: Open University Press.

Altman, W. (1962) 'The rise and fall of the BBC monopoly', in W. Altman, D. Thomas and D. Sawers (eds) *TV: From Monopoly to Competition – And Back?* London: IEA, revised edition, July, pp. 11–40.

Altman, W., Thomas, D. and Sawers, D. (1962) *TV: From Monopoly to Competition – And Back?* London: IEA, revised edition, July.

Annan, The Lord (1981) *The Politics of a Broadcasting Enquiry (The 1981 Ulster Television Lecture, 29 May)* Ulster: Ulster Television Ltd.

Anon (1953) 'Subscription television. Use as alternative service urged', *The Times*, 2 December.

Anon (1983) 'Professor Sir Roy Allen', *The Times*, 3 October.

Anon (1986) 'BBC makes strong plea to retain its licence fee', *UK Press Gazette*, 13 January.

Anon (1986a) 'The BBC at its best, now move on', *Television Today*, 16 January.

Anon (1986b) 'A message for Peacock', *Broadcast*, 17 January.

Anon (2004) 'Watchdog "must make sure Wales doesn't lose out under single ITV"', *The Western Mail*, 17 October.

Anon (2008) Joseph Alois Schumpeter (1883–1950), *The Concise Encyclopedia of Economics*, http://www.econlib.org/library/Enc/bios/Schumpeter.html, accessed 1 September 2009.

Arts Council of Great Britain (1970) *A Report on Orchestral Resources in Great Britain, Chairman: A. T. Peacock* London: Arts Council of Great Britain.

Baker, C. (2002) *Media, Markets, and Democracy* Cambridge: Cambridge University Press.

Barlow, D., Mitchell, P. and O'Malley, T. (2005) *The Media in Wales: Voices of a Small Nation*, Cardiff: University of Wales Press.

Barnard, N. (1985) *The Price of Television Airtime* London: London Business School, October.

Barnett, S. (2004), 'Which end of the telescope? From market failure to cultural value', in J. Tambini and T. Damian (eds) *From Public Service Broadcasting to Public Service Communications* London: IPPR, pp. 34–45.

Barwise, P. (1985) *BBC Television–No Rich Prizes for Advertisers* London: London Business School, October.

Bazalgette, P. (2008) 'Re-imagining PSB', *Television, The Journal of The Royal Television Society*, May: 4–7.

BBC (2005) *Review of the BBC's Royal Charter: BBC response to a strong BBC, independent of government* London: BBC, http://www.bbc.co.uk/thefuture/pdfs/green_paper_response.pdf, accessed 28 December 2005.

BBC (2008) *The BBC Trust Impartiality Report: BBC Network News and Current Affairs Coverage of the Four UK Nations* London: BBC, http://www.bbc.co.uk/bbctrust/

assets/files/pdf/review_report_research/impartiality/uk_nations_impartiality. pdf, accessed 21 July 2008.

BBC Wales (2007) 'Challenges and opportunities for BBC Wales', *Press Release 18 October*, www.bbc.co.uk/pressoffice/pressrelease/stories/2007/10_october/18/ wales.shtml, accessed 21 February.

Belfrage, B. (1952) 'Letter', *The Times*, 26 March.

Berlin, I. (1998) *The Proper Study of Mankind: An Anthology of Essays* London: Pimlico.

Berlin, I. (1998a) 'Two concepts of liberty', in I. Berlin (1998) *The Proper Study of Mankind: An Anthology of Essays* London: Pimlico, pp. 191–242.

Bessborough (1952) 'Letter', *The Times*, 25 March.

Birt, J. and Jay, P. (1975) 'Television journalism: the child of an unhappy marriage between newspapers and film', *The Times*, 30 September.

Birt, J. and Jay, P. (1975a) 'The radical changes needed to remedy TV's bias against understanding', *TheTimes*, 1 October.

Black, L. (2003) *The Political Culture of the Left in Affluent Britain, 1951-64* London: Palgrave Macmillan.

Blain, N. and Hutchinson, D. (eds) (2008) *The The Media in Scotland* Edinburgh: Edinburgh University Press.

Blanchard, S. and Morley, D. (eds) (1982) *What is This Channel Fo(u)r?* London: Comedia.

Bodden, T. (2008) 'Wales has to build on Gavin and Stacey', *Daily Post*, 3 June.

Bonner, P. with Ashton, L. (1998) *Independent Television in Britain.Volume 5. ITV and the IBA 1981-92: The Old Relationship Changes.* London: Palgrave.

Bonner, P. with Ashton, L. (2003) *Independent Television in Britain.Volume 6. New Developments in Independent Television, 1981-9. Channel 4, TVam, Cable and Satellite* London: Palgrave.

Booth, P. (ed.) (2005) *Towards a Liberal Utopia?* London: IEA.

Born, G. (2005) *Uncertain Vision: Birt, Dyke and the Reinvention of the BBC* London: Verso.

Born, G. (2005a) 'Digitising democracy', *The Political Quarterly*, Vol. 76, No. 1: 102–23.

Bracken, M. and Balfour, A. (2004) ' Public service interactivity and the BBC', in J. Cowling and D. Tambini (eds) *From Public Service Broadcasting to Public Service Communications* London: IPPR, pp. 100–15.

Briggs, A. (1961) *The History of Broadcasting in the United Kingdom Volume 1. The Birth of Broadcasting* Oxford: Oxford University Press.

Briggs, A. (1965) *The History of Broadcasting in the United Kingdom Volume 2. The Golden Age of the Wireless* London: Oxford University Press.

Briggs, A. (1970) *The History of Broadcasting in the United Kingdom Volume 3. The War of Words* London: Oxford University Press.

Briggs, A. (1979) *The History of Broadcasting in the United Kingdom Volume 4. Sound and Vision* Oxford: Oxford University Press.

Briggs, A. (1995) *The History of Broadcasting in the United Kingdom Volume 5. Competition* Oxford: Oxford University Press.

Brinkmann, C. (1959 [1930]) 'Citizenship', in R. A. Seligman and A. Johnson (eds) *Encyclopaedia of the Social Sciences* New York: Macmillan, pp. 471–4.

Brittan, S. (1968) *Left or Right: The Bogus Dilemma* London: Secker and Warburg.

Brittan, S. (1973) *Capitalism and the Permissive Society* London: Macmillan.

Brittan, S. (1973a) 'Conservatism and the Market Economy', in S. Brittan (ed.) (1973) *Capitalism and the Permissive Society* London: Macmillan pp. 233–74 (original version published as a Hobart Paperback, by IEA in 1971 under title, *Government and the Market Economy*).

Brittan, S. (1986) 'Bird's eye view of Peacock', *Financial Times*, 5 July.

Brittan, S. (1987) 'The fight for freedom in broadcasting', *The Political Quarterly*, Vol. 58, No. 1: 1–20.

Brittan, S. (1996) 'Introduction: footfalls in the memory', in S. Brittan *Capitalism with a Human Face* London: Fontana pp. 1–25.

Brittan, S. (2004) 'Hayek, Freidrich August (1899–1992)', *Oxford Dictionary of National Biography* Oxford: Oxford University Press, http://oxforddnb.com/view/article/51095/, accessed 26 June 2008.

Broadcast (2004) 'Uprising in the Regions' Letters, 24 October.

Bromley, M. (ed.) (2001) *No News is Bad News* London: Longman.

Budd, A. (1986) 'The Peacock Committee and the BBC: Liberal Values Versus Regulation', *Public Money*, Vol. 6, No. 3: 29–33.

Caine, S. (1968) *Paying for TV?* London: Institute for Economic Affairs, Hobart Paper 43.

Cairncross, A. (2004) 'John Maynard, Baron Keynes (1883–1946)', *Oxford Dictionary of National Biography* Oxford: Oxford University Press, online edn, January 2008, http://www.oxforddnb.com/view/article/34310, accessed 1 September 2008.

Calabrese, A. and Burgelman J. C. (eds) (1999) *Communication, Citizenship and Social Policy* Lanham, MA: Rowman and Littlefield.

Calhoun, C. (ed.) (1992) *Habermas and the Public Sphere* Cambridge: MIT Press.

Callaghan, J. (1987) *Time and Chance* London: Fontana.

Campbell, J. (2003) *Margaret Thatcher: The Iron Lady* London: Jonathan Cape.

Cannandine, D. (2004) 'Annan, Noel Gilroy, Baron Annan (1916–2000)', *Oxford Dictionary of National Biography* Oxford: Oxford University Press, online edn, January 2008, http://www.oxforddnb.com/view/article/73716, accessed 1 September 2008.

Carrell, S. (2007) 'Salmond demands control of broadcasters in Scotland', *The Guardian*, 9 August.

Cathcart, R. (1984) *The Most Contrary Region: The BBC in Northern Ireland 1924–1984* Belfast: Blackstaff.

Chapman, R. (1992) *Selling the Sixties- The Pirates and Pop Music Radio* London: Routledge.

Clarke, P. (2004) *Hope and Glory. Britain 1900-2000* London: Penguin.

Coase, R. (1946) 'B.B.C. Enquiry?, *The Spectator*, Vol. 176: 446–7.

Coase, R. H. (1947) 'The origin of the monopoly of broadcasting in Great Britain', *Economica*, New Series, Vol. 14, No. 55: 189–210.

Coase, R. H. (1948) 'Wire broadcasting in Great Britain', *Economica*, New Series, Vol. 15, No. 59: 194–220.

Coase, R. H. (1950) *British Broadcasting. A Study in Monopoly* London: Longmans Green and Co.

Coase, R. H. (1950a) 'British television policy. Questions of control and finance', *The Times*, 9 September.

Coase, R. (1950b) 'The B.B.C. monopoly', *Time and Tide*, 7 October: pp. 991–2.

Coase, R. (1951) 'Report on the B.B.C', *Time and Tide*, 20 January : p. 51.

Coase, R. (1951a) 'The Beveridge Report and private enterprise in broadcasting' *The Owl*, Quarterly, No. 2, April: 31–6.

Coase, R. H. (1954) 'The development of the British television service', *Land Economics*, Vol. 30, No. 3: 207–22.

Coase, R. H. (1959) 'The Federal Communications Commission', *Journal of Law and Economics*, Vol. 2: 1–40.

Coase, R. H. (1961) 'Why not use the pricing system in the broadcasting industry?', *The Freeman*, Vol. 11, July: 52–7.

Coase, R. (1966) 'The economics of broadcasting and government policy', *American Economic Review*, Vol. 56, No. 1/2: 440–7.

Coase, R. (1998) 'Comment on Thomas W. Hazlett, assigning property rights to radio spectrum users: why did FCC license auctions take 67 years?', *Journal of Law and Economics*, Vol. 41: 577–80.

Cockett, R. (1995) *Thinking the Unthinkable. Think-Tanks and the Economic Counter-Revolution, 1931-1983* London: Fontana.

Coleman, S. (2004) 'From service to commons: reinventing a space for public communication', in J. Cowling and D. Tambini (eds) *From Public Service Broadcasting to Public Service Communications* London: IPPR, pp. 89–99.

Coleman, S. (2005) 'New mediation and direct representation: reconceptualising representation in a digital age', *New Media and Society*, Vol. 7, No. 2: 177–98.

Collins, R. (2006) *Taking the High Ground: the struggle for ideas in UK broadcasting policy CRESC Working Paper Series* No 20, http://www.cresc.ac.uk/publications/papers.html, accessed 15 November 2007.

Collins, R. and Purnell, J. (1995) *The Future of the BBC: Commerce, Consumers and Governance* London: IPPR.

Communications Act (2003) *Communications Act: Chapter 21*. Norwich: TSO, http://www.legislation.hmso.gov.uk/acts/acts2003/20030021.html, accessed 29 March 2005.

Conference Transcripts (2005) 'Opening Plenary', National Library of Wales.

Conference Transcripts (2005) 'Establishing Peacock', National Library of Wales.

Conference Transcripts (2005) 'Conduct of the Committee', National Library of Wales.

Conference Transcripts (2005) 'View from the BBC', National Library of Wales.

Conference Transcripts (2005) 'Influence', National Library of Wales.

Conference Transcripts (2005) 'Closing Plenary', National Library of Wales.

Conservative Party (1983) *The Conservative Manifesto 1983* London: Conservative Party.

Cook, J. (2008) 'Three ring circus: television drama about, by and for Scotland', in N. Blain and D. Hutchinson (eds) *The Media in Scotland* Edinburgh: Edinburgh University Press, pp. 107–23.

Coopey, R. and Woodward, N. (1996) *Britain in the 1970s.The Troubled Economy* London: UCL Press.

Coopey, R. and Woodward, N. (1996a) 'The British economy in the 1970s: an overview', in R. Coopey and N. Woodward (eds) (1996) *Britain in the 1970s. The Troubled Economy* London: UCL Press, pp. 1–33.

Corner, J., Harvey, S. and Lury, K. (1994) 'Culture, quality and choice: the re-regulation of TV 1989-91, in S. Hood (ed.) *Behind the Scenes: The Structure of British Television in the Nineties* London: Lawrence & Wishart, pp. 1–20.

Cowling, J. and Tambini, D. (eds) (2004) *From Public Service Broadcasting to Public Service Communications* London: IPPR.

Crick, B. (1980) *George Orwell. A Life* London: Penguin.

Crissell, A. (2002) *An Introductory History of British Broadcasting* London: Routledge, 2nd edn.

Crossman, R. (1979) *The Crossman Diaries* London: Hamish Hamilton and Jonathan Cape.

Crowther, G. (1962) 'Letter', *The Times*, 3 July.

Curran, C. (1969) *Money, Management and Programmes* London: BBC.

Curran, J. (1986) 'The different approaches to media reform', in J. Curran, J. Ecclestone, G. Oakely and A. Richardson (eds) *Bending Reality. The State of the Media* London: Pluto, CPBF, pp. 89–135.

Curran, J. (2002) *Media and Power* London: Routledge.

Curran, J. and Seaton, J. (2003) *Power Without Responsibility* London: Routledge, 6th edn.

Dahlgren, P. (1995) *Television and the Public Sphere: Citizenship, Democracy and the Media* London: Sage.

Darlow, M. (2004) *Independents Struggle. The Programme Makers who Took on the TV Establishment* London: Quartet.

Davidson, A. (1992) *Under the Hammer: The ITV Franchise Battle* London: Heinemann.

Davies, G. (2004) *The BBC and Public Value* London: Social Market Foundation.

Davies, G. et al. (1999) *The Future Funding of the BBC* London: DCMS.

Davies, H. (1990) 'Bill can dash all our hopes', *The Western Mail*, 2 February.

Davies, J. (1994) *Broadcasting and the BBC in Wales* Cardiff: University of Wales Press.

Davis, J. (1993) 'BBC regional policy: network television and the regions', in S. Harvey and K. Robins (eds) *The Regions, the Nations and the BBC* London: British Film Institute, pp. 72–81.

Dawes, S. (2007) *Reducing the difference between citizens and consumers: a critical discourse analysis of the Communications White Paper 2000.* Paper presented at the MeCCSA Graduate Conference, University of the West of England, July 2007.

Denham, A. and Garnett, M. (2006) ' "What works?" British think tanks and the "end of ideology" ', *The Political Quarterly*, Vol. 77, No. 2: 156–65.

DTI (2000) *Communications White Paper. A New Future for Communications* London: Department of Trade and Industry , Cm 5010, http://www.communicationswhitepaper.gov.uk, accessed 20 July 2005.

Dunkley, C. (1986) 'Auntie and the golden goose', *Financial Times*, 11 January.

Dyke, G. (2004) *Inside Story* London: Harper Collins.

Dyke, G. (2004a) 'ITV has lost interest in making programmes - but not money', *Independent*, 18 April.

Eccleshall, R. (ed.) (1986) *British Liberalism. Liberal Thought from the 1640s to the 1980s* London: Longman.

Ehrenberg A. S. C. (1986) 'Advertisers or viewers paying?' London: Admap Monograph, February.

Eliot, T. S. (1940) *The Waste Land and Other Poems* London: Faber and Faber.

Ellis, C. (2004) 'Durbin, Evan Frank Mottram (1906-1948)', *Oxford Dictionary of National Biography* Oxford: Oxford University Press, http://www.oxforddnb.com/view/article/39462, accessed 29 November 2007.

Fielding, S., Thompson, P. and Tiratsoo, N. (1995) *"England Arise" The Labour Party and Popular Politics in 1940s Britain* Manchester: Manchester University Press.

Fraser, N. (1992) 'Rethinking the public sphere: a contribution to the critique of actually existing democracy', in C. Calhoun (ed.) *Habermas and the Public Sphere* Cambridge: MIT Press, pp. 109–42.

Freedman, D. (2003) *Television Policies of the Labour Party 1951-2001* London: Frank Cass.

Gabriel, R.P. (1970) 'R. P. Gabriel' in University of Manchester: 10–11.

Gibson, O. (2008) *'Ofcom's Blueprint leaked'*, *Guardian*, 28 July, http://www.guardian.co.uk/media/2008/jul/28/ofcom.channel4, accessed 8 August 2008.

Goodhart, C. (2006) *'Obituary: Milton Friedman'*, *Guardian*, 17 November.

Goodwin, A. and Whannel, G. (eds) (1990) *Understanding Television* London: Routledge.

Graham, A. (1999) 'Broadcasting policy in the multimedia age', in A. Graham et al. (eds) *Public Purposes in Broadcasting* Luton: University of Luton Press, pp. 17–46.

Graham, A. and Davies, G. (1997) *Broadcasting, Society and Policy in the Multimedia Age* Luton: University of Luton Press.

Graham, A. et al. (1999) *Public Purposes in Broadcasting* Luton: University of Luton Press.

Greene, H. (1967) *What price culture? An examination of broadcasting finance* London: BBC – speech delivered to Association for Literature and Art, Duisberg, Germany, on 11 October 1966.

Greenleaf, W. H. (1983) *The British Political Tradition. Volume One. The Rise of Collectivism* London: Routledge.

Gripsrud, J. (ed.) (1999) *Television and Common Knowledge* London: Routledge.

Growth Company Investor (2008) 'Trends favour TV producer Tinopolis – BUY', 31 March.

Habermas, J. (1996) *Between Facts and Norms* Cambridge: Polity.

Hall, S. (1993) 'Which public, whose service?', in W. Stevenson (ed.) *All Our Futures: The Changing Role and Purpose of The BBC* London: BFI, pp. 36–47.

Hanson, F. (1993) 'The BBC, the regions and the nations, and independent production', in S. Harvey and K. Robins (eds) *The Regions, the Nations and the BBC* London: British Film Institute, pp. 65–71.

Harris, R. (1974) 'Letter', *The Times*, 14 August.

Harris, R. (2005) 'An independent station', in P. Booth (ed.) *Towards a Liberal Utopia?* London: IEA, pp. 235–47.

Harris, R. (2005a) 'Playing the fool with inflation', in P. Booth (ed.) (2005) *Towards a Liberal Utopia?* London: IEA, pp. 248–57.

Harris, M. and Wegg-Prosser, V. (1998) 'The BBC and producer choice: a study of public service broadcasting and managerial change , *Wide Angle*, Vol. 20, No. 2: 150–63.

Harrison, B. (2004) 'Joseph, Keith Sinjohn, Baron Joseph (1918-1994)', *Oxford Dictionary of National Biography* Oxford: Oxford University Press, online edn, May 2008, http://www.oxforddnb.com/view/article/55063, accessed 1 September 2008.

Hartley, J. (1999) *Uses of Television* London: Routledge.

Harvey, S. (2006) 'Ofcom's first year and the neo-liberalism's blind spot: attacking the culture of production', *Screen*, Vol. 47, No. 1: 91–105.

Harvey, S. and Robins, K. (eds) (1993) *The Regions, the Nations and the BBC* London: British Film Institute.

Hayek, F. (1997 [1944]) *The Road to Serfdom* London: Routledge.

Heller, C. (1978) *Broadcasting and Accountability* London: British Film Institute.

Helm, D. (2005) 'Consumers, citizens and members: public service broadcasting and the BBC', in D. Helm et al. (eds) (2005a) *Can the Market Deliver? Funding Public Service Television in the Digital Age* Eastleigh: John Libbey, pp. 1–21.

Helm, D. et al. (2005a) *Can the Market Deliver? Funding Public Service Television in the Digital Age* Eastleigh: John Libbey.

Hibberd, L. (2007) 'Devolution in policy and practice: a study of River City and BBC Scotland', *Westminster Papers in Communication and Culture*, Vol. 4, No. 3: 108–27.

Hirschman, A. (1970) *Exit, Voice and Loyalty: Responses to Decline in Firms, Organizations, and States* Cambridge: Harvard University Press.

Hollins, T. (1984) *Beyond Broadcasting: Into the Cable Age* London: BFI for the Broadcasting Research Unit.

Holmes, D. (2005) *Communication Theory: Media, Technology and Society* London: Sage.

Home Office (1978) *Broadcasting* London: HMSO, Cmnd.7294.

Home Office (1987) *Radio. Choices and Opportunities* London: HMSO.

Home Office (1988) *Broadcasting in the 1990s: Competition, Choice and Quality* London: HMSO, cm517.

Home Office (2004) *Building Communities, Beating Crime: A Better Police Service for the 21st Century* London: TSO, Cm 6360, http://police.homeoffice.gov.uk/news-and-publications/publication/police-reform/wp04_complete.pdf?view=Binary, accessed 14 August 2006.

Hood, S. (ed) (1994) *Behind the Scenes: The Structure of British Television in the Nineties* London: Lawrence & Wishart.

Horrocks, P. (2006) *The Future of News* London: BBC, http://www.bbc.co.uk/blogs/theeditors/2006/11/the_future_of_news.html, accessed 12 December 2006.

Horrocks, P. (2008) *The Value of Citizen Journalism* London: BBC, http://www.bbc.co.uk/blogs/theeditors/2008/01/value_of_citizen_journalism.html, accessed 9 January 2008.

House of Commons Library Research Paper (2003) 'An introduction to devolution in the UK' London: House of Commons, http://www.parliament.uk/commons/lib/research/rp2003/rp03-084.pdf., accessed 30 July 2008.

Howson, S. (2004) 'Meade, James Edward (1907-1995)', *Oxford Dictionary of National Biography* Oxford: Oxford University Press, September; online edn, January 2008, http://www.oxforddnb.com/view/article/60333, accessed 16 April 2008.

Hume, D. (1759) 'Letter to Adam Smith, 12 April 1759', in E. C. Mossner and I. S. Ross (eds) (1977) *Correspondence of Adam Smith* Oxford: Clarendon Press.

Ignatieff, M. (2000) *Isaiah Berlin* London: Verso.

Ingham, B. (1991) *Kill the Messenger* London: Harper Collins.

ITV Wales (2008) Memorandum submitted to the Welsh Affairs Select Committee enquiry, *Globalisation and its Impact on Wales*, http://www.publications.parliament.uk/pa/cm/cmwelaf.htm, accessed 21 February 2008.

Jay, P. (1970) 'Peter Jay' in University of Manchester, 1970: 68–70.

Jay, P. (1970a) 'Broadcasting laissez-faire', *The Times*, 27 November.

Jay, P. (1975) 'Politics-proofing the BBC's finances', *The Times*, 23 January.

Jay, P. (1975a) 'Lord Annan's Committee on the Future of Broadcasting. Evidence by Peter Jay Economics Editor of *The Times*', National Library of Wales, Aberystwyth, Future of Broadcasting Annan Committee. Files of Evidence, Box 6 File 376.

Jay, P. (1981) 'Electronic publishing', in P. Jay (1984) *The Crisis of Western Political Economy* London: Andre Deutsch, pp. 219–36.

Jay, P. (1984) *The Crisis of Western Political Economy* London: Andre Deutsch.

Jay, P. (2003) 'Interview', 30 September. Interview conducted by J. Jones and T. O'Malley.

Jay, P. (2004) 'Interview', 30 March. Interview conducted by J. Jones and T. O'Malley.

Jenkins, H. (2006) *Convergence Culture: Where Old and New Media Collide* New York: NYU Press.

Johnson, C. and Turnock, R. (eds) (2005) *ITV Cultures: Independent Television over Fifty Years* Milton Keynes: Open University Press.

Johnson, C. and Turnock, R. (2005a) 'From start-up to consolidation: institutions, regions and regulation over the history of ITV', in C. Johnson and R. Turnock (eds), *ITV Cultures: Independent Television over Fifty Years* Milton Keynes: Open University Press, pp. 14–35.

Jones, J. (forthcoming 2009) 'Changing Auntie – a case study in managing and regulating user generated news content at the BBC', in G. Monaghanand S. Tunney (eds) *Web Journalism: A New Form of Citizenship?* Sussex: Sussex Academic Press.

Jones, R. (2008) Memorandum submitted to Welsh Affairs Select Committee enquiry, *Globalisation and its Impact on Wales*, http://www.publications.parliament.uk/pa/cm/cmwelaf.htm, accessed 21 February 2008.

Lawson, N. (1992) *The View from Number11: Memoirs of a Tory Radical* London: Bantam Press.

Leapman, M. (1986) *The Last Days of the Beeb* London: Allen and Unwin.

Leys, C. (2001) *Market-Driven Politics* London: Verso.

Lipsey, R. G. (1966) *An Introduction to Positive Economics* London: Weidenfeld and Nicholson, 2nd edn.

Little, T. (2006) '£180m a year… and the best that we get for it is *Happy Birthday Broons*', *Scotland on Sunday*, 18 November.

Livingstone, S. and Lunt, P. (2007) 'Representing citizens and consumers in media and communication regulation', *Annals of the American Academy of Political and Social Science*, Vol. 611: 51–65.

Livingstone, S., Lunt, P. and Miller, L. (2007) 'Citizen, consumers and the citizen-consumer: articulating the citizen interest in media and communications regulation', *Discourse and Communication*, Vol. 1, No. 1: 85–111.

Local Radio Workshop (1983) *Capital. Local Radio and Private Profit* London: Comedia/LRW.

Lowe, G. F. and Jauert, P. (eds) (2005) *Cultural Dilemmas in Public Service Broadcasting* Goteborg: Nordicom.

Lunt, P. and Livingstone, S. (2007) 'Regulation in the public interest', *Consumer Policy Review*, Vol. 17, No. 2: 42–7.

Mackay, H. and O'Sullivan, T. (eds) (1999) *The Media Reader: Continuity and Transformation* London: Sage.

MacWhirter, I. (2007) 'The BBC is giving up on Scotland', *Sunday Herald*, 19 July.

MacWhirter, I. (2007a) 'Switching off Scotland's window on the world', *The Herald*, 23 July.

Mair, A. (2008) 'Ioan's a superhero', *Wales on Sunday*, 4 April.

Marshall, T. (1950) *Citizenship and Social Class* Cambridge: Cambridge University Press.

Marshall, T. (1981 [1972]) *The Right to Welfare* London: Heinemann Educational.

Marshall, T. (1981a [1972]) 'Welfare in the context of social policy', in T. Marshall (1981 [1972]) *The Right to Welfare* London: Heinemann Educational, pp. 67–82.

Marshall, T. (1981b [1972]) 'The right to welfare', in T. Marshall (1981 [1972]) *The Right to Welfare* London: Heinemann Educational, pp. 83–103.

Mason, T. (2001) 'Morgan hits at London media', *The Western Mail*, 10 February.

Mayhew, C. (1953) *Dear Viewer* London: Lincolns Praeger Publishers.

McChesney, R. (2000) *Rich Media, Poor Democracy. Communication Politics in Dubious Times* New York: New Press.

McDowell, W. (1992) *The History of BBC Broadcasting in Scotland 1923-83* Edinburgh: Edinburgh University Press.

McLoone, M. (1996) Broadcasting in a Divided Community: Seventy Years of the BBC in Northern Ireland Belfast: Queen's University.

Medhurst, J. (2005) 'Mammon's Television? ITV in Wales, 1959-63', in C. Johnson and R. Turnock (eds) *ITV Cultures: Independent Television over Fifty Years* Milton Keynes: Open University Press, pp. 88–107.

Milland, J. (2004) 'Courting Malvolio: the background to the Pilkington Committee on broadcasting, 1960-62', *Contemporary British History*, Vol. 18, No. 2: 76–102.

Milland, J. (2004a) 'Feeding the Hungry Properly: The Pilkington Report and the BBC', paper given at conference at the University of Westminster, *Media in Post-war Britain: Film, Television and Radio in the 1950s and1960s*, 31 July.

Milland, J. (2005) *Paternalists, Populists and Pilkington: The struggle for the soul of British television 1958-1963* Bristol: University of Bristol: PhD thesis.

Miller, D. (1994) *Don't Mention The War. Northern Ireland, Propaganda, and the Media* London: Pluto.

Miller, D. and Dinan, W. (2008) *A Century of Spin. How Public Relations Became the Cutting Edge of Corporate Power* London: Pluto.

Moran, M. (2003) *The British Regulatory State. High Modernism and Hyper-Innovation* Oxford: OUP.

Morgan, J. and Hoggart, R.(eds) (1982) *The Future of Broadcasting* London: Macmillan.

Mulgan, G. (2006) 'Thinking in tanks: the changing ecology of political ideas', *The Political Quarterly*, Vol.77, No. 2: 147–55.

Murdock, G. (1999) 'Rights and representations: public discourse and cultural citizenship', in J. Gripsrud (ed.) *Television and Common Knowledge* London: Routledge, pp. 7–17.

Murdock, G. (1999a) 'Corporate dynamics and broadcasting futures', in H. Mackay and T. O'Sullivan (eds) (1999) *The Media Reader: Continuity and Transformation* London: Sage, pp. 28–42.

Murdock, G. (2004) *Building the Digital Commons: Public Broadcasting in the Age of the Internet*, The 2004 Graham Spry Memorial Lecture, http://www.com. umontreal.ca/spry/spry-gm-lec.htm, accessed 12 January 2005.

Musgrave, A. and Musgrave, B. (1973) *Public Finance in Theory and Practice* London: McGraw-Hill.

National Board (1970), *Report No 156 Costs and Revenues of Independent Television Companies* London: HMSO.

NERA (1985) *The Effects on ITV and Other Media of the Introduction of Advertising on the BBC in Various Amounts. Report to the Peacock Committee* London: NERA.

Nielson, J. (2006) *Participation Inequality: Encouraging More Users to Contribute*, http://www.useit.com/alertbox/participation_inequality, accessed 2 September 2006.

Ofcom (2004) *Speech of 25/5/2004 to the Westminster Media Forum by Ed Richards, Senior Partner, Strategy & Market Developments, Ofcom on Ofcom's Review of Public Service Television Broadcasting* http://www.ofcom.org.uk/media_office/speeches_ presentations/richards_20040525?a=87101, accessed 16 November 2004.

Ofcom (2005) *Review of Public Service Television Phase 3, Competition for Quality* London: Ofcom.

Ofcom (2005a) *The Communications Market Quarterly Update* London: Ofcom, http://www.ofcom.org.uk/research/cm/jan2005_update/update.pdf, accessed 3 May 2005.

Ofcom (2007a) *Mission Statement*, London: Ofcom, http://www.ofcom.org.uk/ consult/condocs/mis-selling/, accessed 1 November 2007.

Ofcom (2007b) *Discussion Paper, A New Approach to Public Service Content in the Digital Media Age: The Potential Role of the Public Service Publisher* London: Ofcom, http://www.ofcom.org.uk/consult/condocs/pspnewapproach/ accessed 13 November 2007.

Ofcom (2008) *Second Public Service Broadcasting Review Phase One: The Digital Opportunity* London: Ofcom.

Ofcom (2008a) *Submission Welsh Affairs Committee Inquiry 'Globalisation and its Impact on Wales'* London: Ofcom, http://www.publications.parliament.uk/pa/ cm/cmwelaf.htm, accessed 21 February 2008.

Ogilvie, F. (1946) 'Letter', *The Times*, 26 June.

O'Malley, T. (1994) *Closedown? The BBC and Government Broadcasting Policy 1979-1994* London: Pluto.

O'Malley, T. (2001) 'The decline of Public Service Broadcasting in the UK', in M. Bromley (ed.) *No News is Bad News* London: Longman, pp 28–45.

O'Malley, T. (2007) ' "Typically anti-American"? The Labour Movement, America and Broadcasting in Britain from Beveridge to Pilkington, 1949-62', in J. Weiner and M. Hampton (eds) *Anglo American Media Interaction, 1850-2000* London: Palgrave Macmillan, pp. 234–53.

Owen, B., Beebe, J. H. and Manning, W. G. (1974) *Television Economics* Lexington, MA: Lexington Books.

PACT (2007) *Production Trend Report for Out of London* London: Pact.

Peacock, A. (1982) 'LSE and postwar economic policy', *Atlantic Monthly Journal*, Vol. 10, Part I: 35–50.

Peacock, A. (1986) *Making Sense of Broadcasting Finance* Stirling: University of Stirling, Robbins Lecture.

Peacock, A. (1987) 'The "politics" of investigating broadcasting finance', *Royal Bank of Scotland Review*, Vol. 153: 3–16.

Peacock, A. (1993) *Paying the Piper: Culture, Music and Money* Edinburgh: Edinburgh University Press.

Peacock, A. (ed.) (2004) *Public Service Broadcasting Without the BBC?* London: Institute of Economic Affairs.

Peacock, A. (2004) 'Public Service Broadcasting Without the BBC', in A. Peacock (ed.) *Public Service Broadcasting Without the BBC?* London: Institute of Economic Affairs, pp. 33–53.

Peacock, A. (2006) 'Review of "Can the Market Deliver? Funding Television in the Digital Age"', *Journal of Economic Affairs*, Vol. 26, No. 1: 81–2.

Peacock, A. and Weir, R. (1975) *The Composer in the Market Place* London: Faber Music, pp. 106–20.

Pearce, E. (2006) 'Obituary: Lord Merlyn Rees', *Guardian*, 6 January.

Pegg, M. (1983) *Broadcasting and Society 1918-1939* London: Croom Helm.

Picone, I. (2007) 'Conceptualising Online News Use', *Observatorio Journal*, Vol. 1, No. 3: 93–114.

Plant, A. (1953) *The New Commerce in Ideas and Intellectual Property* London: University of London, Athlone Press.

Plant, A. (1958) 'Pay as you view', *The Listener*, 25 September.

Political Correspondent (1962) 'Pilkington verdict angers cabinet', *The Times*, 28 June.

Potter, J. (1988) 'Consumerism and the public sector: how well does the coat fit?', *Public Administration*, 66: 149–64.

Potter, J. (1989) *Independent Television in Britain: Volume 3: Politics and control, 1968-80* London: Macmillan.

Potter, J. (1990) *Independent Television in Britain: Volume 4: Companies and Programmes, 1968-80* London: Macmillan.

Pugh, A. (2004) 'Remote Control', *The Western Mail*, 12 August.

Pugh, P. M. (2004) 'Caine, Sir Sydney (1902-1991)', *Oxford Dictionary of National Biography* Oxford: Oxford University Press, http://www.oxforddnb.com/view/article/4958, accessed 29 Nov 2007.

Purnell, J. (2007) 'Television remains at the centre of attention', *Television: The Magazine of the Royal Television Society*, March: 8–11.

Report (1923) *The Broadcasting Committee Report* London: HMSO, Cmd 1951.

Report (1926) *Report of the Committee on Broadcasting 1925* London: HMSO, Cmd 2599.

Report (1936) *Report of the Committee on Broadcasting 1935* London: HMSO, Cmnd 5091.

Report (1951) *Report of the Broadcasting Committee, 1949* London: HMSO, Cmnd 8116.

Report (1962) *Report of the Committee on Broadcasting 1960* London: HMSO, Cmnd 1753, reprinted 1974.

Report, Appendix E (1962) *Report of the Committee on Broadcasting 1960. Volume 1. Appendix E. Memoranda Submitted to the Committee (Papers 1-103)* London: HMSO, Cmnd.

Report (1977) *Report of the Committee on the Future of Broadcasting* London: HMSO, Cmnd. 6753.

Report (1986) *Report of the Committee on Financing the BBC* London: HMSO, Cmnd 9824.

Report (2002) *The Joint Committee on the Draft Communications Bill* London: The Stationary Office.

Richards, E. (2008) 'Challenging thoughts', *Television: The Magazine of the Royal Television Society*, April, http://www.rts.org.uk/magazine_det.asp?id=35151&sec_id=946, accessed 8 August 2008.

Rogers, B. J. (1970) 'B. J. Rogers' in University of Manchester, 1970: 12–14.

Ronald Coase Institute (2007) 'Curriculum Vitae of Ronald Coase', Ronald Coase Institute, http://coase.org/coasecv.htm, accessed 17 October 2007.

Ross, S. (2002) 'ITV charter ushers in a new dawn for Scottish', *Sunday Herald*, 2 June.

Rudin, R. (2007) 'Revisiting the pirates', *Media History*, Vol.13, No. 2 & 3: 235–55.

Sandbrook, D. (2005) *Never Had it So Good. A History of Britain from Suez to the Beatles* London: Abacus.

Sandbrook, D. (2006), *White Heat. A History of Britain in the Swinging Sixties* London: Abacus.

Sargant, N. (1992) *Broadcasting Policy: Listening to the Consumer* London: Consumers' Association.

Sargant, N. (1993) 'Listening to the consumer' *Consumer Policy Review*, 3.3: 159–66.

Sawers, D. (1962) 'The sky's the limit', in W. Altman, D. Thomas and D. Sawers (eds) *TV: From Monopoly to Competition – And Back?* London: IEA, revised edition, July, pp. 71–119.

Scannell, P. (1990) 'Public service broadcasting: the history of a concept', in A. Goodwin and G. Whannel (eds) *Understanding Television* London: Routledge, pp. 11–29.

Scannell, P. (2005) 'The meaning of broadcasting in the digital era', in G. F. Lowe and P. Jauert (eds) *Cultural Dilemmas in Public Service Broadcasting* Goteborg: Nordicom, pp. 129–43.

Scannell, P. and Cardiff, D. (1991) *A Social History of British Broadcasting* London: Basil Blackwell.

Seligman, R. A. and Johnson, A. (eds) (1959) *Encyclopaedia of the Social Sciences* New York: Macmillan.

Sendall, B. (1982) *Independent Television in Britain. Volume 1: Origin and Foundation, 1946-62* London: Macmillan.

Sendall, B. (1983) *Independent Television in Britain: Volume, 2: Expansion and Change, 1958-68* London: Macmillan.

Shipton, M. (2007) 'BBC network criticised over Wales coverage', *Western Mail*, 16 July.

Shonfield, A. (1967) 'The pragmatic illusion', *Encounter*, June.

Slim, (1962) 'Letter', *The Times*, July 13.

Smith, A. (1812) *An Inquiry into the Nature and Causes of the Wealth of Nations* London: Ward Lock and Co., 3 volumes.

Stage, Screen and Radio (1995) 'A policy from Wonderland', April.

Steiner, P. O. (1961) 'Monopoly and competition in television: some policy issues', *The Manchester School of Economic and Social Studies*, Vol. XXIX, No. 2: 107–31.

Stevenson, N. (2003) *Cultural Citizenship* Maidenhead: Open University Press.

Stevenson, W. (ed.) (1993) *All Our Futures: The Changing Role And Purpose Of The BBC* London: BFI.

Strachan, D. (2007) 'ITV is failing the regions', *Broadcast*, 15 July.

Sturgess, B. (1985) *An Investigation Into The Potential For Advertising On The BBC* London: SRW Forecasting, October.

Sturgess, B. (1985a) *A Free Market Supply of Television?* London: SRW Forecasting, October.

Suenson-Taylor, A. (1951) 'Foreword', *The Owl*, Quarterly, No. 1, January: 2.

Summers, S. (1985) 'Swearing in the jury', *Sunday Times*, 26 May.

TAC (2008) Memorandum submitted to Broadcasting Committee, National Assembly for Wales, http://www.publications.parliament.uk/pa/cm/cmwelaf. htm, accessed 15 April 2008.

Talfan-Davies, G. (1999) *Not By Bread Alone: Information, Media and the National Assembly* Cardiff: Wales Media Forum.

Tambini, J. and Damian, T. (eds) (2002) *From Public Service Broadcasting to Public Service Communications* London: IPPR.

Thatcher, M. (1993) *The Downing Street Years* London: Harper Collins.

Thomas, D. (1962) 'Commercial TV and after', in W. Altman, D. Thomas and D. Sawers (eds) *TV: From Monopoly to Competition – And Back?* London: IEA, revised edition, July, pp. 43–68.

Thomas, D. (1966) *Competition in Radio* London: Institute of Economic Affairs, Occasional Paper 5, 2nd edn, August, First published in May 1965.

Thomas, L. (2008) 'Behind the news: ITV regional output', 25 March, http://www.broadcastnow.co.uk/technology/indepth/2008/03/behind_the_news_itv_regional_output.html, accessed 19 June.

Thompson, M. (2006) *BBC Creative Future* London, BBC, Press Briefing, http://www.bbc.co.uk/pressoffice/pressreleases/stories/2006/04_april/25/creative_detail.shtml, accessed 14 March 2008.

Thompson, M. (2008) 'Keynote address at Television from the Nations and Regions conference, Salford Quays, 22 January', www.bbc.co.uk/pressoffice/speeches/stories/thompson_salford.shtml, accessed 19 June 2008.

Thompson, N. (1996) 'Economic ideas and the development of economic opinion', in R. Coopey and N. Woodward (eds) *Britain in the 1970s. The Troubled Economy* London: UCL Press,) pp. 55–80.

Thorne, B. (1970) *The BBC's Finances and Cost Control* London: BBC.

Thorpe, A. (1997) *A History of the British Labour Party* London: Macmillan.

Tomlinson, J. (1990) *Hayek and the Market* London: Pluto.

Tomlinson, J. (2007) 'Tale of a death exaggerated: how Keynesian policies survived the 1970s', *Contemporary British History*, Vol. 21, No. 4: 429–48.

Tomos, A. (1982) 'Realising a dream', in S. Blanchard and D. Morley (eds) *What is This Channel Fo(u)r?* London: Comedia, pp. 37–53.

Towse, R. (2005) 'Alan Peacock and cultural economics', *The Economic Journal*, 115 (June): 262–76.

Toynbee, P. (2008) 'A top sliced licence fee will trigger the BBC's destruction', *Guardian*, 22 January, http://www.guardian.co.uk/commentisfree/2008/jan/22/media.politicalcolumnists, accessed 8 August 2008.

Tribe, K. (2004) 'Plant, Sir Arnold (1898-1978), *Oxford Dictionary of National Biography* Oxford: Oxford University Press, http://oxforddnb.com/view/article/66814, accessed 26 June 2008.

Trollope, A. (1951) *The Way We Live Now* (The World's Classics Edition) Oxford: Oxford University Press.

Tulberg, R. M. (2004) 'Marshall, Alfred (1842-1924)', *Oxford Dictionary of National Biography* Oxford: Oxford University Press, online edn, May 2005, http://www.oxforddnb.com/view/article/34893, accessed 1 September 2008.

Tunstall, J. (1983) *The Media in Britain* London: Constable.

University of Manchester (1970) *Second Symposium of Broadcasting: Determinants of Broadcasting Policy November 1970* Manchester: University of Manchester, Department of Extra-Mural Studies, F. S. Badley (ed.).

Vass, S. (2007) 'Grade: Scottish TV suffering from shortage of talent', *Sunday Herald*, 1 July.

Veljanovski, C. (ed.) (1989) *Freedom in Broadcasting* London: Institute of Economic Affairs.

Veljanovski, C. and Bishop, W. (1983) *Choice By Cable* London: Institute of Economic Affairs, Hobart Paper 96.

Wales Screen Commission (2008) 'Rondo Media: The Birth of a New Welsh Indie', Wales Screen Commission: press release, 18th March, at www.walesscreencommission.co.uk/news/more/?id=5041, accessed 21 March.

Warnock, M. (1974) 'Accountability, responsibility – or both?', *Independent Broadcasting* 2, November 2–3.

Webb, S. and Webb, B. (1920) *Constitution for a Socialist Commonwealth of Great Britain* London: Longmans Green.

Weiner, J. and Hampton, M. (eds) (2007) *Anglo American Media Interaction, 1850-2000* London: Palgrave Macmillan.

Wells, M. (2002) 'ITV cuts regional content to raise ratings', *The Guardian*, 28 May.

Whyte, J. S. (1970) 'The Technological Determinants' in University of Manchester, 1970: 5–9.

Wiles, P. (1963) 'Pilkington and the theory of value', *The Economic Journal*, Vol. 73, No. 290: 183–200.

Williams, R. (1974) *Television: Technology and Cultural Form* London: Routledge.

Willis, J. (2000) 'Strength in Numbers', *The Guardian*, 24 April.

Wilson, H. H. (1961) *Pressure Group. The Campaign for Commercial Television* London: Secker and Warburg.

Winch, D. (2004) 'Smith, Adam (*bap.* 1723, d.1790)', *Oxford Dictionary of National Biography* Oxford: Oxford University Press, online edn, October 2007, http://www.oxforddnb.com/view/article/25767, accessed 1 September 2008.

Winston, B. (1998) *Media, Technology and Society: A History - From the Printing Press to the Superhighway* London: Routledge.

Wooton, Baroness (1962) 'Letter', *The Times*, 17 July.

Index